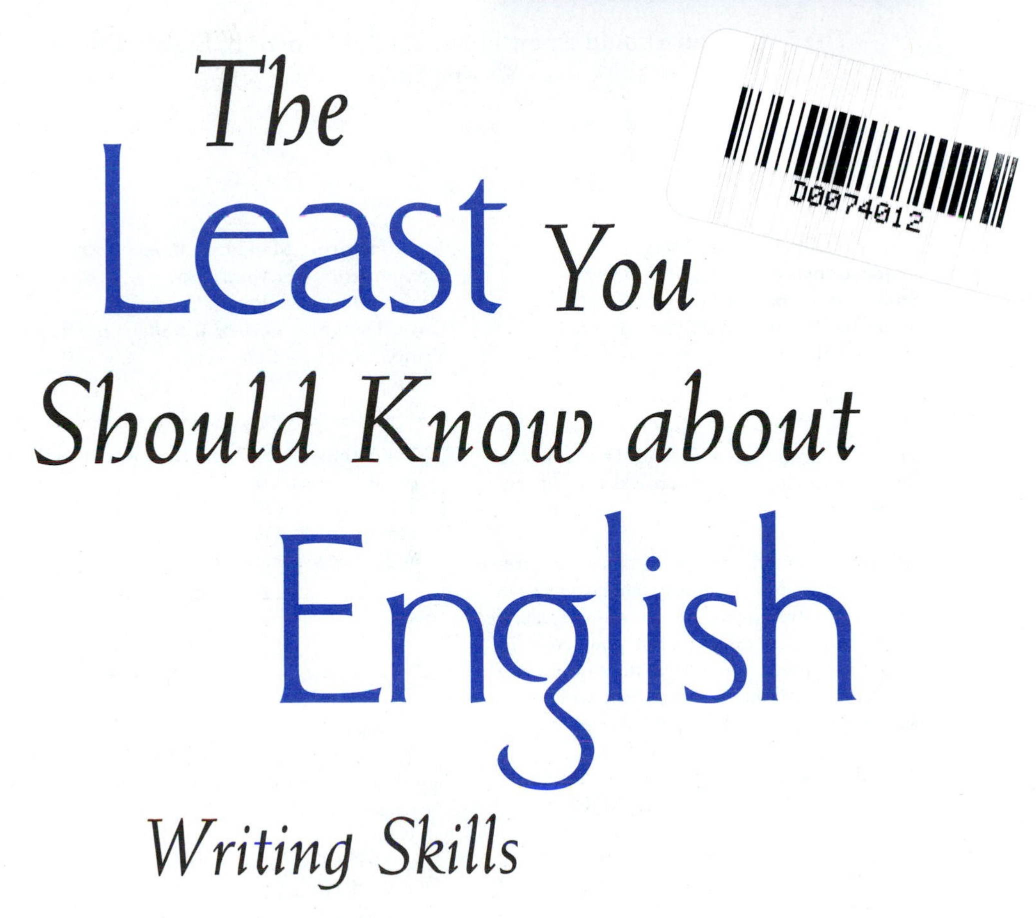

The Least You Should Know about English

Writing Skills

Paige Wilson
Pasadena City College
Teresa Ferster Glazier

Australia Canada Mexico Singapore Spain United Kingdom United States

Benko

THOMSON
HEINLE

The Least You Should Know about English, Form B, Eighth Edition
Writing Skills
Wilson • Glazier

Publisher: *Michael Rosenberg*
Acquisitions Editor: *Stephen Dalphin*
Senior Development Editor: *Michell Phifer*
Associate Production Editor: *Matt Drapeau*
Director of Marketing: *Lisa Kimball*
Manufacturing Manager: *Marcia Locke*
Compositor: *WestWords, Inc.*
Project Manager: *Pat McCutcheon*
Cover Designer: *Dutton and Sherman Design*
Printer: *Phoenix Color Corp.*

Printed in the United States of America.
1 2 3 4 5 6 7 8 9 10 06 05 04 03

For information contact Heinle, 25 Thomson Place, Boston, Massachusetts 02210 USA, or you can visit our Internet site at http://www.heinle.com

For permission to use material from this text or product contact us:
Tel 1-800-730-2214
Fax 1-800-730-2215
Web www.thomsonrights.com

Library of Congress Cataloging-in-Publication Data

Wilson, Paige.
The least you should know about English : writing skills : form B / Paige Wilson, Teresa Ferster Glazier.— 8th ed.
p. cm.
Includes index.
ISBN 0-8384-0771-4
1. English language—Rhetoric—Problems, exercises, etc. 2. English language—Grammar—Problems, exercises, etc. 3. Report writing—Problems, exercises, etc. I. Glazier, Teresa Ferster. II. Title.

PE1413 .W64 2003
808'.042—dc21

2003044767

To the Instructor/Acknowledgments

This book is for students who need to review basic English skills and who may profit from a simplified "least you should know" approach. Parts 1 to 3 cover the essentials of word choice and spelling, sentence structure, punctuation and capitalization. Part 4 on writing teaches students the basic structures of the paragraph and the essay, along with the writing skills necessary to produce them.

Throughout the book, we try to avoid the use of linguistic terminology whenever possible. Students work with words they know instead of learning a vocabulary they may never use again.

There are abundant exercises, including practice with writing sentences and proofreading paragraphs—enough so that students learn to use the rules automatically and *thus carry their new skills over into their writing.* Exercises consist of sets of ten thematically related, informative sentences on such subjects as the oldest tree in the world, the cat that walked 350 miles to rejoin her family, the man who put two million miles on his Volvo, and so on. Such exercises reinforce the need for coherence and details in student writing. With answers provided at the back of the book, students can correct their own work and progress at their own pace.

For the eighth edition, we have added a section on parts of speech to Part 1 and have continued to enhance Part 4 on writing. Part 4 introduces students to the writing process and stresses the development of the student's written "voice." Writing assignments follow each discussion, and there are samples by both student and professional writers. Part 4 ends with a section designed to help students with writing assignments based on readings. It includes articles to read, react to, and summarize. Students improve their reading by learning to spot main ideas and their writing by learning to write meaningful reactions and concise summaries.

The Least You Should Know about English functions equally well in the classroom and at home as a self-tutoring text. The simple explanations, ample exercises, and answers at the back of the book provide students with everything they need to progress on their own. Students who have previously been overwhelmed by the complexities of English should, through mastering simple rules and through writing and rewriting simple papers, gain enough competence to succeed in further composition courses.

For their thoughtful commentary on the book, we would like to thank the following reviewers: Brenda Freaney, *Bakersfield College*; Ann George, *Northwestern Michigan College*; Bronwyn Jones, *Northwestern Michigan College*; Kaye Kolkmann, *Modesto Junior College*; Rosella Miller, *North Idaho College*; Carol Miter, *Riverside Community College*; Brigid Murphy, *Pima Community College*; Barbara Perry, *Northwest Indian College*; and Jane Wilson, *Modesto Junior College*.

For their specific contributions to Form B, we extend our gratitude to the following student writers: Christian Magdaleno, Maggie Wong, and Xia Zhang.

In addition, we would like to thank our publishing team for their expertise and hard work: Stephen Dalphin, Acquisitions Editor; Michell Phifer, Senior Development Editor; Matt Drapeau, Associate Production Editor; and Pat McCutcheon, Project Manager.

As always, we are indebted to Herb and Moss Rabbin, Kenneth Glazier, and the rest of our families and friends for their support and encouragement.

Paige Wilson and Teresa Ferster Glazier

As in all previous editions, **Form B** differs from **Form A** in its exercises, writing samples, and assignments; however, the explanatory sections are the same as in Form A.

A **Test Packet** with additional exercises and ready-to-photocopy tests accompanies this text and is available to instructors.

Contents

2. SENTENCE STRUCTURE 55

What Is the Least You Should Know?

Most English textbooks try to teach you more than you need to know. This book will teach you the least you should know—and still help you learn to write clearly and acceptably. You won't have to deal with grammatical terms like *gerund, modal auxiliary verb,* or *demonstrative pronoun.* You can get along without knowing such technical labels if you learn a few key concepts. You *should* know about the parts of speech and how to use and spell common words; you *should* be able to recognize subjects and verbs; you *should* know the basics of sentence structure and punctuation—but rules, as such, will be kept to a minimum.

The English you'll learn in this book is sometimes called Standard Written English, and it may differ slightly or greatly from the spoken English you use. Standard Written English is the form of writing accepted in business and the professions. So no matter how you speak, you will communicate better in writing when you use Standard Written English. You might *say* something like "That's a whole nother problem," and everyone will understand, but you would probably want to *write,* "That's a completely different problem." Knowing the difference between spoken English and Standard Written English is essential in college, in business, and in life.

Until you learn the least you should know, you'll probably have difficulty communicating in writing. Take this sentence for example:

> Since I easily past my driving test, I deserve a car of my own.

We assume that the writer used the *sound,* not the meaning, of the word *past* to choose it and in so doing used the wrong word. If the sentence had read

> Since I easily *passed* my driving test, I deserve a car of my own.

then the writer would have communicated clearly. Or take this sentence:

> The tigers clawed each other and their trainer and I watched from outside the cage.

This sentence includes two statements and therefore needs punctuation, a comma in this case:

> The tigers clawed each other, and their trainer and I watched from outside the cage.

But perhaps the writer meant

> The tigers clawed each other and their trainer, and I watched from outside the cage.

Punctuation makes all the difference, especially for the trainer. With the help of this text, we hope you'll learn to make your writing so clear that no one will misunderstand it.

As you make your way through the book, it's important to remember information after you learn it because many concepts and structures build upon others. For example, once you can identify subjects and verbs, you'll be able to recognize fragments, understand subject-verb agreement, and use correct punctuation. Explanations and examples are brief and clear, and it shouldn't be difficult to learn from them—*if you want to.* But you have to want to!w

How to Learn the Least You Should Know

1. Read each explanatory section carefully (aloud, if possible).
2. Do the first exercise. Compare your answers with those at the back of the book. If they don't match, study the explanation again to find out why.
3. Do the second exercise and correct it. If you miss a single answer, go back once more to the explanation. You must have missed something. Be tough on yourself. Don't just think, "Maybe I'll get it right next time." Reread the examples, and *then* try the next exercise. It's important to correct each group of ten sentences before moving on so that you'll discover your mistakes early.
4. You may be tempted to quit after you do one or two exercises perfectly. Instead, make yourself finish another exercise. It's not enough to *understand* a concept or structure. You have to *practice* using it.
5. If you're positive, however, after doing several exercises, that you've learned a concept or structure, take the next exercise as a test. If you miss even one answer, you should do all the rest of the questions. Then move on to the proofreading and sentence composing exercises so that your understanding carries over into your writing.

Learning the basics of word choice and spelling, sentence structure, and punctuation does take time. Generally, college students spend a couple of hours outside of class for each hour in class. You may need more. Undoubtedly, the more time you spend, the more your writing will improve.

PART 1

Word Choice and Spelling

Anyone can learn to use words more effectively and become a better speller. You can eliminate most of your word choice and spelling errors if you want to. It's just a matter of deciding you're going to do it. If you really intend to improve your word choice and spelling, study each of the following eight sections until you make no mistakes in the exercises.

Your Own List of Misspelled Words

On the inside cover of your English notebook or in some other obvious place, write correctly all the misspelled words from your previously graded papers. Review the correct spellings until you're sure of them, and edit your papers to find and correct repeated errors.

Words Often Confused (Set 1)

Learning the differences between these often-confused words will help you overcome many of your spelling problems. Study the words carefully, with their examples, before trying the exercises.

a, an

Use *an* before a word that begins with a vowel *sound* (*a, e, i,* and *o,* plus *u* when it sounds like *uh*) or silent *h.* Note that it's not the letter but the *sound* of the letter that matters.

an apple, *an* essay, *an* inch, *an* onion

an umpire, *an* ugly design (The *u*'s sound like *uh.*)

an hour, *an* honest person (The *h*'s are silent.)

Use *a* before a word that begins with a consonant sound (all the sounds except the vowels, plus *u* or *eu* when they sound like *you*).

a chart, *a* pie, *a* history book (The *h* is not silent in *history.*)

a union, *a* uniform, *a* unit (The *u*'s sound like *you.*)

a European vacation, *a* euphemism (*Eu* sounds like *you.*)

accept, except

Accept means "to receive willingly."

I *accept* your apology.

Except means "excluding" or "but."

Everyone arrived on time *except* him.

advise, advice

Advise is a verb. (The *s* sounds like a *z*).

I *advise* you to take your time finding the right job.

Advice is a noun. (It rhymes with *rice.*)

My counselor gave me good *advice.*

affect, effect

Affect is a verb and means "to alter or influence."

All quizzes will *affect* the final grade.

The happy ending *affected* the mood of the audience.

Effect is most commonly used as a noun and means "a result." If *a, an,* or *the* is in front of the word, then you'll know it isn't a verb and will use *effect.*

The strong coffee had a powerful *effect* on me.

We studied the *effects* of sleep deprivation in my psychology class.

all ready, already If you can leave out the *all* and the sentence still makes sense, then *all ready* is the form to use. (In that form, *all* is a separate word and could be left out.)

We're *all ready* for our trip. (*We're ready for our trip* makes sense.)

The banquet is *all ready.* (*The banquet is ready* makes sense.)

But if you can't leave out the *all* and still have a sentence that makes sense, then use *already* (the form in which the *al* has to stay in the word).

They've *already* eaten. (*They've ready eaten* doesn't make sense.)

We have seen that movie *already.*

are, our *Are* is a verb.

We *are* residents of Colorado Springs.

Our shows we possess something.

We painted *our* fence to match the house.

brake, break *Brake* used as a verb means "to slow or stop motion." It's also the name of the device that slows or stops motion.

I *brake* to avoid squirrels.

Luckily I just had my *brakes* fixed.

Break used as a verb means "to shatter" or "to split." It's also the name of an interruption, as in "a coffee break."

She never thought she would *break* a world record.

I will enjoy my spring *break.*

choose, chose The difference here is one of time. Use *choose* for present and future; use *chose* for past.

I will *choose* a new major this semester.

We *chose* the best time of year to get married.

clothes, cloths *Clothes* are something you wear; *cloths* are pieces of material you might clean or polish something with.

I love the *clothes* that characters wear in movies.

The car wash workers use special *cloths* to dry the cars.

coarse, course

Coarse describes a rough texture.

I used *coarse* sandpaper to smooth the surface of the board.

Course is used for all other meanings.

Of *course* we saw the golf *course* when we went to Pebble Beach.

complement, compliment

The one spelled with an *e* means to compl*e*te something or bring it to perfection.

Use a color wheel to find a *complement* for purple.

Juliet's personality *complements* Romeo's; she is practical, and he is a dreamer.

The one spelled with an *i* has to do with praise. Remember "*I* like compl*i*ments," and you'll remember to use the *i* spelling when you mean praise.

My evaluation included a really nice *compliment* from my coworkers.

We *complimented* them on their new home.

conscious, conscience

Conscious means "aware."

They weren't *conscious* of any problems before the accident.

Conscience means that inner voice of right and wrong. The extra *n* in conscience should remind you of *No,* which is what your conscience often says to you.

My *conscience* told me not to keep the expensive watch I found.

dessert, desert

Dessert is the sweet one, the one you like two helpings of. So give it two helpings of *s.*

We had a whole chocolate cheesecake for *dessert.*

The other one, *desert,* is used for all other meanings and has two pronunciations.

I promise that I won't *desert* you at the party.

The snake slithered slowly across the *desert.*

do, due

Do is a verb, an action. You *do* something.

I always *do* my best work at night.

But a payment or an assignment is *due;* it is scheduled for a certain time.

Our first essay is *due* tomorrow.

Due can also be used before *to* in a phrase that means *because of.*

The outdoor concert was canceled *due to* rain.

feel, fill

Feel describes *feel*ings.

Whenever I stay up late, I *feel* sleepy in class.

Fill describes what you do to a cup or a gas tank.

Did they *fill* the pitcher to the top?

fourth, forth

The word *fourth* has four in it. (But note that *forty* does not. Remember the word *forty-fourth.*)

That was our *fourth* quiz in two weeks.

My grandparents celebrated their *forty-fourth* anniversary.

If you don't mean a number, use *forth.*

We wrote back and *forth* many times during my trip.

have, of

Have is a verb. Sometimes, in a contraction, it sounds like *of.* When you say *could've,* the *have* may sound like *of,* but it is not written that way. Always write *could have, would have, should have,* and *might have.*

We should *have* planned our vacation sooner.

Then we could *have* used our coupon for a free one-way ticket.

Use *of* only in a prepositional phrase (see p. 62).

She sent me a box *of* chocolates for my birthday.

hear, here

The last three letters of *hear* spell "ear." You *hear* with your ear.

When I listen to a sea shell, I *hear* ocean sounds.

The other spelling *here* tells "where." Note that the three words indicating a place or pointing out something all have *here* in them: *here, there, where.*

I'll be *here* for three more weeks.

it's, its *It's* is a contraction and means "it is" or "it has."

It's hot. (*It is* hot.)

It's been hot all week. (*It has* been hot all week.)

Its is a possessive. (Words such as *its, yours, hers, ours, theirs,* and *whose* are already possessive forms and never need an apostrophe. See p. 38.)

The jury had made *its* decision.

The dog pulled at *its* leash.

knew, new *Knew* has to do with knowledge (both start with *k*).

New means "not old."

They *knew* that she wanted a *new* bike.

know, no *Know* has to do with knowledge (both start with *k*).

By Friday, I must *know* all the state capitals.

No means "not any" or the opposite of "yes."

My boss has *no* patience. *No,* I need to work late.

EXERCISES

Underline the correct word. Don't guess! If you aren't sure, turn back to the explanatory pages. When you've finished ten sentences, compare your answers with those at the back of the book. Correct each set of ten sentences before continuing so you'll catch your mistakes early.

Exercise 1

1. (It's, Its) finally been proved to be true!
2. People (do, due) weigh more when standing on carpet.
3. (A, An) unique (affect, effect) of most standard scales makes them add as much as ten percent to people's weight when the scales are placed on thick carpet.
4. David MacKay, (a, an) physicist at the University of Cambridge, studied the inner workings of scales to prove whether carpet did (affect, effect) them or not.

5. Many weight-loss services (all ready, already) (knew, new) about the carpet (affect, effect).
6. The difference in weight is (do, due) to the way certain parts bend when a person stands on the scale.
7. When (a, an) typical scale leaves the scale factory, (it's, its) designed to be placed on a hard floor.
8. (It's, Its) parts are calibrated to bend when someone stands on it.
9. The (affect, effect) of plush carpet eliminates the bending, and the scale shows the wrong weight.
10. Experts now (advise, advice) people who weigh themselves on carpet to (choose, chose) a digital scale to help avoid the problem.

Source: New Scientist, June 2, 2002

Exercise 2

1. Did you (know, no) that the tin can was invented before the can opener?
2. When first introduced in the early 1800s, canning was (accepted, excepted) as a great new way to preserve food.
3. But the invention was not (complemented, complimented) by a tool to open the cans.
4. Originally, food cans were made of iron with a coating of tin, so they were extremely difficult to (brake, break) into.
5. (Do, Due) to their construction, the heavy cans had to be pierced and then cut around the top somehow.
6. Labels on the first cans gave the (advise, advice) to use a hammer and chisel to get at the food inside.
7. (Conscious, Conscience) of the dangers, many people asked storeowners to open the cans.
8. Bayonets helped the earliest troops with canned rations (feel, fill) their stomachs.

9. During the Civil War, desperate soldiers (choose, chose) to shoot the tops off their food cans.
10. Of (coarse, course), lighter steel eventually replaced the iron in cans, and can-opening devices became less dangerous and more effective over time.

Source: Invention & Technology, Summer 2000

Exercise 3

1. You probably (know, no) something about Stonehenge, but did you ever (hear, here) of Seahenge?
2. (It's, Its) like Stonehenge, (accept, except) (it's, its) made of wood, and it was discovered in 1998 at the edge of the sea on the coast of England.
3. (It's, Its) shape is similar to Stonehenge's in that they (are, our) both circular.
4. Stonehenge is (a, an) ancient stone circle—one of many nearly 4000-year-old stone structures found throughout Great Britain and that still baffle scientists.
5. Seahenge is (a, an) timber circle from even earlier in the Bronze Age, but (it's, its) the very first wooden circle to be found intact.
6. Previous to (it's, its) discovery, scientists (knew, new) about timber circles only from the indentations the wooden posts had left in the earth.
7. Seahenge became visible after (a, an) especially severe storm removed the peat it had been buried under for thousands of years.
8. At the center of Seahenge's circle of wooden posts was (a, an) huge upside down tree trunk that many (feel, fill) must (have, of) been used as (a, an) alter of some kind.
9. Almost against their (conscious, conscience), British experts decided to dig up Seahenge (do, due) to the vulnerable nature of (it's, its) newly exposed wood.

10. This (brake, break) with the traditional preservation instinct angered many but has (all ready, already) led to several scientific discoveries about the people and tools that created one of the world's newest mysteries—Seahenge.

Source: Smithsonian, July 2002

Exercise 4

1. I've lived on my own for two years, and I'm (all ready, already) tired of trying to decide what to (do, due) for dinner every night.
2. When I lived at home, I used to come home from school, change my (clothes, cloths), and (choose, chose) from all of the things my mom, dad, or siblings were eating for dinner.
3. I could (have, of) taken a plate of Dad's famous macaroni and cheese back to my room and then gone downstairs later for a slice of Mom's lemon pie with (it's, its) fluffy meringue on top.
4. Now I have to come up with a main (coarse, course) and a (dessert, desert) all by myself.
5. (Do, Due) to my lack of cooking experience, dinners of my own are either burned or bought.
6. I'm beginning to (feel, fill) a little self-(conscience, conscious) about my limitations in the kitchen.
7. I could call my parents for (advise, advice), but I don't want them to worry about me.
8. Without a doubt, I should (have, of) paid more attention when both my parents were cooking, not just have (complemented, complimented) them on the results.
9. I guess I could take a cooking (coarse, course) or get a roommate to (do, due) the cooking for reduced rent.
10. I like everything about living away from home (accept, except) making my own dinner.

Exercise 5

1. There is (a, an) old, commonly held belief that if you (choose, chose) to wash your car today, it will rain tomorrow.
2. Of (coarse, course), that's just a saying; (it's, its) not true.
3. However, if you take my (advise, advice) and wash your car at home, you will at least save the cost of (a, an) expensive car wash should this happen to you.
4. To avoid the undesirable (affect, effect) of clouding or streaking of the finish, never wash your car in direct sunlight.
5. But don't park your car under a tree to take advantage of (it's, its) shade, or you may be sorry later (do, due) to the possibility of sap falling from the tree.
6. Also, be sure that the (clothes, cloths) you use to wipe the surface are clean and have (know, no) (coarse, course) stitching or texture that might scratch the finish.
7. You don't want to (brake, break) your antenna, so it should be removed if possible.
8. Once your car is (all ready, already) to be washed, use circular motions and (feel, fill) the surface with your hand every now and then to be sure (it's, its) been thoroughly cleaned.
9. Take the time to dry the whole surface of the car with a chamois if you want to get a lot of (complements, compliments) from your friends.
10. If you've done a good job, the (clothes, cloths) you're wearing will be wet, but your car will be dry and as shiny as it was the day you bought it.

PROOFREADING EXERCISE

Find and correct the ten errors contained in the following student paragraph. All of the errors involve Words Often Confused (Set 1).

I'm enjoying all of my classes this semester accept my speech class. Its not a bad class. The teacher is knowledgeable and supportive. My classmates and I have a good attitude, and we all complement each other when we due a good job. It's just that I don't no how to calm my nerves. Everyone has given me advise, but I can't seem to relax enough to speak without turning red. At the beginning of the semester, everyone was a little nervous and shy at the podium. But now that everyone else has conquered the problem, I fill even more self-conscience whenever I give a speech. I hope my classmates don't dessert me before I can conquer my embarrassment too. I guess I couldn't of picked a worse time in my life to take a speech class.

SENTENCE WRITING

The surest way to learn these Words Often Confused is to use them immediately in your own writing. Choose the five pairs of words that you most often confuse from Set 1. Then use each of them correctly in a new sentence. No answers are provided at the back of the book, but you can see if you are using the words correctly by comparing your sentences to the examples in the explanations.

Words Often Confused (Set 2)

Study this second set of words carefully, with their examples, before attempting the exercises. Knowing all of the word groups in these two sets will take care of many of your spelling problems.

lead, led

Lead is the metal that rhymes with *head.*

Old paint is dangerous because it may contain *lead.*

The past form of the verb "to lead" is *led.*

What factors *led* to your decision?

I *led* our school's debating team to victory last year.

If you don't mean past time, use *lead,* which rhymes with *bead.*

I will *lead* the debating team again this year.

loose, lose

Loose means "not tight." Note how *l o o s e* that word is. It has plenty of room for two *o*'s.

My dog has a *loose* tooth.

Lose is the opposite of win.

If we *lose* this game, we will be out for the season.

passed, past

The past form of the verb "to pass" is *passed.*

She easily *passed* her math class.

The runner *passed* the baton to her teammate.

I *passed* your house on my way to the store.

Use *past* when it's not a verb.

I drove *past* your house. (meaning "I drove *by* your house.")

I try to learn from *past* experiences.

In the *past,* he worked for a small company.

personal, personnel

Pronounce these two correctly, and you won't confuse them—*pérsonal, personnél.*

She shared her *personal* views as a parent.

Personnel means "a group of employees."

I had an appointment in the *personnel* office.

piece, peace

Remember "piece of pie." The one meaning "a *piece* of something" always begins with *pie.*

Many children asked for an extra *piece* of candy.

The other one, *peace,* is the opposite of war.

The two sides finally signed a *peace* treaty.

principal, principle

Principal means "main." Both words have *a* in them: princip*a*l, m*a*in.

Their *principal* concern is safety. (main concern)

He paid both *principal* and interest. (main amount of money)

Also, think of a school's "princi*pal*" as your "*pal.*"

An elementary school *principal* must be kind. (main administrator)

A *principle* is a "rule." Both words end in *le:* princip*le,* ru*le.*

I am proud of my high *principles.* (rules of conduct)

We value the *principle* of truth in advertising. (rule)

quiet, quite

Pronounce these two correctly, and you won't confuse them. *Quiet* means "free from noise" and rhymes with *diet.*

Tennis players need *quiet* in order to concentrate.

Quite means "very" and rhymes with *bite.*

It was *quite* hot in the auditorium.

right, write

Right means "correct" or "proper."

You will find your keys if you look in the *right* place.

It also means in the exact location, position, or moment.

Your keys are *right* where you left them.

Let's go *right* now.

Write means to compose sentences, poems, essays, and so forth.

I asked my teacher to *write* a letter of recommendation for me.

than, then

Than compares two things.

I am taller *than* my sister.

Then tells when (*then* and *when* rhyme, and both have *e* in them).

I always write a rough draft of a paper first; *then* I revise it.

their, there, they're

Their is a possessive, meaning belonging to them.

Their cars have always been red.

There points out something. (Remember that the three words indicating a place or pointing out something all have *here* in them: *here, there, where.*)

> I know that I haven't been *there* before.
>
> *There* was a rainbow in the sky.

They're is a contraction and means "they are."

> *They're* living in Canada now. (*They are* living in Canada now.)

threw, through

Threw is the past form of "to throw."

> We *threw* snowballs at each other.
>
> I *threw* away my chance at a scholarship.

If you don't mean "to throw something," use *through.*

> We could see our beautiful view *through* the new curtains.
>
> They worked *through* their differences.

two, too, to

Two is a number.

> We have written *two* papers so far in my English class.

Too means "extra" or "also," and so it has an extra *o.*

> The movie was *too* long and *too* violent. (extra)
>
> They are enrolled in that biology class *too.* (also)

Use *to* for all other meanings.

> They like *to* ski. They're going *to* the mountains.

weather, whether

Weather refers to conditions of the atmosphere.

> Snowy *weather* is too cold for me.

Whether means "if."

> I don't know *whether* it is snowing there or not.
>
> *Whether* I travel with you or not depends on the weather.

were, wear, where

These words are pronounced differently but are often confused in writing.

Were is the past form of the verb "to be."

> We *were* interns at the time.

Wear means to have on, as in wearing clothes.

I always *wear* a scarf in winter.

Where refers to a place. (Remember that the three words indicating a place or pointing out something all have *here* in them: *here, there, where.*)

Where is the mailbox? There it is.

Where are the closing papers? Here they are.

who's, whose *Who's* is a contraction and means "who is" or "who has."

Who's responsible for signing the checks? (*Who is* responsible?)

Who's been reading my journal? (*Who has* been reading my journal?)

Whose is a possessive. (Words such as *whose, its, yours, hers, ours,* and *theirs* are already possessive forms and don't need an apostrophe. See p. 38.)

Whose keys are these?

woman, women The difference here is one of number: wo*man* refers to one adult female; wo*men* refers to two or more adult females.

I know a *woman* who won $8,000 on a single horse race.

I bowl with a group of *women* from my work.

you're, your *You're* is a contraction and means "you are."

You're as smart as I am. (*You are* as smart as I am.)

Your is a possessive meaning "belonging to you."

I borrowed *your* lab book.

EXERCISES

Underline the correct word. When you've finished ten sentences, compare your answers with those at the back of the book. Do only ten sentences at a time so that you will catch your mistakes early.

Exercise 1

1. You've probably been (threw, through) this experience.
2. (You're, Your) in a theater, auditorium, or intimate restaurant, and someone's cell phone rings.

3. The person (who's, whose) phone it is becomes (two, to, too) embarrassed (two, to, too) answer it.
4. In the (passed, past), (their, there, they're) was no way to keep this unfortunate event from happening.
5. Now scientists in Japan have invented a type of magnetic wood paneling that will maintain the (piece, peace) and (quiet, quite) of public places even if people still refuse to turn off (their, there, they're) cell phones.
6. This new wood will block radio signals and therefore keep such calls from going (threw, through) the walls of a theater, auditorium, restaurant, or anywhere else (their, there, they're) not wanted.
7. Of course, (their, there, they're) are people who do not want to (loose, lose) (their, there, they're) (right, write) to make (personal, personnel) calls wherever they want.
8. One of the best uses of magnetic wood will be to protect areas (were, wear, where) signals interfere with each other.
9. (Than, Then) wooden panels will be used (two, too, to) divide wireless signals rather (than, then) block calls altogether.
10. (Weather, Whether) (you're, your) for it or against it, magnetic wood will probably be used worldwide (quiet, quite) soon.

Source: New Scientist, June 27, 2002

Exercise 2

1. The three days following the September 11, 2001, attacks on America (were, wear, where) unique.
2. (Their, There, They're) was an unprecedented opportunity to study an aspect of the (whether, weather) that could not be studied under normal conditions.
3. The situation that (lead, led) to the study was the temporary ban on nearly all airline flights over America.

4. In the (passed, past), scientists had wondered (whether, weather) the artificial clouds produced by airplane engine exhaust affected temperatures on land.
5. These man-made clouds, called contrails, are the streaks left behind after an airplane has (passed, past) across the sky.
6. Never in the recent (passed, past) had (their, there, they're) been days when the skies were clear of contrails.
7. The absence of air traffic also produced an eerie kind of (quiet, quite).
8. Not wanting to (loose, lose) the chance to discover the effects of contrails, (two, too, to) scientists went (right, write) to work.
9. David Travis and Andrew Carleton discovered, (threw, through) comparisons of temperatures from the three days without air traffic and the same days for the (passed, past) thirty years, that the contrails do cause temperatures to cool slightly.
10. This (piece, peace) of scientific data may (lead, led) to a greater understanding of our impact on the planet's (whether, weather) overall.

Source: Discover, August 2002

Exercise 3

1. Many details about Emily Dickinson's life make her one of the most interesting (woman, women) in American literary history.
2. Every (piece, peace) of information about her life is fascinating.
3. First, she managed to (right, write) nearly 1800 poems that (were, wear, where) both (personal, personnel) and universal at the same time.
4. But she followed her own (principal, principle) that "Publication is the auction of the mind of man."
5. More comfortable writing (than, then) publishing, Dickinson saw only a handful of her poems in print during her lifetime—most without her consent and all anonymously.

6. Dickinson included poems in letters to special friends but kept the remainder of her poems hidden in a chest in her bedroom, (were, wear, where) they (were, wear, where) discovered after her death.
7. While she lived, Dickinson took her (right, write) to privacy to an extreme.
8. One frequent visitor to the Dickinson home for years, a (woman, women) named Mabel Loomis Todd, never actually saw the poet until after Dickinson died.
9. Until (than, then), Dickinson had allowed friends and acquaintances to speak with her only from the bottom of the stairs, from behind doors, or from distant rooms.
10. For some of the children in her neighborhood, Dickinson (passed, past) baskets full of treats (threw, through) the curtains of her upstairs window and lowered them to the youngsters while she remained unseen.

Sources: The Life of Emily Dickinson (Harvard University Press, 1974) and *Emily Dickinson: A Poet's Grammar* (Harvard University Press, 1987)

Exercise 4

1. I don't know (weather, whether) I should (right, write) my own resume or pay a service to do it for me.
2. I have a friend (who's, whose) just been hired by a law firm; he told me, "(You're, Your) crazy if you don't let an expert put together (you're, your) resume."
3. Maybe he's (right, write); he's been (threw, through) the process already and was (quiet, quite) satisfied with the result.
4. He has never (lead, led) me astray before, and I'm not (two, too, to) sure I know how to (right, write) all of my (personal, personnel) information in a clear format.
5. For instance, I can't decide how much of my (passed, past) experience I should include.

6. (Personal, Personnel) offices do have strict requirements about the length and styles of documents.
7. (Their, There, They're) often harder to get (passed, past) (than, then) the people on the hiring committees.
8. In fact, the one (woman, women) who helped me last time I tried to get a job told me that the (principal, principle) problem with my file was the poor quality of my resume.
9. I think I'll ask my friend (were, wear, where) he got his resume done and how much it cost.
10. I would rather (loose, lose) a little money (than, then) (loose, lose) another job opportunity.

Exercise 5

1. Lately, it seems people have forgotten the (principal, principle) "Mind (you're, your) own business, and let other people mind theirs."
2. Private moments are becoming more public (than, then) ever, especially when it comes (two, too, to) marriage proposals.
3. In the (passed, past), people asked each other the big question in the secure setting of a home or perhaps in a (quiet, quite) corner of a restaurant.
4. Now a stadium full of baseball fans, the readership of a whole newspaper, or a whole TV audience must be (their, there, they're) to witness the event.
5. One man decided to (right, write) a crossword puzzle that would spell out the question "Will you marry me?" for his beloved to discover.
6. The (woman, women) he wanted to marry did the puzzle in the newspaper every morning.
7. On the morning of the proposal, she went (threw, through) the clues, answered all of them correctly, and when she saw the proposal and her name spelled out in the puzzle, she looked up at her boyfriend and said, "Yes!"

8. Some men and (woman, women) don't think it's (right, write) to be put on the spot in public, however.
9. In one instance, the intended (threw, through) the ring overboard after being asked in front of the entire population of a cruise ship.
10. (Weather, Whether) it's other people's cell phone calls or marriage proposals, we (loose, lose)—or maybe we give away—a little more privacy every day.

PROOFREADING EXERCISE

See if you can correct the ten errors in this student paragraph. All errors involve Words Often Confused (Set 2).

Now that the whether is nice, my kids and I have decided to repaint the outside of our house. We are going to paint it ourselves. But it isn't going to be an easy job since many of the shingles have come lose over the years. In the passed before we moved in, the house had been repainted without the scraping and sanding necessary, so big chunks of paint have just started falling off onto the grass. We worry that their is led in the old paint, but we can't decide weather to call in a professional. One of our neighbors, a woman who's house was just remodeled, told us, "Your going to regret doing it yourselves. After what I've been threw, I would strongly recommend hiring a professional. That's the only way to guarantee your piece of mind."

SENTENCE WRITING

Write several sentences using any words you missed in doing the exercises for Words Often Confused (Set 2).

Sentence writing is a good idea not only because it will help you remember these Words Often Confused but also because it will be a storehouse for ideas you can later use in writing papers. Here are some topics you might consider writing your sentences about:

— Your study habits

— Your favorite actor/actress

— One of your best qualities

— Something you would like to change

— Your favorite sport to watch on TV

The Eight Parts of Speech

Choosing the right word is an important aspect of writing. Some words sound alike but are spelled differently and have different meanings (*past* and *passed,* for instance), and some words are spelled the same but sound different and mean different things (*lead,* for the action of "leading," and *lead,* for the stuff inside pencils).

One way to choose words more carefully is to understand the roles that words play in sentences. Just as one actor can play many different parts in movies (a hero, a villain, a humorous sidekick), single words can play different parts in sentences (a noun, a verb, an adjective). These are called the *eight parts of speech,* briefly defined with examples below.

1. **Nouns** name some*one, thing, place,* or *idea* and are used as subjects and objects in sentences.

    The **technician** fixed the **computers** in the **lab.**

2. **Pronouns** are special words that replace nouns to avoid repeating them.

    She (the technician) fixed **them** (the computers) in **it** (the lab).

3. **Adjectives** add description to nouns and pronouns—telling *which one, how many,* or *what kind, color,* or *shape* they are.

    The **new** technician fixed **thirty old** computers in the **writing** lab.

4. **Verbs** show action or state of being.

   The new technician **fixed** the old computers in the writing lab; Terri **is** the technician's name.

5. **Adverbs** add information—such as *when, where, why,* or *how*—to verbs, adjectives and other adverbs, or whole sentences.

   Yesterday the new technician **quickly** fixed the **very** old computers in the writing lab.

6. **Prepositions** show position in *space* and *time* and are followed by nouns to form prepositional phrases.

   The technician fixed the computers **in** the writing lab **at** noon.

7. **Conjunctions** are connecting words—such as *and, but,* and *or*—and words that begin dependent clauses—such as *because, since, when, while,* and *although.*

   Students still visited the lab **and** the media center **while** the computers were broken.

8. **Interjections** interrupt a sentence to show surprise or other emotions and are rarely used in Standard Written English.

   Wow, Terri is a valuable new employee.

To find out what parts of speech an individual word can play, look it up in a good dictionary (see p. 50). A list of definitions beginning with an abbreviated part of speech (n, adj, prep, and so on) will catalog its uses. However, seeing how a word is used in a particular sentence is the best way to identify its part of speech.
Look at these examples:

The **train** of a wedding gown flows elegantly behind it.

(*Train* is a noun in this sentence, naming the part of a gown we call a "*train.*")

Sammy and Helen **train** dolphins at Sea World.

(*Train* is a verb in this example, expressing the action of teaching skills we call "*training.*")

Doug's parents drove him to the **train** station.

(*Train* is an adjective here, adding description to the noun "station," telling what *kind* of station it is.)

All of the words in a sentence work together to create meaning, but each one serves its own purpose by playing a part of speech. Think about how each of the words in the following sentence plays the particular part of speech labeled:

adj adj n v prep n conj pro adv v n prep n
Many college students work during the day, so they usually take classes at night.

Familiarizing yourself with the parts of speech will help you spell better now and understand phrases and clauses better later. Each of the eight parts of speech has characteristics that distinguish it from the other seven, but it takes practice to learn them.

EXERCISES

Label the parts of speech above all of the words in the following sentences using the abbreviations n, pro, adj, v, adv, prep, conj, and interj. For clarity's sake, the sentences here are very brief, and you may ignore the words *a, an,* and *the.* These words are actually special forms of adjectives (called articles), but they are so numerous that there's no need to mark them. Refer back to the definitions and examples of the parts of speech whenever necessary. When in doubt, leave a word unmarked until you check the answers at the back of the book after each set of ten sentences. You'll find that many of the ones you found difficult to label will be *adverbs,* the most versatile of the parts of speech.

Exercise 1

1. I really love cookies.
2. They are my favorite snack.
3. I prefer the ones with chocolate chips or nuts.
4. Cookies taste best when they are fresh.
5. Sometimes, I have cookies and milk for breakfast.
6. Now some fast-food restaurants offer fresh-baked cookies.
7. Oatmeal cookies are delicious when they are still warm.
8. Companies release new versions of traditional cookies.
9. One variety of Oreos now has chocolate centers.
10. Wow, are they yummy!

Exercise 2

1. Tall office buildings are dangerous for migrating birds at night.
2. The buildings' lighted windows confuse the birds.
3. They fly toward the glowing windows and lose their way.

4. Bird experts studied this phenomenon.
5. McCormick Place is a tall building in Chicago.
6. Scientists counted the number of bird deaths there for two years.
7. Hundreds of birds flew into the lighted windows.
8. Only one fifth of that number hit the dark windows.
9. Scientists suggest a lights-out policy for tall buildings from midnight to dawn during migration periods.
10. Birds migrate from March to May and from August to November.

Source: Discover, August 2002

Exercise 3

1. Jan Demczur recently donated several objects to the Smithsonian Institution.
2. Demczur was a window washer at One World Trade Center.
3. He was in an elevator of the building when terrorists attacked the tower.
4. With the help of his squeegee handle, Demczur saved several people's lives.
5. Demczur and the others in the elevator used the handle as an ax.
6. They cut an opening from the elevator shaft into the building.
7. Demczur and his five elevator-mates escaped just before the tower fell.
8. Such survival stories give people hope.
9. The Smithsonian is the nation's place for rare artifacts.
10. Demczur's squeegee handle and his dusty clothes are now on display at the Smithsonian.

Source: Smithsonian, July 2002

Exercise 4

1. Plants need water and sunlight.
2. Sometimes house plants wither unexpectedly.

3. People often give them too much water or not enough water.
4. I saw an experiment on a television show once.
5. It involved two plants.
6. The same woman raised both plants with water and sunlight.
7. The plants grew in two different rooms.
8. She yelled at one plant but said sweet things to the other.
9. The verbally praised plant grew beautifully, but the other one died.
10. Plants have feelings too.

Exercise 5

1. I recently read some facts about movie kisses.
2. The first one occurs in a film by Thomas Edison in 1896.
3. The title of that short film is *The Kiss.*
4. A longer movie kiss holds the record for time.
5. In a 1941 film, Jane Wyman kisses Regis Toomey for three full minutes.
6. Mae West flirts with many men in her movies although she never kisses one of them.
7. *Don Juan* (1926) is a movie with many kisses in it.
8. John Barrymore delivers nearly two hundred of them.
9. In that movie, one kiss occurs for each minute of film.
10. Gee, I love trivial facts like these.

Source: I Was a Fugitive from a Hollywood Trivia Factory (Contemporary Books, 2000)

PARAGRAPH EXERCISE

Here is a brief excerpt from a book called *The Question and Answer Book of Everyday Science,* by Ruth A. Sonneborn. This excerpt answers the question "Why do our eyes blink?" We have modified some of the phrasing in the excerpt for this exercise. Label the parts of speech above as many of the words as you can before checking your answers at the back of the book.

Your eyelids blink regularly all day long. They stop only when you sleep. Blinking protects your delicate eyes from injury. When something flies toward you, usually your lids shut quickly and protect your eyes.

Blinking also does a kind of washing job. It keeps your eyelids moist. If a speck of dirt gets past your lids, your moist eyeball traps it. Then your eyes fill with water, your lids blink, and the speck washes out of your eye.

SENTENCE WRITING

Write ten sentences imitating those in Exercise 1 above. Instead of beginning with "I really love cookies," you may begin with "Kids usually order pizza" or "Pets always enjoy treats," then continue to imitate the rest of the sentences in Exercise 1. Label the parts of speech above the words in your imitation exercise.

The next two sections on contractions and possessives involve spelling words correctly through the use of apostrophes.

Contractions

When two words are shortened into one, the result is called a *contraction:*

is not ········➤ isn't   you have ········➤ you've

The letter or letters that are left out are replaced with an apostrophe. For example, if the two words *do not* are condensed into one, an apostrophe is put where the *o* is left out.

do not   don't

Note how the apostrophe goes in the exact place where the letter or letters are left out in these contractions:

I am	I'm
I have	I've
I shall, I will	I'll
I would	I'd
you are	you're
you have	you've
you will	you'll
she is, she has	she's
he is, he has	he's
it is, it has	it's
we are	we're
we have	we've
we will, we shall	we'll
they are	they're
they have	they've
are not	aren't
cannot	can't
do not	don't
does not	doesn't
have not	haven't
let us	let's
who is, who has	who's
where is	where's
were not	weren't
would not	wouldn't
could not	couldn't
should not	shouldn't
would have	would've

could have	could've
should have	should've
that is	that's
there is	there's
what is	what's

One contraction does not follow this rule: *will not* becomes *won't.*

In all other contractions that you're likely to use, the apostrophe goes exactly where the letter or letters are left out. Note especially *it's, they're, who's,* and *you're.* Use them when you mean two words. (See p. 38 for the possessive forms—*its, their, whose,* and *your*—which don't contain apostrophes.)

EXERCISES

Put an apostrophe in each contraction. Then compare your answers with those at the back of the book. Be sure to correct each set of ten sentences before going on so you'll catch your mistakes early.

Exercise 1

1. Charles F. Brannock is someone whos not as well-known as the machine he invented.
2. Im sure you remember having your foot measured at some point in your life.
3. Youre in a shoe store, and the salesperson wants to sell you a shoe that fits perfectly.
4. So the clerk grabs a metal device thats behind the counter and plops it on the floor.
5. Its a silver and black metal tray, ruler, and vice all in one.
6. My parents wouldnt let anyone sell us a pair of shoes when I was young unless wed been measured using one of these contraptions.
7. Theyre called Brannock Devices, named for Charles F. Brannock, the man who invented them.

8. He got the idea while he was still in college and working in his father's shoe store, where he noticed that the wooden stick they used to measure customers' feet wasnt practical.
9. Brannock spent countless hours in his dorm room designing a metal device thats able to measure three parts of a person's foot at once.
10. The Brannock Device is still used and manufactured today, and its design hasnt been greatly altered since its original patent in 1928.

Source: Invention & Technology, Summer 2000

Exercise 2

1. Recently, a species of unknown squids has been discovered, and theyve amazed just about everyone whos seen them.
2. Theyre over twenty feet long; theyve got elbows; and their images have been captured by submersible-craft cameras in the deepest parts of three different oceans (Pacific, Atlantic, Indian) and the Gulf of Mexico.
3. These squids have two other unusual characteristics: theyve got big fins that flap as they swim and ten really long, equal-size thin arms that make a bend at the top.
4. Scientists speculate that the squids' arms are covered with little suckers after one squid became stuck to an underwater camera and couldnt easily pull itself free.
5. Theres no name for the new species of squid yet.
6. Scientists say its not that rare to find a new species.
7. Weve only just begun to explore the deep ocean.
8. Submersible cameras may have been used for nearly fifty years.
9. But theyve only observed about sixty square miles of the deep sea in that time.
10. Theres a lot more ocean out there and probably many more surprises in store.

Sources: New York Times, December 21, 2001, and *Science News,* December 22–29, 2001

Exercise 3

1. My friends and I needed some extra money for a trip wed planned, so we decided to have a group yard sale.
2. I didnt think that Id find very many items to sell in my own house.
3. But I couldnt believe how much stuff I discovered that I hadnt ever used.
4. There wasnt any reason to hang onto an old exercise bicycle, for instance.
5. And I knew I didnt want to keep the cat-shaped clock that hung in my room when I was a kid.
6. My parents werent willing to part with the clock, though; I guess theyre more sentimental than I am right now.
7. It isnt easy to get rid of some things, and my friends didnt have any better luck with their parents than Id had.
8. Still, since there were so many of us, we ended up with a yard full of merchandise.
9. We spent the weekend selling a cup here and a bike there until wed made over three hundred dollars.
10. Now were convinced that without our yard-sale profits, we couldnt have had such a fun-filled trip.

Exercise 4

1. Leonardo da Vinci's mural *The Last Supper* hasnt been treated well over the years.
2. If hed known, in the 1490s when he created the mural, that it would suffer so, da Vinci mightve reconsidered doing it at all.
3. In the past, its been painted over and even covered with glue in unsuccessful efforts to preserve it.
4. Often there wasnt any attempt to protect the mural; at one time, the room containing the masterpiece was even used as a stable for horses.
5. Napoleon's soldiers didnt treat it any better; in fact, theyre known to have vandalized it on purpose.

6. Although the room hasnt held horses or soldiers recently, its been filled with the exhaust from nearby cars and moisture from the breath of too many visitors.
7. In the late 1970s, Italy decided that it wouldnt allow the mural to suffer any further abuse.
8. The Italian government enlisted a team of experts to clean and repair da Vinci's famous painting, and theyd been working for more than twenty years on the project before it was finished in 1999.
9. Whats on the wall now that theyve finished hasnt been universally well received.
10. Its hard to tell how much of da Vinci's work remains after layers and chunks of grime and coverings have been removed.

Source: Newsweek, June 7, 1999

Exercise 5

1. Every semester, theres a blood drive at my school, and usually I tell myself Im too busy to participate.
2. But this time, Ive decided to give blood with a couple of my friends.
3. Weve all wanted to donate before, but individually we havent had the nerve.
4. Well visit the "blood-mobile" together and support each other if any of us cant do it.
5. My friend Carla has donated before, so shes the one weve asked about how it feels.
6. She described the whole process and assured us that its easy and painless.
7. First, a volunteer asks us some questions and takes a small blood sample from one of our earlobes to see if we are or arent able to give blood.
8. Once were cleared to donate, well be asked to lie down and have one of our arms prepared for the actual donation.

9. Thats the part Ill be dreading, but Carla says its just the first stick that stings a little.
10. After that, she says that theres no sensation at all except the satisfaction of helping with such a worthy cause.

PROOFREADING EXERCISE

Can you correct the ten errors in this student paragraph? They could be from any of the areas we have studied so far.

Ive just learned about a new web site created to allow people to share there books with complete strangers. Its called BookCrossing.com, and when your finished reading a book, it can be past on to a knew reader just by leaving it on a park bench, at a cafe, or wherever you like. Before you pass it on, you just register the book on the web site, get its ID number, and tell wear you're going to leave it. Then you place a note or a sticker in the book with a identification number and the web address telling the person whose going to find it what to do next. This way, people can keep track of the books they decide to "release into the wild," which is how the web site phrases it. The best part about "bookcrossing" is it's anonymous, and its free!

Source: Book, March/April 2002

SENTENCE WRITING

Doing exercises will help you learn a rule, but even more helpful is using the rule in writing. Write ten sentences using contractions. You might write about your reaction to this week's big news story, or you can choose your own subject.

Possessives

Words that clarify ownership are called *possessives.* The trick in writing possessives is to ask the question "Who (or what) does the item belong to?" Modern usage has made *who* acceptable when it begins a question. More correctly, of course, the phrasing should be "*Whom* does the item belong to?" or even "*To whom* does the item belong?"

In any case, if the answer to this question does not end in *s* (e.g., *girl, person, people, children, month*), simply add an apostrophe and *s* to show the possessive. Look at the first five examples in the following chart.

However, if the answer to the question already ends in *s* (e.g., *girls, Brahms*), add only an apostrophe after the *s* to show the possessive. See the next two examples in the chart and say them aloud to hear that their sound does not change.

Finally, some *s*-ending words need another sound to make the possessive clear. If you need another *s* sound when you *say* the possessive (e.g., *boss* made possessive is *boss's*), add the apostrophe and another *s* to show the added sound.

a girl (uniform)	Whom does the uniform belong to?	a girl	Add '*s*	a girl's uniform
a person (clothes)	Whom do the clothes belong to?	a person	Add '*s*	a person's clothes
people (clothes)	Whom do the clothes belong to?	people	Add '*s*	people's clothes
children (games)	Whom do the games belong to?	children	Add '*s*	children's games
a month (pay)	What does the pay belong to?	a month	Add '*s*	a month's pay
girls (uniforms)	Whom do the uniforms belong to?	girls	Add '	girls' uniforms
Brahms (Lullaby)	Whom does the Lullaby belong to?	Brahms	Add '	Brahms' Lullaby
my boss (office)	Whom does the office belong to?	my boss	Add '*s*	my boss's office

The trick of asking "Whom does the item belong to?" will always work, but you must ask the question every time. Remember that the key word is *belong.* If you ask the question another way, you may get an answer that won't help you. Also, notice that the trick does not depend on whether the answer is *singular* or *plural,* but on whether it ends in *s* or not.

To Make a Possessive

1. Ask "Whom (or what) does the item belong to?"
2. If the answer doesn't end in *s*, add an apostrophe and *s*.
3. If the answer already ends in *s*, add just an apostrophe *or* an apostrophe and *s* if you need an extra sound to show the possessive (as in *boss's office*).

EXERCISES

Follow the directions carefully for each of the following exercises. Because possessives can be tricky, we include explanations in some exercises to help you understand them better.

Exercise 1

Cover the right column and see if you can write the following possessives correctly. Ask the question "Whom (or what) does the item belong to?" each time. Don't look at the answer before you try!

1. the men (reaction)	______________	the men's reaction
2. an umpire (decision)	______________	an umpire's decision
3. Jess (remarks)	______________	Jess's remarks
4. Alice (company)	______________	Alice's company
5. the Porters (cat)	______________	the Porters' cat
6. Mr. Deeds (ears)	______________	Mr. Deeds' ears
7. parents (values)	______________	parents' values
8. a butterfly (wings)	______________	a butterfly's wings
9. two butterflies (wings)	______________	two butterflies' wings
10. a novel (success)	______________	a novel's success

(You may have noticed a couple of options when a word ends in *s*. *Jess's remarks* was given an extra *s*, but *Mr. Deeds' ears* was not. The choice depends on whether *you* want your reader to say the possessive with or without an extra *s* sound. Think of how the result will "sound" when given such choices, and be consistent.)

CAUTION - Don't assume that every word that ends in *s* is a possessive. The *s* may indicate more than one of something, a plural noun. Make sure the word actually possesses something before you add an apostrophe.

A few commonly used words have their own possessive forms and don't need apostrophes added to them. Memorize this list:

our, ours	its
your, yours	their, theirs
his, her, hers	whose

Note particularly *its, their, whose,* and *your.* They are already possessive and don't take an apostrophe. (These words sound just like *it's, they're, who's,* and *you're,* which are *contractions* that use an apostrophe in place of their missing letters.)

Exercise 2

Cover the right column and see if you can write the required form. The answer might be a *contraction* or a *possessive.* If you miss any, go back and review the explanations.

1. (She) the best friend I have.	She's
2. (They) remodeling next door.	They're
3. Does (you) computer work?	your
4. (Who) traveling with us?	Who's
5. My parrot enjoys (it) freedom.	its
6. (They) car needs new tires.	Their
7. (Who) shoes are those?	Whose
8. My apartment is noisy; (it) by the airport.	it's
9. (He) going to give his speech today.	He's
10. (There) someone at the gate.	There's

Exercise 3

Here's another chance to check your progress with possessives. Cover the right column again as you did in Exercises 1 and 2, and add apostrophes correctly to any possessives. Each answer is followed by an explanation.

1. My cousins spent the weekend at my parents mountain cabin.	parents' (You didn't add an apostrophe to *cousins,* did you? The cousins don't possess anything.)
2. The border guard collected all of the tourists passports.	tourists' (Whom did the passports belong to?)
3. I attended my sisters graduation.	sister's (if it is one sister) sisters' (two or more sisters)
4. Two of my friends borrowed the camp directors boat.	director's (The friends don't possess anything.)
5. Patricks salad tasted better than hers.	Patrick's (*Hers* is already possessive and doesn't take an apostrophe.)
6. After a moments rest, the dog wagged its tail again.	moment's (*Its* is already possessive and doesn't take an apostrophe.)
7. Overnight, someone covered the Smiths house with tissue.	Smiths' (The house belongs to the Smiths.)
8. Childrens shoe sizes differ from adults sizes.	children's, adults' (Did you use the "Whom do they belong to" test?)
9. The sign read, "Buses only."	No apostrophe, no possessive.
10. A toothpastes flavor affects its sales.	toothpaste's (*Its* is already possessive and doesn't take an apostrophe.)

Exercises 4 and 5

Now you're ready to add apostrophes to the possessives that follow. But be careful. *First,* make sure the word really possesses something; not every word ending in *s* is a possessive. *Second,* remember that certain words already have possessive forms and don't use apostrophes. *Third,* even though a word ends in *s,* you can't tell where the apostrophe goes until you ask the question, "Whom (or what) does the item belong to?" The apostrophe or apostrophe and *s* should follow the answer to that question. Check your answers at the back of the book after the first set.

Exercise 4

1. President Theodore Roosevelts hunting experience one hundred years ago led to the creation of the teddy bear.
2. Teddy Roosevelt had refused to shoot a weary bear whose helpless position was captured in numerous political cartoons of the time.
3. Clifford Berrymans most famous drawing of Teddys bear showed a cute little cub with round ears and a wide-eyed expression that delighted the public.
4. The teddy bears life as a stuffed animal supposedly began when toymaker Morris Michtom asked for the Presidents permission to name a toy bear after him.
5. Roosevelts reaction was positive, according to legend.
6. Richard Steiffs family business would argue a bit with the legend, however.
7. As early as 1908, the Steiff companys teddy bear production was up to one million bears a year.
8. The Smithsonians celebration of the teddy bears centennial and the post offices issue of four commemorative stamps with teddies on them add to its rich history as a nearly universally loved toy.
9. William H. Taft took office after Teddy Roosevelt, and he tried to create a toy of his own after witnessing the teddy bears popularity.
10. Unfortunately, Tafts idea for a toy called "Billy Possum" failed miserably.

Source: Smithsonian, October 2001

Exercise 5

1. Nearly everyone knows of *The Simpsons* success as an animated television program.
2. At the height of the shows popularity in 1998, several products participated in the promotion of a contest called "The Simpsons House Giveaway."

3. Each of the contestants was hoping to win the following prize: a full-scale, exact duplicate of Homer, Marge, Bart, Lisa, and Maggies beloved home.
4. The prize houses color scheme would even match the cartoon series hues of bright yellow, pink, orange, blue, and green—inside and out.
5. The contests winner was a woman from Kentucky, 63-year-old Barbara Howard.
6. Howards entry form came from a box of iced tea mix, but she never expected to hold the big yellow key to The Simpsons Houses front door.
7. For one thing, the 2,200-square-foot, four-bedroom prize propertys location was far from Kentucky.
8. It was built in Henderson, Nevada, not far from Las Vegas bright lights and casinos.
9. The sponsoring house builder named the area Springfield after the Simpsons own cartoon town, but there were no other similarities.
10. Howard and her family didn't find Ned Flanders house, Principal Skinners elementary school, Apus Kwik-E-Mart, or Chief Wiggums police station anywhere nearby.

PROOFREADING EXERCISE

Find the five errors in this student paragraph. All of the errors involve possessives.

My brothers' friends are nicer to me than he is. When Wes had a party for his birthday last weekend, his friend's Jonathan and Chris tried to convince Wes to let me stay home instead of making me go to our moms' bowling tournament. Wes's reaction surprised them. He stormed out of the living room and slammed the door so hard it nearly came off it's hinges. Of course, I ended up watching a bowling tournament, but I appreciated Jonathan and Chris efforts on my behalf.

SENTENCE WRITING

Write ten sentences using the possessive forms of the names of your family members or the names of your friends. You could write about a recent event where your family or friends got together. Just tell the story of what happened that day.

REVIEW OF CONTRACTIONS AND POSSESSIVES

Here are two review exercises. First, add the necessary apostrophes to the following sentences. Try to get all the correct answers. Don't excuse an error by saying, "Oh, that was just a careless mistake." A mistake is a mistake. Be tough on yourself.

1. Theres a popular tradition most of us celebrate on Valentines Day.
2. We give each other little candy hearts with sayings on them, such as "Im Yours," "Youre Cute," and "Be Mine."
3. Americas largest maker of these candies is Necco; thats short for New England Confectionery Company.
4. Necco calls its version of the candies "Sweethearts Brand Conversation Hearts," and Neccos sayings have only two basic requirements: theyve got to be short and "sweet."

5. The candy hearts recipe is very sweet indeed—its ninety percent sugar.
6. The companys history goes back to the mid-1800s, and at first the sayings were printed on paper and placed inside a shell-shaped candy, more like a fortune cookies design than the tiny printed hearts we buy now.
7. In 1902, the candys shape was changed to a heart, and the sayings were printed directly on the candy.
8. Necco now makes eight billion of its candy hearts each year to satisfy the countrys desire to continue the hundred-year-old tradition.
9. Stores may begin stocking boxes of conversation hearts as early as New Years Day, but statistics show that over seventy-five percent of each years boxes are purchased in the three days before Valentines Day.
10. And if a couple of boxes are left over after February 14th, theyll stay fresh for up to five years.

Source: The Washington Post, February 11, 1998

Second, add the necessary apostrophes to the following short student essay.

Bowling for Values

Growing up as a child, I didnt have a set of values to live by. Neither my mother nor my father gave me any specific rules, guidelines, or beliefs to lead me through the complicated journey of childhood. My parents approach was to set me free, to allow me to experience lifes difficulties and develop my own set of values.

They were like parents taking their young child bowling for the first time. They hung their values on the pins at the end of the lane. Then they put up the gutter guards and hoped that Id hit at least a few of the values theyd lived by themselves.

If I had a son today, Id be more involved in developing a set of standards for him to follow. Id adopt my mom and dads philosophy of letting him discover on his own what hes interested in and how he feels about life. But Id let him bowl in other lanes or even in other bowling alleys. And, from the start, hed know my thoughts on religion, politics, drugs, sex, and all the ethical questions that go along with such subjects.

Now that Im older, I wish my parents wouldve shared their values with me. Being free wasnt as comfortable as it mightve been if Id had some basic values to use a foundation when I had tough choices to make. My childrens lives will be better, I hope. At least theyll have a base to build on or to remodel—whichever they choose.

Words That Can Be Broken into Parts

Breaking words into their parts will often help you spell them correctly. Each of the following words is made up of two shorter words. Note that the word then contains all the letters of the two shorter words.

chalk board	. . .	chalkboard	room mate	. . .	roommate
over due	. . .	overdue	home work	. . .	homework
super market	. . .	supermarket	under line	. . .	underline

Becoming aware of prefixes such as *dis, inter, mis,* and *un* is also helpful. When you add a prefix to a word, note that no letters are dropped, either from the prefix or from the word.

dis appear	disappear	mis represent	misrepresent
dis appoint	disappoint	mis spell	misspell
dis approve	disapprove	mis understood	misunderstood
dis satisfy	dissatisfy	un aware	unaware
inter act	interact	un involved	uninvolved

inter active	interactive	un necessary	unnecessary
inter related	interrelated	un sure	unsure

Have someone dictate the preceding list for you to write and then mark any words you miss. Memorize the correct spellings by noting how each word is made up of a prefix and a word.

Rule for Doubling a Final Letter

Most spelling rules have so many exceptions that they aren't much help. But here's one worth learning because it has very few exceptions (see boxes on page 46).

Double a final letter (consonants only) when adding an ending that begins with a vowel (such as *ing, ed, er*) if all three of the following are true:

1. The word ends in a single consonant,
2. which is preceded by a single vowel (the vowels are *a, e, i, o, u*),
3. and the accent is on the last syllable (or the word has only one syllable).

We'll try the rule on a few words to which we'll add *ing, ed,* or *er.*

begin
1. It ends in a single consonant—*n,*
2. preceded by a single vowel—*i,*
3. and the accent is on the last syllable—be *gin'*.
   Therefore, we double the final consonant and write *beginning, beginner.*

stop
1. It ends in a single consonant—*p,*
2. preceded by a single vowel—*o,*
3. and the accent is on the last syllable (only one).
   Therefore, we double the final consonant and write *stopping, stopped, stopper.*

filter
1. It ends in a single consonant—*r,*
2. preceded by a single vowel—*e,*
3. but the accent isn't on the last syllable. It's on the first—*fil'*ter.
   Therefore, we don't double the final consonant. We write *filtering, filtered.*

keep
1. It ends in a single consonant—*p,*
2. but it isn't preceded by a single vowel. There are two *e*'s.
   Therefore, we don't double the final consonant. We write *keeping, keeper.*

NOTE 1 - Be aware that *qu* is treated as a consonant because *q* is almost never written without *u*. Think of it as *kw*. In words like *equip* and *quit*, the *qu* acts as a consonant. Therefore, *equip* and *quit* both end in a single consonant preceded by a single vowel, and the final consonant is doubled in *equipped* and *quitting*.

NOTE 2 - The final consonants *w*, *x*, and *y* do not follow this rule and are not doubled when adding *ing*, *ed*, or *er* to a word (as in *bowing*, *fixing*, and *enjoying*).

EXERCISES

Add *ing* to these words. Correct each group of ten before continuing so you'll catch any errors early.

Exercise 1

1. top
2. clip
3. intend
4. meet
5. pick
6. buy
7. ask
8. call
9. map
10. target

Exercise 2

1. dig
2. review
3. deal
4. clog
5. click
6. unhook
7. quiz
8. push
9. aim
10. deliver

Exercise 3

1. snip
2. buzz
3. mix
4. flap
5. tamper
6. perform
7. confer
8. gleam
9. clip
10. permit

Exercise 4

1. pat
2. span
3. feed
4. play
5. occur
6. brush
7. gather
8. knot
9. offer
10. hog

Exercise 5

1. help
2. flex
3. assist
4. need
5. select
6. wish
7. cook
8. construct
9. polish
10. lead

PROGRESS TEST

This test covers everything you've studied so far. One sentence in each pair is correct. The other is incorrect. Read both sentences carefully before you decide. Then write the letter of the incorrect sentence in the blank. Try to isolate and correct the error if you can.

1. _____ **A.** Have you decided whether your transferring or not?
   B. Your grades are good enough to be accepted almost anywhere.
2. _____ **A.** She lives by her own set of principles.
   B. She would be a good high school principle.
3. _____ **A.** The Woods family seems very close.
   B. That makes Tiger Wood's career even more fun to watch.
4. _____ **A.** Weather effects satellite dish reception.
   B. The effects of wind are the worst.
5. _____ **A.** A sports car's color should complement it's design.
   B. For most cars, it's best to avoid yellow.
6. _____ **A.** The game show contestant had a choice between money and a room full of furniture.
   B. I would of taken the money.
7. _____ **A.** The test was easier then we thought it would be.
   B. Then we saw our grades and were stunned.
8. _____ **A.** Whose going to tell the landlord that we'll be late with the rent?
   B. You're the one whose name is on the lease.
9. _____ **A.** After the hike, my feet felt as heavy as lead.
   B. I shouldn't have lead the rest of the hikers up that last hill.
10. _____ **A.** My parents didn't give me too much advice about money.
    B. They did advice me to pay cash for everything until I lived on my own.

Using a Dictionary

Some dictionaries are more helpful than others. A tiny pocket-sized dictionary or one that fits on a single sheet in your notebook might help you find the spelling of very common words, but for all other uses, you will need a complete, recently published dictionary. Spend some time at a bookstore looking through the dictionaries to find one that you feel comfortable reading. Look up a word that you have had trouble with in the past, and see if you understand the definition. Try looking the same word up in another dictionary and compare. If all else fails, stick with the big names, and you probably can't go wrong.

Complete the following exercises using a good dictionary. Then you will understand what a valuable resource it is.

1. Pronunciation

Look up the word *jeopardize* and copy the pronunciation here.

____

____

For help with pronunciation of the syllables, you'll probably find key words at the bottom of one of the two dictionary pages open before you. Note especially that the upside-down *e* (ə) always has the sound of *uh* like the *a* in *ago* or *about.* Remember that sound because it's found in many words.

Slowly pronounce *jeopardize,* giving each syllable the same sound as its key word.

Note which syllable has the heavy accent mark. (In most dictionaries the accent mark points to the stressed syllable, but in others it is in front of the stressed syllable.) The stressed syllable in *jeopardize* is *je.* Now say the word, letting the full force of your voice fall on that syllable.

When more than one pronunciation is given, the first is preferred. If the complete pronunciation of a word isn't given, look at the word above it to find the pronunciation.

Find the pronunciation of these words, using the key words at the bottom of the dictionary page to help you pronounce each syllable. Then note which syllable has the heavy accent mark, and say the word aloud.

depot syncopation ambivalence reciprocity

2. Definitions

The dictionary may give more than one meaning for a word. Read all the meanings for each italicized word and then write a definition appropriate to the sentence.

1. People used to drink *phosphates* for fun. ____________________

____

2. The archer hit the *wand* every time. ____________________

____

3. The audience listened to the lovely *bagatelle.* ____________________

____

4. We didn't mean to *gloss* over his accomplishment. ____________________

____

3. Spelling

By making yourself look up each word you aren't sure how to spell, you'll soon become a better speller. When two spellings are given in the dictionary, the first one (or the one with the definition) is preferred.

Use a dictionary to find the preferred spelling for each of these words.

catalog, catalogue ______________ canceled, cancelled ______________

millennium, millenium ______________ judgement, judgment ______________

4. Parts of Speech

English has eight parts of speech: noun, pronoun, verb, adjective, adverb, preposition, conjunction, and interjection. At the beginning of each definition for a word, you'll find an abbreviation for the part of speech that the word is performing when so defined (n, pron, v, adj, adv, prep, conj, interj). For more discussion of parts of speech, see page 24.

Identify the parts of speech listed in all the definitions for each of the following words.

hit ______________________ mean ______________________

each ______________________ calico ______________________

5. Compound Words

If you want to find out whether two words are written separately, written with a hyphen between them, or written as one word, consult your dictionary. Look at these examples:

half sister	two words
father-in-law	a hyphenated word
stepson	one word

Write each of the following as listed in the dictionary (as two words, as a hyphenated word, or as one word):

part time ____________________ card board ____________________

hand made ____________________ in laws ____________________

6. Capitalization

If a word is capitalized in the dictionary, that means it should always be capitalized. If it is not capitalized in the dictionary, then it may or may not be capitalized, depending on how it is used (see p. 199). For example, *American* is always capitalized, but *college* is capitalized or not, according to how it is used.

Last year, she graduated from college.

Last year, she graduated from Monterey Peninsula College.

Write the following words as they're given in the dictionary (with or without a capital) to show whether they must always be capitalized or not. Take a guess before looking them up.

calculus ____________________ russian ____________________

president ____________________ moon ____________________

7. Usage

Just because a word is in the dictionary doesn't mean that it's in standard use. The following labels indicate whether a word is used today and, if so, where and by whom.

obsolete	no longer used
archaic	not currently used in ordinary language but still found in some biblical, literary, and legal expressions
colloquial, informal	used in informal conversation but not in formal writing
dialectal, regional	used in some localities but not everywhere
slang	popular but nonstandard expression
nonstandard, substandard	not used in Standard Written English

Look up each italicized word and write the label indicating its usage. Dictionaries differ. One may list a word as slang whereas another will call it colloquial. Still another may give no designation, thus indicating that that particular dictionary considers the word in standard use.

1. Some TV shows specialize in exposing *two-timing* spouses.________________

2. That last pitch was a *duster,* wasn't it? ________________

3. Her new job comes with plenty of *perks.* ________________

4. I'm just going to *scoot* down to the store for a minute.________________

5. The substitute teacher was a real *softie.* ________________

8. Derivations

The derivations or stories behind words will often help you remember the current meanings. For example, if you read that someone is *narcissistic* and you consult your dictionary, you'll find that *narcissism* is a condition named after Narcissus, who was a handsome young man in Greek mythology. One day Narcissus fell in love with his own reflection in a pool, but when he tried to get closer to it, he fell in the water and drowned. A flower that grew nearby is now named for Narcissus. And *narcissistic* has come to mean "in love with oneself."

Look up the derivation of each of these words. You'll find it in square brackets either just before or just after the definition.

Pollyanna ________________

Luddite ________________

jovial ________________

Florida ________________

9. Synonyms

At the end of a definition, a group of synonyms is sometimes given. For example, at the end of the definition of *injure,* you'll find several synonyms, such as *damage* or *harm.* And if you look up *damage* or *harm,* you'll be referred to the same synonyms listed under *injure.*

List the synonyms given for the following words.

destroy ________________

remember ____________________

agree ____________________

10. Abbreviations

Find the meaning of the following abbreviations.

BL ____________________ IQ ____________________

POW ____________________ UN ____________________

11. Names of People

The names of famous people will be found either in the main part of your dictionary or in a separate biographical names section at the back.

Identify the following famous people.

Christina Rossetti ____________________

John Venn ____________________

Margaret Mead ____________________

Thorstein Veblen ____________________

12. Names of Places

The names of places will be found either in the main part of your dictionary or in a separate geographical names section at the back.

Identify the following places.

Rostock ____________________

Flushing ____________________

Tabasco ____________________

Reindeer Lake ____________________

13. Foreign Words and Phrases

Find the language and the meaning of the italicized expressions.

1. We walked around the *piazza* before we decided to have lunch. ____________________

   ____

2. For an example of *deus ex machina*, just watch the end of that new movie. ____

____

3. We used *tromp l'œil* to paint a doorway on the garden wall. ____

____

4. Let's go back to the *hacienda*. ____

____

14. Miscellaneous Information

Find these miscellaneous bits of information in a good dictionary. Don't just guess; look them up.

1. What is someone involved in *sciamachy* doing? ____

____

2. What kind of animal is a *koala*? ____

____

3. A *gadroon* is what kind of decoration? ____

____

4. How long did the *Boer War* last? ____

____

5. How often does *bimonthly* mean? ____

____

PART 2

Sentence Structure

Sentence structure refers to the way sentences are built using words, phrases, and clauses. Words are single units, and words link up in sentences to form clauses and phrases. Clauses are word groups *with* subjects and verbs, and phrases are word groups *without* subjects and verbs. Clauses are the most important because they make statements—they tell who did what (or what something is) in a sentence. Look at the following sentence for example:

We bought oranges at the farmer's market on Main Street.

It contains ten words, each playing its own part in the meaning of the sentence. But which of the words together tell who did what? *We bought oranges* is correct. That word group is a clause. Notice that *at the farmer's market* and *on Main Street* also link up as word groups but don't have somebody (subject) doing something (verb). Instead, they are phrases to clarify *where* we bought the oranges.

Importantly, you could leave out one or both of the phrases and still have a sentence—*We bought oranges.* However, you cannot leave the clause out. Then you would just have *At the farmer's market on Main Street.* Remember, every sentence needs at least one clause that can stand by itself.

Learning about the structure of sentences helps you control your own. Once you know more about sentence structure, you can understand writing errors and learn how to correct them.

Among the most common errors in writing are fragments, run-ons, and awkward phrasing.

Here are some fragments:

Wandering around the mall all afternoon.

Because I tried to do too many things at once.

By interviewing the applicants in groups.

They don't make complete statements—not one has a clause that can stand by itself. Who was *wandering?* What happened *because you tried to do too many things at once?* What was the result of *interviewing the applicants in groups?* These incomplete sentence structures fail to communicate a complete thought.

In contrast, here are some run-ons:

Computer prices are dropping they're still beyond my budget.

The forecast calls for rain I'll wait to wash my car.

A truck parked in front of my driveway I couldn't get to school.

Unlike fragments, run-ons make complete statements, but the trouble is they make *two* complete statements; the first *runs on* to the second without correct punctuation. The reader has to go back to see where there should have been a break.

So fragments don't include enough information, and run-ons include too much. Another problem occurs when the information in a sentence just doesn't make sense.

Here are a few sentences with awkward phrasing:

The problem from my grades started to end.

It was a time at the picnic.

She won me at chess.

Try to find the word groups that show who did what, that is, the clauses. Once you find them, try to put the clauses and phrases together to form a precise meaning. It's difficult, isn't it? You'll see that many of the words themselves are misused or unclear, such as *from, it,* and *won.* These sentences don't communicate clearly because the clauses, phrases, and even words don't work together. They suffer from awkward phrasing.

Fragments, run-ons, awkward phrasing, and other sentence structure errors confuse the reader. Not until you get rid of them will your writing be clearer and easier to read. Unfortunately, there is no quick, effortless way to learn to avoid errors in sentence structure. First, you need to understand how clear sentences are built. Then you will be able to avoid common errors in your own writing.

This section will describe areas of sentence structure one at a time and then explain how to correct errors associated with the different areas. For instance, we start by helping you find subjects and verbs and understand dependent clauses; then we show you how to avoid fragments. You can go through the whole section yourself to learn all of the concepts and structures. Or your teacher may assign only parts based on errors the class is making.

Finding Subjects and Verbs

The most important words in sentences are those that make up its independent clause—the subject and the verb. When you write a sentence, you write about *something* or *someone.* That's the *subject.* Then you write what the subject *does* or *is.* That's the *verb.*

Lightning strikes.

The word *Lightning* is the thing you are writing about. It's the subject, and we'll underline all subjects once. *Strikes* tells what the subject does. It shows the action in the sentence. It's the verb, and we'll underline all of them twice. Most sentences do not include only two words (the subject and the verb). However, these two words still make up the core of the sentence even if other words and phrases are included with them.

> Lightning strikes back and forth from the clouds to the ground very quickly.
>
> Often lightning strikes people on golf courses or in boats.

When many words appear in sentences, the subject and verb can be harder to find. Because the verb often shows action, it's easier to spot than the subject. Therefore, always look for it first. For example, take this sentence:

> The neighborhood cat folded its paws under its chest.

Which word shows the action? The action word is folded. It's the verb, so we'll underline it twice. Now ask yourself, who or what folded? The answer is cat. That's the subject, so we'll underline it once.

Study the following sentences until you understand how to pick out subjects and verbs.

> Tomorrow our school celebrates its fiftieth anniversary. (Which word shows the action? The action word is celebrates. It's the verb, so we'll underline it twice. Who or what celebrates? The school does. It's the subject. We'll underline it once.)
>
> The team members ate several boxes of chocolates. (Which word shows the action? Ate shows the action. Who or what ate? Members ate.)
>
> Internet users crowd the popular services. (Which word shows the action? The verb is crowd. Who or what crowd? Users crowd.)

Often the verb doesn't show action but merely tells what the subject *is* or *was*. Learn to spot such verbs—*is, am, are, was, were, seems, feels, appears, becomes, looks. . . .* (For more information on these special verbs, see the discussion of sentence patterns on p. 135).

> Marshall is a neon artist. (First spot the verb is. Then ask who or what is? Marshall is.)
>
> The bread appears moldy. (First spot the verb appears. Then ask who or what appears? Bread appears.)

Sometimes the subject comes after the verb, especially when a word like *there* or *here* begins the sentence without being a real subject. It's best not to start sentences with "There is . . ." or "There are . . ." for this reason.

> In the audience were two reviewers from the *Times.* (Who or what were in the audience? Two reviewers from the *Times* were in the audience.)
>
> There was a fortune-teller at the carnival. (Who or what was there? A fortune-teller was there at the carnival.)
>
> There were name tags for all the participants. (Who or what were there? Name tags were there for all the participants.)
>
> Here are the contracts. (Who or what are here? The contracts are here.)

> **Note -** Remember that *there* and *here* (as used in the last three sentences) are not subjects. They simply point to something.

In commands, often the subject is not expressed. An unwritten *you* is understood by the reader.

> Sit down. (You sit down.)
>
> Place flap A into slot B. (You place flap A into slot B.)
>
> Meet me at 7:00. (You meet me at 7:00.)

Commonly, a sentence may have more than one subject.

> Toys and memorabilia from the 1950s are high-priced collectibles.
>
> Celebrity dolls, board games, and even cereal boxes from that decade line the shelves of antique stores.

A sentence may also have more than one verb.

> Water boils at a consistent temperature and freezes at another.
>
> The ice tray fell out of my hand, skidded across the floor, and landed under the table.

EXERCISES

Underline the subjects once and the verbs twice in the following sentences. When you've finished the first set, compare your answers carefully with those at the back of the book.

Exercise 1

1. Cats are extremely loyal and determined pets.
2. They form strong attachments to their families.
3. One cat recently showed her love for the Sampson family very clearly.
4. The Sampsons made a temporary move and took Skittles, the cat, with them.
5. The Sampsons and Skittles spent several months 350 miles away from home.
6. Before the end of their stay, Skittles disappeared.
7. The family returned home without their beloved cat and considered her lost.
8. Seven months later, there was a surprise on their doorstep.
9. Skittles somehow navigated her way home but barely survived the 350-mile trip.
10. This incredible story proves the loyalty and determination of cats.

Source: Current Science, May 3, 2002

Exercise 2

1. There are a number of world-famous trees in California.
2. One of them is the oldest tree on the planet.
3. This tree lives somewhere in Inyo National Forest.
4. The type of tree is a bristlecone pine.
5. Scientists call it the Methuselah Tree.
6. They place its age at five thousand years.

7. The soil and temperatures around it seem too poor for a tree's health.
8. But the Methuselah Tree and its neighbors obviously thrive in such conditions.
9. Due to its importance, the Methuselah Tree's exact location is a secret.
10. Such important natural specimens need protection.

Source: Current Science, May 3, 2002

Exercise 3

1. Your brain has two halves—a right side and a left side.
2. But one side of your brain is stronger in different ways.
3. Scientists refer to this fact as "hemispheric lateralization" and test it this way.
4. Open your eyes and hold up your thumb with your arm far out.
5. Next, point your thumb at something on the other side of the room.
6. Keep both eyes open but cover the thing with the image of your thumb.
7. One at a time, shut one eye and then the other.
8. Your thumb moves to the right or left or stays the same.
9. For most people, the thumb jumps to the right with a closed right eye.
10. Very few people experience the opposite effect and are left-eyed.

Source: Discover, June 1999

Exercise 4

1. Amateur talent shows celebrate the performer or "ham" in all of us.
2. Schools and charities organize these events and raise funds for their organizations.
3. There are singers, dancers, comics, and acrobats in nearly every community.
4. They are not always good singers, dancers, comics, and acrobats, however.

5. In fact, crowds often love the worst performers in talent shows.
6. A sense of humor in the audience and the performers helps enormously.
7. Otherwise, participants feel embarrassment instead of encouragement.
8. Laughing with someone is not the same as laughing at someone.
9. Amateur performers need courage and support.
10. Every celebrity started somewhere, perhaps even in a talent show.

Exercise 5

1. The word *toast* has a couple of different meanings.
2. We toast pieces of bread and eat them with butter and jam.
3. People also make toasts to the bride and groom at weddings.
4. There are Old French and Latin word roots for *toast.*
5. Both *toster* (Old French) and *torrere* (Latin) refer to cooking and drying.
6. *Toast* as the word for cooked bread slices arrived in the 1400s.
7. The story of *toast*'s other meaning makes sense from there.
8. In the 1600s, there was a tradition in taverns.
9. Revelers placed spicy croutons in their drinks for added flavor.
10. Then they drank to the health of various ladies and invented the other meaning of *toast.*

Source: Dictionary of Word Origins (Arcade Publishing, 1990)

PARAGRAPH EXERCISE

Underline the subjects once and the verbs twice in the following student paragraph.

My most valuable possession at the moment is a pair of chopsticks. These chopsticks are not worth a lot of money. In fact, they are the disposable kind and still have the white paper wrapper on them. Their value lies in my memories of an evening with someone very special. It happened almost a year ago. As a favor to my friend Tressa, I agreed to a blind date with her cousin Marcus. Marcus and I met at a restaurant, ate sushi, and talked for hours. That night was the start of a wonderful relationship. On my way out of the restaurant that evening, I looked for a souvenir. There was a tall glass of take-out chopsticks by the door. I grabbed a pair and treasure it to this day.

SENTENCE WRITING

Write ten sentences about any subject—your favorite dessert, for instance. Keeping your subject matter simple in these sentence-writing exercises will make it easier to find your sentence structures later. After you have written your sentences, go back and underline your subjects once and your verbs twice.

Locating Prepositional Phrases

Prepositional phrases are among the easiest structures in English to learn. Remember that a phrase is just a group of related words (at least two) without a subject and a verb. And don't let a term like *prepositional* scare you. If you look in the middle of that long word, you'll find a familiar one—*position.* In English, we tell the *positions* of people and things in sentences using prepositional phrases.

Look at the following sentence with its prepositional phrases in parentheses:

Our field trip (to the desert) begins (at 6:00) (in the morning) (on Friday).

One phrase tells where the field trip is going (*to the desert*), and three phrases tell when the trip begins (*at 6:00, in the morning,* and *on Friday*). As you can see, prepositional phrases show the position of someone or something in space or in time.

Here is a list of some prepositions that can show positions in space:

under	across	with	against
around	by	inside	at
through	beyond	over	beneath
above	among	on	in
below	near	behind	past
between	without	from	to

Here are some prepositions that can show positions in time:

before	throughout	past	within
after	by	until	in
since	at	during	for

These lists include only individual words, *not phrases.* Remember, a preposition must be followed by an object—someone or something—to create a prepositional phrase. Notice that in the added prepositional phrases that follow, the position of the balloon in relation to the object, *the clouds,* changes completely.

The hot-air balloon floated *above the clouds.*
below the clouds.
within the clouds.
between the clouds.
past the clouds.
around the clouds.

Now notice the different positions in time:

The balloon landed *at 3:30.*
by 3:30.
past 3:30.
before the thunderstorm.
during the thunderstorm.
after the thunderstorm.

Note - A few words—such as *of, as,* and *like*—are prepositions that do not fit neatly into either the space or time category, yet they are very common prepositions (box *of candy,* note *of apology,* type *of bicycle*—act *as a substitute,* use *as an example,* testified *as an expert*—vitamins *like A, C, and E,* acts *like a child,* moves *like a snake*).

By locating prepositional phrases, you will be able to find subjects and verbs more easily. For example, you might have difficulty finding the subject and verb in a long sentence like this:

> After the rainy season, one of the windows in the attic leaked at the corners of its molding.

But if you put parentheses around all the prepositional phrases like this

> (After the rainy season), one (of the windows) (in the attic) leaked (at the corners) (of its molding).

then you have only two words left—the subject and the verb. Even in short sentences like the following, you might pick the wrong word as the subject if you don't put parentheses around the prepositional phrases first.

> Two (of the characters) lied (to each other) (throughout the play).
>
> The waves (around the ship) looked real.

Note - Don't mistake *to* plus a verb for a prepositional phrase. Special forms of verbals always start with *to,* but they are not prepositional phrases (see p. 124). For example, in the sentence "I like to run to the beach," *to run* is a verbal, not a prepositional phrase. However, *to the beach* is a prepositional phrase because it begins with a preposition (to), ends with a noun (beach), and shows position in space.

EXERCISES

Put parentheses around the prepositional phrases in the following sentences. Be sure to start with the preposition itself (*in, on, to, at, of . . .*) and include the word or words that go with it (*in the morning, on our sidewalk, to Hawaii . . .*). Then underline the sentences' subjects once and verbs twice. Remember that subjects and verbs are not found inside prepositional phrases, so if you locate the prepositional phrases *first,* the subjects and verbs will be much easier to find. Review the answers given at the back for each set of ten sentences before continuing.

Exercise 1

1. In New Zealand, Maurice Bennett is a man with a strange claim to fame.
2. During the summer of 2002, Bennett created a portrait of Elvis for the twenty-fifth anniversary of Presley's death.
3. At sixty-two square feet, Bennett's rendition of the King was unusual enough due to its size.
4. Adding to the portrait's interest, Bennett made it from 4,000 pieces of toasted bread.
5. The toast varied in color from burned black toast to warmed white toast and four other shades in between these two extremes.
6. The burned toast was perfect for Presley's black hair.
7. The lighter pieces formed the features of Elvis's face.
8. Bennett worked on his Elvis portrait for a couple of months.
9. He used a special oven, toasting nearly one hundred pieces of bread at a time.
10. Now back to his normal life, Bennett is the owner of a supermarket.

Source: Washington Post, August 15, 2002

Exercise 2

1. Most of us remember playing with Frisbees in our front yards in the early evenings and at parks or beaches on weekend afternoons.
2. Fred Morrison invented the original flat Frisbee for the Wham-O toy company in the 1950s.
3. Ed Headrick, designer of the professional Frisbee, passed away at his home in California in August of 2002.

4. Working at Wham-O in the 1960s, Headrick improved the performance of the existing Frisbee with the addition of ridges in the surface of the disc.
5. Headrick's improvements led to increased sales of his "professional model" Frisbee and to the popularity of Frisbee tournaments.
6. After Headrick's redesign, Wham-O sold 100 million of the flying discs.
7. Headrick also invented the game of disc golf.
8. Like regular golf but with discs, the game is played on specially designed disc golf courses like the first one at Oak Grove Park in California.
9. Before his death, Headrick asked for his ashes to be formed into memorial flying discs for select family and friends.
10. Donations from sales of the remaining memorial discs went toward the establishment of a museum on the history of the Frisbee and disc golf.

Source: Los Angeles Times, August 14, 2002

Exercise 3

1. My family and I live in a house at the top of a hilly neighborhood in Los Angeles.
2. On weekday mornings, nearly everyone drives down the steep winding roads to their jobs or to school.
3. In the evenings, they all come back up the hill to be with their families.
4. For the rest of the day, we see only an occasional delivery van or compact school bus.
5. But on Saturdays and Sundays, there is a different set of drivers on our roads.
6. On those two days, tourists in minivans and prospective home buyers in convertibles cram our narrow streets.
7. For this reason, most of the neighborhood residents stay at home on weekends.

8. Frequently, drivers unfamiliar with the twists and turns of the roads in this area cause accidents.
9. The expression "Sunday driver" really means something to those of us on the hill.
10. In fact, even "Saturday drivers" are a nuisance for us.

Exercise 4

1. Through NASA's space-exploration projects, we learn more about everything from our fellow planets to our sun and moon.
2. *Galileo* already discovered a layer of ice on Europa, Jupiter's moon, and in 2003 will look for signs of life beneath the ice's surface.
3. With the help of the *Hubble Space Telescope,* NASA retrieved pictures of the planet Uranus—its system of rings and its weather patterns.
4. NASA launched *Cassini* in 1997 to study Saturn, with an expected arrival time of 2004.
5. In an effort to put an American on Mars by 2020, NASA will use information from *Mars Surveyor 2001.*
6. NASA's *Pluto-Kuiper Express* will study Pluto, the most distant planet in our solar system.
7. With the *Contour Mission* in 2002, NASA hopes to learn about the origin of comets.
8. The *Terra* satellite will look at changes in Earth's weather as part of NASA's Earth Observing System.
9. The *Genesis* probe will fly around the sun and gather new information about its unique properties.
10. Finally, the mission for the *Lunar Prospector* is to discover habitable places on the moon.

Source: George, June 1999

Exercise 5

1. An engraved likeness of Pocahontas, the famous Powhatan Indian princess, is the oldest portrait on display at the National Portrait Gallery.
2. In 1607, Pocahontas—still in her early teens—single-handedly helped the British colonists in Virginia to survive.
3. Later, in 1616, Pocahontas traveled to England after her marriage to John Rolfe and after the birth of their son.
4. She visited the court of King James I and impressed the British with her knowledge of English and with her conversion to Christianity.
5. For her new first name, Pocahontas chose Rebecca.
6. During her seven-month stay in England, she became extremely ill.
7. At some point before or during her illness, Simon Van de Passe engraved her portrait on copper.
8. The portrait shows Pocahontas in a ruffled collar and ornate Anglicized clothes but with very strong Indian features.
9. Successful sales of prints from the portrait illustrate her fame abroad.
10. Pocahontas died on that trip to England at the age of twenty-two.

Source: Smithsonian, January 1999

PARAGRAPH EXERCISE

Put parentheses around the prepositional phrases in the following paragraphs from *Let's Travel in Hawaii,* a vintage tourist book published in 1960 soon after Hawaii had become a U.S. state:

In the broad blue reaches of the Pacific Ocean lies a strand of islands like small green gems strung on a wavering line. From northwest to southeast they stretch for about 1,500 miles, following the course of an ancient cleft in the ocean floor thousands of feet below.

In the warm Pacific waters, coral reefs have formed on some of the lava rock, and there is a sprinkle of small coral islets, mostly uninhabited, among the larger volcanic islands. . . . Now the fiftieth state in the Union, with a total area of 6,407 square miles, Hawaii adds a new and shining star to the flag of the United States.

SENTENCE WRITING

Write ten sentences describing your favorite place to relax—or choose any topic you like. When you go back over your sentences, put parentheses around your prepositional phrases and underline your subjects once and your verbs twice.

Understanding Dependent Clauses

All clauses contain a subject and a verb, yet there are two kinds of clauses: *independent* and *dependent.* Independent clauses have a subject and a verb and make complete statements by themselves. Dependent clauses have a subject and a verb but don't make complete statements because of the words they begin with. Here are some of the words (conjunctions) that begin dependent clauses:

after	since	where
although	so that	whereas
as	than	wherever
as if	that	whether
because	though	which
before	unless	whichever
even if	until	while
even though	what	who
ever since	whatever	whom
how	when	whose
if	whenever	why

When a clause starts with one of these dependent words, it is usually a dependent clause. To show you the difference between an independent and a dependent clause, look at this example of an independent clause:

We ate dinner together.

It has a subject (We) and a verb (ate), and it makes a complete statement. But as soon as we put one of the dependent words in front of it, the clause becomes dependent because it no longer makes a complete statement:

After we ate dinner together . . .

Although we ate dinner together . . .

As we ate dinner together . . .

Before we ate dinner together . . .

Since we ate dinner together . . .

That we ate dinner together . . .

When we ate dinner together . . .

While we ate dinner together . . .

Each of these dependent clauses leaves the reader expecting something more. Each would depend on another clause—an independent clause—to make a sentence. For the rest of this discussion, we'll place a broken line beneath dependent clauses.

After we ate dinner together, we went to the evening seminar.

We went to the evening seminar *after* we ate dinner together.

The speaker didn't know *that* we ate dinner together.

While we ate dinner together, the restaurant became crowded.

As you can see in these examples, *when a dependent clause comes before an independent clause, it is followed by a comma.* Often the comma prevents misreading, as in the following sentence:

When he returned, the DVD was on the floor.

Without a comma after *returned,* the reader would read *When he returned the DVD* before realizing that this was not what the author meant. The comma prevents misreading. Sometimes if the dependent clause is short and there is no danger of misreading, the comma can be left out, but it's safer simply to follow the rule that a dependent clause coming before an independent clause is followed by a comma. You'll learn more about the punctuation of dependent clauses on page 179, but right now just remember the previous rule.

Note that a few of the dependent words (*that, who, which, what*) can do "double duty" as both the dependent word and the subject of the dependent clause:

Thelma wrote a book *that* sold a thousand copies.

The manager saw *what* happened.

Sometimes the dependent clause is in the middle of the independent clause:

The book *that* sold a thousand copies was Thelma's.

The events *that* followed the parade delighted everyone.

The dependent clause can even be the subject of the entire sentence:

What you do also affects me.

How your project looks counts for ten percent of the grade.

Also note that sometimes the *that* of a dependent clause is omitted:

I know *that* you feel strongly about this issue.

I know you feel strongly about this issue.

Everyone received the classes *that* they wanted.

Everyone received the classes they wanted.

Of course, the word *that* doesn't always introduce a dependent clause. It may be a pronoun and serve as the subject or object of the sentence:

That was a long movie.

We knew *that* already.

That can also be an adjective, a descriptive word telling *which one:*

That movie always upsets me.

We took them to *that* park last week.

EXERCISES

Draw a broken line beneath any dependent clauses in the following sentences. Some sentences have no dependent clauses, and others have more than one. The best way to begin is to look for the dependent words (*when, since, that, because, after . . .*) and be sure they are followed by subjects and verbs. Finally, underline the subjects once and the verbs twice in both the independent and dependent clauses. Compare your underlines with those at the back of the book carefully after each set.

Exercise 1

1. The Breathalyzer is a machine that measures a person's blood alcohol level.
2. Police officers use the device when they suspect that a driver is drunk.
3. Robert F. Borkenstein was the man who invented the Breathalyzer.
4. Before Borkenstein created the portable measuring device, officers took suspects' breath samples in balloons back to a laboratory where the samples went through a series of tests, but that process had too many variables to be reliable.
5. Borkenstein's Breathalyzer solved the problem because all testing occurred at the scene.
6. The Breathalyzer was so reliable and became so feared that one man went to extremes to avoid its results.
7. While this man waited in the back of the police car, he removed his cotton underwear and ate them.
8. He hoped that the cotton cloth would soak up all the alcohol that he had in his system.
9. When the desperate man's case went to court, the judge acquitted him.
10. The judge's decision came after whole rows of spectators in the court laughed so hard and for so long that they could not stop.

Source: Los Angeles Times, August 18, 2002

Exercise 2

1. The world is a miserable place when you have an upset stomach.
2. Whether you get carsick, airsick, or seasick, you probably welcome any advice that comes your way.
3. Did you know that motion sickness is most common when people are between the ages of seven and twelve?
4. Motion sickness happens to some people whenever the brain receives mixed messages.
5. If the inner ear feels movement but the eyes report that there is no movement, the brain gets confused.
6. This confusion results in dizziness and the feeling that all is not well.
7. Experts suggest that you sleep well and eat lightly before you travel if you want to avoid motion sickness.
8. When you travel by car, you should sit in the middle of the back seat and look straight out the windshield.
9. Likewise, the best seat on an airplane or a boat is one that allows a view of the clouds or horizon so that your ears and eyes give your brain the same messages.
10. Whenever the queasy feeling comes in spite of your best efforts, it may dissipate if you sip small amounts of water.

Source: Current Health, April/May 2002

Exercise 3

1. Jo Ann Altsman is a woman who is lucky to be alive.
2. When she had a second heart attack, no other person was there to help her.
3. Because she was in such pain, she couldn't move or easily call for help.

4. She did have two pets that she looked to as she lay on the floor of her home in what she considered her final moments.
5. She wondered if her dog might help, but he only barked at her.
6. Then Altsman's 150-pound potbellied pig LuLu took action when it became obvious that no one else could help her master.
7. The pig somehow made it through the little door that allows smaller pets to go in and out.
8. As she went through the opening, LuLu suffered big scratches on her tummy, but she persisted.
9. While she whined loudly for help, LuLu walked to the nearest highway and waited for a car.
10. The man who stopped followed LuLu to Altsman's house, and he called for an ambulance.

Source: People, November 2, 1998

Exercise 4

1. On June 8, 1924, two British men, George Mallory and Andrew Irvine, disappeared as they climbed to the top of Mount Everest.
2. When a reporter earlier asked Mallory why he climbed Everest, his response became legendary.
3. "Because it is there," Mallory replied.
4. No living person knows whether the two men reached the summit of Everest before they died.
5. Nine years after Mallory and Irvine disappeared, English climbers found Irvine's ice ax.
6. But nothing else of Mallory's or Irvine's was found until a Chinese climber spotted their bodies in 1975.
7. He kept the news of his sighting secret for several years but finally told a fellow climber on the day before he died himself in an avalanche on Everest.

8. In May 1999, a team of mountaineers searched the area where the Chinese man reported seeing something, and they found George Mallory's frozen body still intact after seventy-five years.
9. After they took DNA samples for identification, the mountaineers buried the famous climber on the mountainside where he fell.
10. Mallory and Irvine were the first climbers to try to get to the top of Everest, and the question remains whether they were on their way up or on their way down when they met their fate.

Source: Newsweek, May 17, 1999

Exercise 5

1. I read an article that described the history of all the presidents' dogs.
2. Our first president, George Washington, cared so much about dogs that he bred them; Washington even interrupted a battle to return a dog that belonged to a British general.
3. Abraham Lincoln, whose dog's name was actually Fido, left his loyal pet in Illinois after the Lincolns moved to the White House.
4. Teddy Roosevelt had lots of dogs but met and adopted Skip, the one that he loved best, as the little terrier held a bear at bay in the Grand Canyon.
5. FDR's pooch was always with him; he was a black Scottie named Fala, and they say that Roosevelt was so devoted to this pet that he made a U.S. Navy ship return to the Aleutians to pick Fala up after the diplomatic party accidentally left the dog behind.
6. Warren G. Harding's Laddie Boy was the most pampered of the presidential dogs since the Hardings gave him birthday parties and ordered a specially made chair for Laddie Boy to sit in during presidential meetings.
7. Soviet leader Nikita Khrushchev brought with him Pushinka, a dog that he gave to John F. Kennedy's daughter Caroline.

8. At a filling station in Texas, Lyndon Johnson's daughter Luci found a little white dog, Yuki, whom President Johnson loved to have howling contests with in the Oval Office.
9. Of course, Nixon had his famous Checkers, and George Bush Sr. had a spaniel named Millie, who wrote her own best-selling book with the help of Barbara Bush.
10. And just when it seemed that all presidents prefer dogs, Bill Clinton arrived with Socks, a distinctively marked black-and-white cat.

Source: Smithsonian, June 1997

PARAGRAPH EXERCISE

Underline the subjects once, the verbs twice, and put a broken line under the dependent clauses in these paragraphs from *The Look-It-Up Book of Stars and Planets.*

Years and Months

As the earth orbits the sun, the seasons change. They change from winter to spring to summer and back to winter. The changing seasons were probably the first calendar that people used. The four seasons gave them a length of time that we call a year. One year is the time that it takes the earth to journey once around the sun.

While it orbits the sun, the earth also spins. During one orbit, the earth spins about 365 1/4 times. To put it another way, there are about 365 1/4 days in a year. A fraction of a day is awkward. So we do not use it. In a calendar, there are three years of 365 days. Then there is leap year—a year with 366 days. The extra day is the result of the four fractions.

The seasons were one early calendar. The phases of the moon were another. People saw that the face of the moon changed. It took about 30 days for the moon to go from full moon to full moon. This meant that people could measure time by the moon. They found that during the four seasons, the moon went through its phases 12 times. That is how the year came to be divided into 12 months.

Correcting Fragments

Sometimes a group of words looks like a sentence—with a capital letter at the beginning and a period at the end—but it may be missing a subject, a verb, or both. Such incomplete sentence structures are called *fragments.* Here are a few examples:

> Just ran around with his arms in the air. (*Who* did? There is no subject.)
>
> Paul and his sister with the twins. (*Did* what? There is no verb.)
>
> Nothing to do at night. (This fragment is missing a subject and a real verb. *To do* is a verbal, see p. 124.)

To change these fragments into sentences, we must make sure each has a subject and a real verb:

> The lottery winner just ran around with his arms in the air. (We added a subject.)
>
> Paul and his sister with the twins arrived. (We added a verb.)
>
> The jurors had nothing to do at night. (We added a subject and a real verb.)

Sometimes we can simply attach such a fragment to the previous sentence.

> I want a fulfilling job. A teaching position, for example.
>
> I want a fulfilling job—a teaching position, for example.

Or we can add a subject or a verb to the fragment and make it a complete sentence.

> I want a fulfilling job. A teaching position is one example.

Phrases

By definition, phrases are word groups without subjects and verbs, so whenever a phrase is punctuated as a sentence, it is a fragment. Look at this example of a sentence followed by a phrase fragment beginning with *hoping* (see p. 124 for more about verbal phrases):

> Actors waited outside the director's office. Hoping for a chance at an audition.

We can correct this fragment by attaching it to the previous sentence.

> Actors waited outside the director's office, hoping for a chance at an audition.

Or we can change it to include a subject and a real verb.

> Actors waited outside the director's office. They hoped for a chance at an audition.

Here's another example of a sentence followed by a phrase fragment:

> Philosophy classes are difficult. When taught by great thinkers.

Here the two have been combined into one complete sentence:

> Philosophy classes taught by great thinkers are difficult.

Or a better revision might be

> Philosophy classes are difficult when taught by great thinkers.

Sometimes, prepositional phrases are also incorrectly punctuated as sentences. Here a prepositional phrase follows a sentence, but the word group is a fragment—it has no subject and verb of its own. Therefore, it needs to be corrected.

> I live a simple life. With my family on our farm in central California.

Here is one possible correction:

> I live a simple life with my family on our farm in central California.

Or it could be corrected this way:

> My family and I live a simple life on our farm in central California.

Dependent Clauses

Dependent clauses punctuated as sentences are still another kind of fragment. A sentence needs a subject, a verb, *and* a complete thought. As discussed in the previous section, a dependent clause has a subject and a verb, but it begins with a word that makes its meaning incomplete, such as *after, while, because, since, although, when, if, where, who, which,* and *that.* (See p. 69 for a longer list of these conjunctions.) To correct such fragments, we need to eliminate the word that makes the clause dependent *or* add an independent clause.

Fragment

> *While* some of us wrote in our journals.

Corrected

Some of us wrote in our journals.

or

While some of us wrote in our journals, the fire alarm rang.

Fragment

Which kept me from finishing my journal entry.

Corrected

The fire alarm kept me from finishing my journal entry.

or

We responded to the fire alarm, *which* kept me from finishing my journal entry.

Are fragments ever permissible? Professional writers sometimes use fragments in advertising and other kinds of writing. But professional writers use these fragments intentionally, not in error. Until you're an experienced writer, it's best to write in complete sentences. Especially in college writing, you should avoid using fragments.

EXERCISES

Some—but not all—of the following word groups are sentences. The sentences include subjects and verbs and make complete statements. Write the word "sentence" next to each of the sentences. Any word groups that do *not* include subjects and verbs and make complete statements are fragments. Write the word "fragment" next to each of these incomplete sentence structures. Then change the fragments into sentences by ensuring that each has a subject and a real verb and makes a complete statement.

Exercise 1

1. Most people have at least one couch in their home.
2. Old-fashioned or modern, leather or fabric, comfortable or uncomfortable.
3. Whatever shape a couch is in.

4. There are always slipcovers to cover an ugly couch.
5. And some couches really need slipcovers.
6. A contest by the makers of Sure Fit slipcovers.
7. People submit photos of their couches to Sure Fit headquarters in New York.
8. Hoping to win the company's yearly "Ugly Couch" contest.
9. A $10,000 living room makeover to the person with the ugliest couch.
10. Visitors to the company's website vote for one of ten semi-finalists to receive the big prize.

Source: http://www.surefit.com

Exercise 2

1. One of the amazing abilities of cats.
2. To survive falling from tall trees or the windows, roofs, and balconies of high buildings.
3. Strangely, cats often have fewer injuries when they fall farther.
4. From a height of one or two stories, walking away without injuries.
5. The trouble comes when cats fall between three and six stories.
6. Scientists discovering that at seven stories and above the results are the same as at the lower levels.
7. Meaning that the timing of a cat's fall determines the outcome.
8. Cats' inner ears help them turn themselves right side up while falling.
9. Extremely flexible spines and leg positions too.
10. Some part of the process must be disrupted at the medium heights.

Source: Discover, September 2002

Exercise 3

Correct each phrase fragment by changing or adding words or by attaching the phrase to the complete sentence nearby.

1. Finding a parking space on the first day of classes seems impossible. Driving endlessly around campus and looking for an empty spot.
2. With the hope that the situation will improve. I always spend forty dollars for a parking permit.
3. My old car's engine doesn't like the long periods of idling. Stalling a lot and not starting up again easily.
4. In order to get a space close to my first class. I always follow anyone walking through the parking lot closest to the science building.
5. I am usually disappointed by this method, however. Most people just walking through the parking lot to get to farther lots or to the bus stop.
6. I was really lucky on the first day of classes two semesters ago. Driving right into a spot vacated by a student from an earlier class.
7. Maybe I should get up before dawn myself. A foolproof way to secure a perfect parking place.
8. Every morning, I see these early birds in their cars with their seats back. Sleeping there for hours before class but in a great spot.
9. I don't think I can solve the problem this way. Finding it hard to get out of bed in the dark.
10. Due to the rise in college populations. Campus parking problems will most likely only get worse.

Exercise 4

Correct each dependent clause fragment by eliminating its dependent word or by attaching the dependent clause to the independent clause before or after it.

1. We were writing our in-class essays. When suddenly the emergency bell rang.
2. Everyone in the class looked at each other first and then at the teacher. Who told us to gather up our things and follow him outside.
3. The series of short rings continued. As we left the room and noisily walked out into the parking lot beside the main building.

4. The sunlight was very warm and bright compared to the classroom's fluorescent lights. Which always make everything look more clinical than natural.
5. As we stood in a large group with students and teachers from other classes. We wondered about the reason for the alarm.
6. I have never heard an emergency alarm. That was anything but a planned drill.
7. Without the danger of injury, a party atmosphere quickly developed. Since we all got a break from our responsibilities.
8. I've noticed that the teachers seem the most at ease during these situations. Because they don't have to be in control.
9. After we students and the teachers chatted for ten minutes or so. The final bell rang to signal the end of the drill.
10. When we sat down at our desks again. The teacher asked us to continue writing our essays until the end of the hour.

Exercise 5

All of the following word groups contain subjects and verbs and are therefore clauses. If the clause *does not* begin with a dependent word (a conjunction such as *when, while, after, because, since, as, where, if, who, which,* or *that*), put a period after it. If the clause *does* begin with a dependent word (making it a dependent clause fragment), add an independent clause or revise the dependent clause to make it a sentence. These ten clauses are not about the same topic.

1. Whenever I see a seagull up close
2. After lunch on Tuesdays, our club meets in the gym
3. After we turned in our research assignments
4. Traveling overseas requires a lot of planning
5. The pizza arrived within thirty minutes of our call
6. That was the hardest question on the test
7. That people often stretch the truth
8. Briefly discuss this topic with the person next to you
9. Even though "wet paint" signs were still on the walls

10. How a series of paragraphs becomes an essay

PROOFREADING EXERCISE

Find and correct the five fragments in the following paragraph.

When a ten-year-old girl named Stephanie Taylor heard about the shooting death of a police dog in New Jersey. She decided to do something to protect the dogs. Who worked for the police in Oceanside, California. Where Stephanie lived with her family. Raising enough money to buy bulletproof vests for all of Oceanside PD's K-9 (canine) officers. Stephanie was glad. Knowing that the dogs who served and protected her neighborhood were being protected themselves.

Source: People, August 16, 1999

SENTENCE WRITING

Write ten fragments and then revise them so that they are complete sentences. Or exchange papers with another student and turn your classmate's ten fragments into sentences.

Correcting Run-on Sentences

Any word group having a subject and a verb is a clause. As we have seen, the clause may be independent (making a complete statement and able to stand alone as a sentence), or it may be dependent (beginning with a dependent word and unable to stand alone as a sentence). When two *independent* clauses are written together without proper punctuation between them, the result is called a *run-on sentence.* Here are some examples.

Classical music is soothing I listen to it in the evenings.

I love the sound of piano therefore, Chopin is one of my favorites.

Run-on sentences can be corrected in one of four ways:

1. **Make the two independent clauses into two sentences.**

Classical music is soothing. I listen to it in the evenings.

I love the sound of piano. Therefore, Chopin is one of my favorites.

2. **Connect the two independent clauses with a semicolon.**

Classical music is soothing; I listen to it in the evenings.

I love the sound of piano; therefore, Chopin is one of my favorites.

When a connecting word (transition) such as

also	however	otherwise
consequently	likewise	then
finally	moreover	therefore
furthermore	nevertheless	thus

is used to join two independent clauses, the semicolon comes before the connecting word, and a comma usually comes after it.

Mobile phones are convenient; however, they are very expensive.

Earthquakes scare me; therefore, I don't live in Los Angeles.

Yasmin traveled to London; then she took the "Chunnel" to Paris.

The college recently built a large new library; thus we have more quiet study areas.

Note - The use of the comma after the connecting word depends on how long the connecting word is. If it is only a short word, like *then* or *thus,* the comma is not necessary.

3. **Connect the two independent clauses with a comma and one of the following seven words (the first letters of which create the word *fanboys*): *for, and, nor, but, or, yet, so.***

Classical music is soothing, *so* I listen to it in the evenings.

Chopin is one of my favorites, *for* I love the sound of piano.

Each of the *fanboys* has its own meaning (for example, *so* means "as a result," and *for* means "because").

Swans are beautiful birds, *and* they mate for life.

Students may register for classes by phone, *or* they may do so in person.

I applied for financial aid, *but* I was still working at the time.

Brian doesn't know how to use a computer, *nor* does he plan to learn.

Before you put a comma before a *fanboys,* be sure there are two independent clauses. Note that the first sentence that follows has two independent clauses. However, the second sentence contains one independent clause with two verbs and therefore needs no comma.

The snow began falling at dusk, and it continued to fall through the night.

The snow began falling at dusk and continued to fall through the night.

4. Make one of the clauses dependent by adding a dependent word (such as *since, when, as, after, while,* or *because*—see p. 69 for a longer list of these conjunctions).

Since classical music is soothing, I listen to it in the evenings.

Chopin is one of my favorites *because* I love the sound of piano.

Learn these ways to join two clauses, and you'll avoid run-on sentences.

Ways to Correct Run-on Sentences

They were learning a new song. They needed to practice. (two sentences)

They were learning a new song; they needed to practice. (semicolon)

They were learning a new song; therefore, they needed to practice. (semicolon + transition)

They were learning a new song, so they needed to practice. (comma + *fanboys*)

Because they were learning a new song, they needed to practice. (dependent clause first)

They needed to practice because they were learning a new song. (dependent clause last)

EXERCISES

Exercises 1 and 2

CORRECTING RUN-ONS WITH PUNCTUATION

Most—but not all—of the following sentences are run-ons. If the sentence has two independent clauses, separate them with correct punctuation. For the first two exercises, *don't create any dependent clauses;* use only a period, a semicolon, or a comma to separate the two independent clauses. Remember to insert a comma only when the words *for, and, nor, but, or, yet,* or *so* are used to join two independent clauses.

Exercise 1

1. Mary Mallon is a famous name in American history but she is not famous for something good.
2. Most people know Mary Mallon by another name and that is "Typhoid Mary."
3. Mallon lived during the late nineteenth and early twentieth centuries.
4. At that time, there was little knowledge about disease carriers.
5. Mary Mallon was the first famous case of a healthy carrier of disease but she never believed the accusations against her.
6. Mallon, an Irish immigrant, was a cook she was also an infectious carrier of typhoid.
7. By the time the authorities discovered Mallon's problem, she had made many people ill a few of her "victims" actually died from the disease.
8. A health specialist approached Mallon and asked her for a blood sample she was outraged and attacked him with a long cooking fork.
9. Eventually the authorities dragged Mallon into a hospital for testing but she fought them hysterically the entire time.
10. The lab tests proved Mallon's infectious status and health officials forced Mary Mallon to live on an island by herself for twenty-six years.

Sources: Los Angeles Times, September 2, 2002; and *Long Island: Our History Home Page (www.lihistory.com)*

Exercise 2

1. Frank Epperson invented something delicious and refreshing and it comes on a stick.
2. In 1905, Epperson was an eleven-year-old boy he lived in San Francisco.
3. On the porch outside his house, he was mixing a fruity drink with a stick and forgot to put his drink away before going to bed.
4. The drink sat outside all night with the stick still in it.
5. There was a record-breaking cold snap that evening and the drink froze.
6. In the morning, Frank Epperson ate his frozen juice creation it made a big impression.
7. Epperson grew up and kept making his frozen "Epsicles" they came in seven varieties.
8. Eighteen years after that cold night, Epperson patented his invention but with a different name.
9. Epperson's kids loved their dad's treat and they always called them "pop's sicles."
10. So Popsicles were born and people have loved them ever since.

Source: Biography Magazine, July 1999

Exercises 3 and 4

CORRECTING RUN-ONS WITH DEPENDENT CLAUSES

Most—but not all—of the following sentences are run-ons. Correct any run-on sentences by making one or more of the clauses *dependent.* You may rephrase the clauses, but be sure to use dependent words (such as *since, when, as, after, while, because* or the other conjunctions listed on p. 69) to begin dependent clauses. In some sentences, you will want to put the dependent clauses first; in others, you may want to put them last (or in the middle of the sentence). Since various words can be used to start dependent clauses, your answers may differ from those suggested at the back of the book.

Exercise 3

1. I went to an optometrist for the first time last Tuesday I discovered that I need glasses.
2. I've noticed some blurriness when I read but I thought my eyes were just tired.
3. To my surprise, I need bifocals I consider bifocals something that only old people wear.
4. My insurance policy covers only the lenses I have to pay for the frames myself.
5. Now I have a dilemma I need bifocals, but I don't have the money for good-looking frames.
6. People will start calling me "Ma'am" soon I can't afford "cool" frames.
7. My mother gets a good deal at the glasses place in the mall I definitely don't want to go there.
8. My mom's glasses make her look like an old-time game-show host.
9. Her wire frames start above her eyebrows and end in the middle of her cheeks they are way too big.
10. I want glasses with small frames in a great color that way I can still look my age.

Exercise 4

1. I've been learning about sleep in my psychology class I now know a lot more about it.
2. Sleep has five stages we usually go through all these stages many times during the night.
3. The first stage of sleep begins our muscles relax and mental activity slows down.
4. During stage one, we are still slightly awake.
5. Stage two takes us deeper than stage one we are no longer aware of our surroundings.

6. We spend about half our sleeping time in the second stage.
7. Next is stage three in it we become more and more relaxed and are very hard to awaken.
8. Stage four is the deepest in this stage we don't even hear loud noises.
9. The fifth stage of sleep is called REM (rapid eye movement) sleep our eyes move back and forth quickly behind our eyelids.
10. REM sleep is only about as deep as stage two we do all our dreaming during the REM stage.

Exercise 5

Correct the following run-on sentences using any of the methods studied in this section: adding a period, a semicolon, a semicolon + a transition word, a comma + a *fanboys,* or using dependent words to create dependent clauses.

1. In 1999, the BBC released its documentary series called *The Life of Birds* Sir David Attenborough was the host.
2. The series took nearly three years to complete the crew filmed in more than forty countries they shot about two hundred miles of film.
3. The BBC spent fifteen million dollars making *The Life of Birds* the cost included Attenborough's traveling the equivalent of ten times around the world.
4. The BBC takes such shows very seriously this one about birds comes after the BBC's amazing documentary called *The Private Life of Plants.*
5. For the plant series, BBC filmmakers even invented new ways to film plants and record the sounds they make a lot of the filming had to take place under artificial conditions however, for the bird series, the BBC wanted a more realistic feeling.
6. All of the filming was done in the birds' own habitats it showed their natural behavior some of this behavior had never been seen or filmed before.
7. To capture these rare moments, filmmakers had to live with birds in the wild it was not a very safe environment at times.

8. A tree full of BBC filmmakers was struck by lightning in an Amazon rainforest they were covered with insects in Jamaica and Attenborough had to speak to the camera in total darkness in a cave in Venezuela.
9. Makers of the series were especially proud of their bird of paradise footage they shot it in New Guinea.
10. It turned out to be one of their biggest disappointments the priceless film was erased by an especially powerful X-ray machine at the airport.

Source: Christian Science Monitor, August 3, 1999

REVIEW OF FRAGMENTS AND RUN-ON SENTENCES

If you remember that all clauses include a subject and a verb, but only independent clauses can be punctuated as sentences (since only they can stand alone), then you will avoid fragments in your writing. And if you memorize these six rules for the punctuation of clauses, you will be able to avoid most punctuation errors.

Punctuating Clauses

I am a student. I am still learning.	(two sentences)
I am a student; I am still learning.	(two independent clauses)
I am a student; therefore, I am still learning.	(two independent clauses connected by a word such as *also, consequently, finally, furthermore, however, likewise, moreover, nevertheless, otherwise, then, therefore, thus*)
I am a student, so I am still learning.	(two independent clauses connected by *for, and, nor, but, or, yet, so*)
Because I am a student, I am still learning.	(dependent clause at beginning of sentence)
I am still learning because I am a student.	(dependent clause at end of sentence) The dependent words are *after, although, as, as if, because, before, even if, even though, ever since, how, if, in order that, since, so that, than, that though, unless, until, what, whatever, when, whenever, where, whereas, wherever, whether, which, whichever, while, who, whom, whose, why.*

It is essential that you learn the italicized words in the previous table—which ones come between independent clauses and which ones introduce dependent clauses.

PROOFREADING EXERCISE

Rewrite the following paragraph, making the necessary changes so there will be no fragments or run-on sentences.

With all of the attention on cleanliness lately in advertising for soaps and household cleaning products. People are surprised to hear that we may be too clean for our own good. This phenomenon is called the "hygiene hypothesis" and recent studies support its validity. For instance, one study showing the benefit on children of living with two or more pets. Babies may grow up with healthier immune systems and be less allergic if they live with a dog and a cat or two dogs or two cats. The old thinking was that young children would become more allergic living with many pets but they don't. Somehow the exposure to pets and all their "dirty" habits gives youngsters much-needed defenses. Sometimes as much as a seventy-five percent lower allergy risk, according to this study.

Source: Los Angeles Times, September 2, 2002

SENTENCE WRITING

Write a sample sentence of your own to demonstrate each of the six ways a writer can use to punctuate two clauses. You may model your sentences on the examples used in the preceding review chart.

Identifying Verb Phrases

Sometimes a verb is one word, but often the whole verb includes more than one word. These are called verb phrases. Look at several of the many forms of the verb *speak,* for example. Most of them are verb phrases, made up of the main verb *(speak)* and one or more helping verbs.

speak	is speaking	had been speaking
speaks	am speaking	will have been speaking
spoke	are speaking	is spoken
will speak	was speaking	was spoken
has spoken	were speaking	will be spoken
have spoken	will be speaking	can speak
had spoken	has been speaking	must speak
will have spoken	have been speaking	should have spoken

Note that words like the following are never verbs even though they may be near a verb or in the middle of a verb phrase:

already	finally	now	probably
also	just	often	really
always	never	only	sometimes
ever	not	possibly	usually

Jason has *never* spoken to his instructor before. She *always* talks with other students.

Two verb forms—*speaking* and *to speak*—look like verbs, but neither can ever be the verb of a sentence. No *ing* word by itself can ever be the verb of a sentence; it must be helped by another verb in a verb phrase. (See the discussion of verbal phrases on p. 124.)

Jeanine speaking French. (not a sentence because there is no complete verb phrase)

Jeanine is speaking French. (a sentence with a verb phrase)

And no verb with *to* in front of it can ever be the verb of a sentence.

Ted to speak in front of groups. (not a sentence because there is no real verb)

Ted hates to speak in front of groups. (a sentence with *hates* as the verb)

These two forms, *speaking* and *to speak* may be used as subjects, or they may have other uses in the sentence.

adj

Speaking on stage is scary. To speak on stage is scary. Ted had a *speaking* part in that play.

EXERCISES

Underline the subjects once and the verbs or verb phrases twice in the following sentences. It's a good idea to put parentheses around prepositional phrases first. (See p. 62 if you need help in locating prepositional phrases.) The sentences may contain independent *and* dependent clauses, so there could be several verbs and verb phrases. (Remember that *ing* verbs alone and the *to* ____ forms of verbs are never real verbs in sentences. We will learn more about them on p. 124.)

Exercise 1

1. Kris Kliszewicz, a successful businessman in England, has been raising money and interest around the world for a pet project.
2. Kliszewicz wants to build a theme park which will allow people to immerse themselves for a day in the life and times of Shakespeare.
3. Kliszewicz is planning to call the new history-based theme park "Shakespeare's World."
4. He has decided on the perfect location for the first of these parks—on the outskirts of Shakespeare's hometown, Stratford-upon-Avon.
5. At Shakespeare's World, troupes of roaming actors will perform scenes from Shakespeare's plays.
6. According to Kliszewicz, visitors will see the sights and hear the sounds that Shakespeare saw and heard.
7. There will be cobblestoned streets complete with bakeries and butcheries, fields full of animals and farming peasants, and tradespeople who will demonstrate Tudor crafts.
8. Some Shakespeare scholars are not convinced that a Shakespeare theme park is a good idea.

9. But Kliszewicz believes that people might enjoy learning more about Shakespeare without the purely academic treatment that he is given in classrooms.
10. The idea of Shakespeare's World is also getting some attention in China, Russia, and America, which Kliszewicz plans to make future sites for Shakespeare's World.

Source: London Theatre News, September 8, 2002

Exercise 2

1. Loyal viewers have been devoted to the television series *Star Trek* since its first episode aired in September of 1966.
2. Until recently, no one could have imagined the amount of money that fans would pay for memorabilia from the original series and beyond.
3. In June of 2002, an auction was held for prime pieces of the show's sets, costumes, and documents.
4. Just one memo from Leonard Nimoy to Gene Roddenberry about the portrayal of Spock fetched $9,775 even though the pre-auction estimate was only $400–$600.
5. A command tunic that was worn by the character of Sulu in the first season sold for $16,100.
6. The highest bid of all went to Captain James T. Kirk's command chair and platform that was featured in every episode of the original *Star Trek* series.
7. Estimates of the chair's worth before the auction ranged from $100,000 to $150,000.
8. By the time the auction ended, Kirk's command chair had become the highest-priced object in the history of television.
9. To everyone's surprise, the winning bid for the chair was a phenomenal $304,750.

10. Even the control panel from the bridge of the *U.S.S. Enterprise* sold for over $40,000.

Sources: Antiques & Collecting Magazine, August 2002; and *www.profilesinhistory.com*

Exercise 3

1. I have always wondered how an Etch A Sketch works.
2. This flat TV-shaped toy has been popular since it first arrived in the 1960s.
3. Now I have learned the secrets inside this popular toy.
4. An Etch A Sketch is filled with a combination of metal powder and tiny plastic particles.
5. This mixture clings to the inside of the Etch A Sketch screen.
6. When the pointer that is connected to the two knobs moves, the tip of it "draws" lines in the powder on the back of the screen.
7. The powder at the bottom of the Etch A Sketch does not fill in these lines because it is too far away.
8. But if the Etch A Sketch is turned upside down, the powder clings to the whole underside surface of the screen and "erases" the image again.
9. Although the basic Etch A Sketch has not changed since I was a kid, it now comes in several different sizes.
10. Best of all, these great drawing devices have never needed batteries, and I hope that they never will.

Exercise 4

1. During my last semester of high school, our English teacher assigned a special paper.
2. He said that he was becoming depressed by all the bad news out there, so each of us was assigned to find a piece of good news and write a short research paper about it.

3. I must admit that I had no idea how hard that assignment would be.
4. Finally, I found an article while I was reading my favorite magazine.
5. The title of the article was a pun; it was called "Grin Reaper."
6. I knew instantly that it must be just the kind of news my teacher wanted.
7. The article explained that one woman, Pam Johnson, had started a club that she named The Secret Society of Happy People.
8. She had even chosen August 8 as "Admit You're Happy Day" and had already convinced more than fifteen state governors to recognize the holiday.
9. The club and the holiday were created to support people who are happy so that the unhappy, negative people around will not bring the happy people down.
10. As I was writing my essay, I visited the Society of Happy People web site and, for extra credit, signed my teacher up for their newsletter.

Source: People, August 30, 1999; and *www.sohp.com*

Exercise 5

1. Most people do not connect bar codes and cockroaches in their minds.
2. We do expect to see bar codes on products in supermarkets and shopping malls.
3. And we might not be surprised to see a cockroach by a trash can behind the supermarket or shopping mall.
4. But we would definitely look twice if we saw a cockroach with a bar code on its back.
5. In 1999, however, that is just what exterminator Bruce Tennenbaum wanted everyone to do.
6. Tennenbaum attached bar codes to one hundred roaches and released them in Tucson, Arizona, as a public-awareness campaign.
7. When people found a bar-coded bug, they could return it for a hundred-dollar prize.

8. One of the roaches was tagged with a unique bar code that was worth fifty thousand dollars to any lucky person who found it.
9. Many of the citizens of Tucson were searching for these "prizes," and some of the tagged roaches were found.
10. But Tennenbaum should have put a tracking device on the fifty-thousand-dollar bug because it was never seen again.

Source: Today's Homeowner, May 1999

REVIEW EXERCISE

To practice finding all of the sentence structures we have studied so far, mark the following paragraph from the book *Charlie Brown's 'Cyclopedia, Volume 1,* based on the Charles M. Schulz characters. First, put parentheses around prepositional phrases; then underline subjects once and verbs or verb phrases twice. Finally, put a broken line beneath dependent clauses. Begin by marking the first sentence; then check your answers at the back of the book before going on to the next sentence.

Why Do You Get "Goose Pimples"?

"Goose pimples" are tiny bumps that sometimes come out on your skin when you are cold or frightened. If you look closely at the bumps, you will see a hair in the middle of each one. A tiny muscle is attached to each hair inside your skin. When you get scared or chilled, each of these muscles tightens up and gets short. The muscles pull the hairs and make them stand straight up. The skin around each hair is pulled up, too. The result is little bumps. We call these bumps goose pimples because they look just like the bumps on the skin of a plucked goose!

Using Standard English Verbs

The next two discussions are for those who need to practice using Standard English verbs. Many of us grew up doing more speaking than writing. But in college and in the business and professional world, the use of Standard Written English is essential.

The following charts show the forms of four verbs as they are used in Standard Written English. These forms might differ from the way you use these verbs when you speak. Memorize the Standard English forms of these important verbs. The first verb (*talk*) is one of the regular verbs (verbs that all end the same way according to a pattern); most verbs in English are regular. The other three verbs charted here (*have, be,* and *do*) are irregular and are important because they are used not only as main verbs but also as helping verbs in verb phrases.

Don't go on to the exercises until you have memorized the forms of these Standard English verbs.

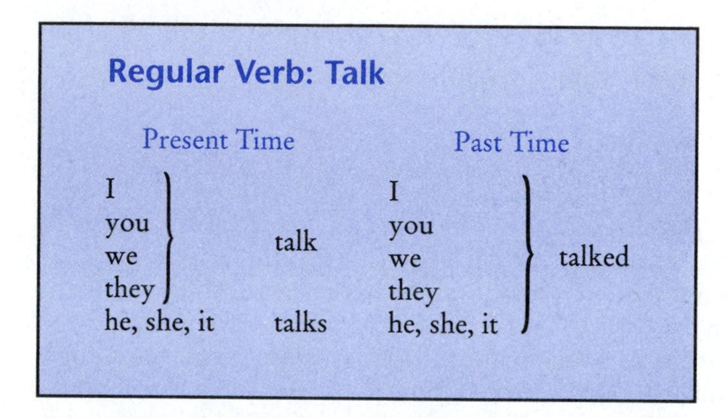

Regular Verb: Talk

Present Time		Past Time	
I, you, we, they	talk	I, you, we, they, he, she, it	talked
he, she, it	talks		

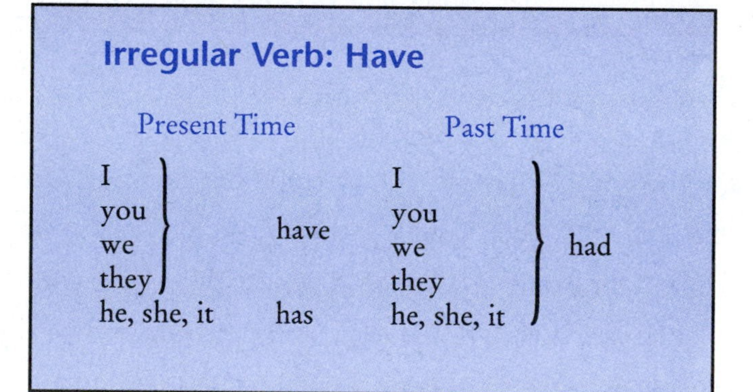

Irregular Verb: Have

Present Time		Past Time	
I, you, we, they	have	I, you, we, they, he, she, it	had
he, she, it	has		

Irregular Verb: Be

Present Time		Past Time	
I	am	I	was
you, we, they	are	you, we, they	were
he, she, it	is	he, she, it	was

Irregular Verb: Do

Present Time		Past Time	
I you we they	do	I you we they he, she, it	did
he, she, it	does		

Sometimes you may have difficulty with the correct endings of verbs because you don't hear the words correctly. Note carefully the *s* sound and the *ed* sound at the end of words. Occasionally, the *ed* is not clearly pronounced, as in *They tried to help,* but most of the time you can hear it if you listen.

Read the following sentences aloud, making sure that you say every sound.

1. He seems satisfied with his new job.
2. She likes saving money for the future.
3. It takes strength of character to control spending.
4. Todd makes salad for every potluck he attends.
5. I used to know all their names.
6. They supposed that they were right.
7. He recognized the suspect and excused himself from the jury.
8. Shao Ming sponsored Dorothy in the school's charity event.

Now read some other sentences aloud from this text, making sure that you say all of the *s*'s and *ed*'s. Reading aloud and listening to others will help you use the correct verb endings automatically.

EXERCISES

In these pairs of sentences, use the *present* form of the verb in the first sentence and the *past* form in the second. All the verbs follow the pattern of the regular verb *talk* except the irregular verbs *have, be,* and *do.* Keep referring to the tables if you're not sure which form to use. Check your answers in the back of the book after each set.

Exercise 1

1. (walk) She _____ people's dogs. She _____ in a marathon last year.
2. (learn) I _____ new languages easily. I _____ Italian in high school.
3. (be) They _____ now team captains. They _____ not happy as teammates.
4. (have) He _____ a temporary crown on his tooth. He _____ a terrible toothache yesterday.
5. (do) We still _____ a lot of gardening for our parents. We even _____ some gardening for our neighbors before.
6. (need) My teenage daughter _____ so many school supplies. She never _____ that many in elementary school.
7. (have) Vera upgraded her computer; now it _____ a DVD player. It only _____ a CD player before.
8. (be) I _____ the manager of a coffee bar. I _____ a waiter before that.
9. (study) She _____ too much. Last week, she _____ for a total of sixty hours.
10. (be) He _____ finally the owner of a credit card. He _____ not qualified to have one before.

Exercise 2

1. (be) They _____ in college this semester. They _____ high school seniors last year.
2. (do) He _____ his best writing at night. He _____ not do well on the first in-class essay.
3. (have) She _____ two weeks left to write her transfer application letter. She originally _____ two months, but she has been putting it off.

4. (open) He _____ a new restaurant every year. He even _____ one in my neighborhood recently.

5. (have) I always _____ fun with my friend Norman. I _____ a great time in Las Vegas with him over spring break.

6. (count) She _____ boxes at the factory part-time. Yesterday she _____ boxes for six hours straight.

7. (be) Many of us _____ left-handed. We _____ unsure at first which hand to use when we played tennis.

8. (do) They _____ everything to make their grandmother's life easier. They _____ her shopping and her laundry yesterday.

9. (look) You _____ like an adult now. You _____ like a kid when your hair was longer.

10. (be) At the moment, she _____ the fastest cashier in the store. She _____ the second-fastest cashier when Carl still worked there.

Underline the Standard English verb forms. All the verbs follow the pattern of the regular verb *talk* except the three irregular verbs *have, be,* and *do.* Keep referring to the tables if you are not sure which form to use.

Exercise 3

1. I (do, does) an exercise routine every morning so that I (don't, doesn't) get out of shape again.
2. A couple of months ago, I (have, had) a bad experience after I (decide, decided) to join some friends for basketball.
3. I (was, were) on my best friend Ana's team, but I (play, played) really badly.
4. Ana (talk, talked) to me after the game.
5. She (ask, asked) me why I (was, were) so slow on the court.
6. I (was, were) really embarrassed.

7. Ana and I (was, were) in high school together, and we (was, were) even in the same P.E. class.
8. We both (enjoy, enjoyed) the track exercises the most and (like, liked) to challenge each other's stamina.
9. Then, after high school, I (start, started) my job as a clerk in an insurance office and (stop, stopped) doing any exercising.
10. Now that I (am, is) back to a good routine, I (plan, planned) to call Ana to set up another game.

Exercise 4

1. I recently (change, changed) my career plans; now I (want, wants) to be a chef.
2. Last year, I (have, had) my mind set on becoming a kindergarten teacher.
3. I (sign, signed) up for several childhood education classes, and they all (turn, turned) out to be disappointing.
4. The class work (was, were) often too easy, and the reading assignments (was, were) too hard.
5. We (does, did) spend part of the semester working in a real kindergarten class where we (was, were) able to observe just what the teacher (does, did).
6. The teacher that I (observes, observed) (have, had) twenty-seven children to look after.
7. I (watch, watched) her as she (help, helped) them learn their numbers and letters.
8. She (have, had) her students, their parents, and the school's administration to worry about all the time.
9. I never (imagine, imagined) that a kindergarten teacher (have, had) so many responsibilities.

10. A chef (need, needs) to worry about the food and the customers, and those (is, are) responsibilities that I (is, am) ready to take.

Exercise 5

Correct any of the following sentences that do not use Standard English verb forms.

1. Yesterday my English teacher assigns a narration essay.
2. Now we have one week to finish a rough draft.
3. Before the assignment, he showed us two sample narration essays.
4. They was about holiday traditions in different families.
5. In one essay, the writer explain the tradition of Thanksgiving at her house.
6. I likes the part about making pies for the adults and candy for the kids.
7. The second essay outline the steps another family goes through to prepare for Chinese New Year.
8. That one have even more details about food and gifts for the children.
9. My teacher asked us to write about a family ritual of our own.
10. I start my rough draft last night; it's about my dad's obsession with Halloween.

PROOFREADING EXERCISE

Correct any sentences in the following paragraph that do not use Standard English verb forms.

Most people believe that they has the best pets. I think that we have the cutest pet hamster in the world. Her name is Toots. We name her after the little dog that die in the movie *Lassie Come Home.* Our Toots don't look like that dog, but she have something about her that reminds us of it. The dog in the movie protect her owner from some really mean men. When the men try to beat the man who own her, Toots is so brave. She jump in front of her owner and saves him. Our hamster is small but fearless too, so we name her Toots.

SENTENCE WRITING

Write ten sentences about a pet that you have (or a friend has). Check your sentences to be sure that they use Standard English verb forms. Try exchanging papers with another student if possible.

Using Regular and Irregular Verbs

All regular verbs end the same way in the past form and when used with helping verbs. Here is a table showing all the forms of some *regular* verbs and the various helping verbs with which they are used.

Regular Verbs

Base Form	Present	Past	Past Participle	*Ing* Form
(Use after can, may, shall, will, could, might, should, would, must, do, does, did.)			*(Use after have, has, had. Some can be used after forms of be.)*	*(Use after forms of be.)*
ask	ask *(s)*	asked	asked	asking
bake	bake *(s)*	baked	baked	baking
count	count *(s)*	counted	counted	counting
dance	dance *(s)*	danced	danced	dancing
decide	decide *(s)*	decided	decided	deciding
enjoy	enjoy *(s)*	enjoyed	enjoyed	enjoying
finish	finish *(es)*	finished	finished	finishing
happen	happen *(s)*	happened	happened	happening
learn	learn *(s)*	learned	learned	learning
like	like *(s)*	liked	liked	liking
look	look *(s)*	looked	looked	looking
mend	mend *(s)*	mended	mended	mending
need	need *(s)*	needed	needed	needing
open	open *(s)*	opened	opened	opening
start	start *(s)*	started	started	starting
suppose	suppose *(s)*	supposed	supposed	supposing
tap	tap *(s)*	tapped	tapped	tapping
walk	walk *(s)*	walked	walked	walking
want	want *(s)*	wanted	wanted	wanting

Note - When there are several helping verbs, the last one determines which form of the main verb should be used: they *should* finish soon; they should *have* finished an hour ago.

When do you write *ask, finish, suppose, use?* And when do you write *asked, finished, supposed, used?* Here are some rules that will help you decide.

Write *ask, finish, suppose, use* (or their *s* forms) when writing about the present time, repeated actions, or facts:

He *asks* questions whenever he is confused.

They always *finish* their projects on time.

I *suppose* you want me to help you move.

Birds *use* leaves, twigs, and feathers to build their nests.

Write *asked, finished, supposed, used*

1. When writing about the past:

He *asked* the teacher for another explanation.

She *finished* her internship last year.

They *supposed* that there were others bidding on that house.

I *used* to study piano.

2. When some form of *be* (other than the word *be* itself) comes before the word:

He was *asked* the most difficult questions.

She is *finished* with her training now.

They were *supposed* to sign at the bottom of the form.

My essay was *used* as a sample of clear narration.

3. When some form of *have* comes before the word:

The teacher has *asked* us that question before.

She will have *finished* all of her exams by the end of May.

I had *supposed* too much without any proof.

We have *used* many models in my drawing class this semester.

All the verbs in the chart on page 105 are *regular.* That is, they're all formed in the same way—with an *ed* ending on the past form and on the past participle. But many verbs are irregular. Their past and past participle forms change spelling instead of just adding an *ed.* Here's a chart of some *irregular* verbs. Notice that the base, present, and *ing* forms end the same as regular verbs. Refer to this list when you aren't sure which verb form to use. Memorize all the forms you don't know.

Irregular Verbs

Base Form	Present	Past	Past Participle	*Ing* Form
(Use after can, may, shall, will, could, might, should, would, must, do, does, did.)			*(Use after have, has, had. Some can be used after forms of be.)*	*(Use after forms of be.)*
be	is, am, are	was, were	been	being
become	become *(s)*	became	become	becoming
begin	begin *(s)*	began	begun	beginning
break	break *(s)*	broke	broken	breaking
bring	bring *(s)*	brought	brought	bringing
buy	buy *(s)*	bought	bought	buying
build	build *(s)*	built	built	building
catch	catch *(es)*	caught	caught	catching
choose	choose *(s)*	chose	chosen	choosing
come	come *(s)*	came	come	coming
do	do *(es)*	did	done	doing
draw	draw *(s)*	drew	drawn	drawing
drink	drink *(s)*	drank	drunk	drinking
drive	drive *(s)*	drove	driven	driving
eat	eat *(s)*	ate	eaten	eating
fall	fall *(s)*	fell	fallen	falling
feel	feel *(s)*	felt	felt	feeling
fight	fight *(s)*	fought	fought	fighting
find	find *(s)*	found	found	finding
forget	forget *(s)*	forgot	forgotten	forgetting
forgive	forgive *(s)*	forgave	forgiven	forgiving
freeze	freeze *(s)*	froze	frozen	freezing
get	get *(s)*	got	got *or* gotten	getting
give	give *(s)*	gave	given	giving
go	go *(es)*	went	gone	going
grow	grow *(s)*	grew	grown	growing
have	have *or* has	had	had	having
hear	hear *(s)*	heard	heard	hearing
hold	hold *(s)*	held	held	holding

Base Form	Present	Past	Past Participle	*Ing* Form
keep	keep *(s)*	kept	kept	keeping
know	know *(s)*	knew	known	knowing
lay (to put)	lay *(s)*	laid	laid	laying
lead (like "bead")	lead *(s)*	led	led	leading
leave	leave *(s)*	left	left	leaving
lie (to rest)	lie *(s)*	lay	lain	lying
lose	lose *(s)*	lost	lost	losing
make	make *(s)*	made	made	making
meet	meet *(s)*	met	met	meeting
pay	pay *(s)*	paid	paid	paying
read (pron. "reed")	read *(s)* (pron. "reeds")	read (pron. "red")	read (pron. "red")	reading
ride	ride *(s)*	rode	ridden	riding
ring	ring *(s)*	rang	rung	ringing
rise	rise *(s)*	rose	risen	rising
run	run *(s)*	ran	run	running
say	say *(s)*	said	said	saying
see	see *(s)*	saw	seen	seeing
sell	sell *(s)*	sold	sold	selling
shake	shake *(s)*	shook	shaken	shaking
shine (give light)	shine *(s)*	shone	shone	shining
shine (polish)	shine *(s)*	shined	shined	shining
sing	sing *(s)*	sang	sung	singing
sleep	sleep *(s)*	slept	slept	sleeping
speak	speak *(s)*	spoke	spoken	speaking
spend	spend *(s)*	spent	spent	spending
stand	stand *(s)*	stood	stood	standing
steal	steal *(s)*	stole	stolen	stealing
strike	strike *(s)*	struck	struck	striking
swim	swim *(s)*	swam	swum	swimming
swing	swing *(s)*	swung	swung	swinging
take	take *(s)*	took	taken	taking
teach	teach *(es)*	taught	taught	teaching
tear	tear *(s)*	tore	torn	tearing
tell	tell *(s)*	told	told	telling
think	think *(s)*	thought	thought	thinking
throw	throw *(s)*	threw	thrown	throwing
wear	wear *(s)*	wore	worn	wearing
win	win *(s)*	won	won	winning
write	write *(s)*	wrote	written	writing

Sometimes verbs from the past participle column are used after some form of the verb *be* (or verbs that take the place of *be* like *appear, seem, look, feel, get, act, become*) to describe the subject or to say something in a passive, rather than an active, way.

She is contented.

You appear pleased. (You *are* pleased.)

He seems delighted. (He *is* delighted.)

She looked surprised. (She *was* surprised.)

I feel shaken. (I *am* shaken.)

They get bored easily. (They *are* bored easily.)

You acted concerned. (You *were* concerned.)

They were thrown out of the game. (Active: *The referee threw them out of the game.*)

We were disappointed by the news. (Active: *The news disappointed us.*)

Often these verb forms become words that describe the subject; at other times they still act as part of the verb in the sentence. What you call them doesn't matter. The only important thing is to be sure you use the correct form from the past participle column.

EXERCISES

Write the correct form of the verbs in the blanks. Refer to the tables and explanations on the preceding pages if you aren't sure which form to use after a certain helping verb. Check your answers after each exercise.

Exercise 1

1. (cook) I ______ for my family and friends whenever I can.
2. (cook) After I have ______ a delicious meal, I feel appreciated.
3. (cook) Sometimes when I am ______, I listen to music.
4. (cook) Then I can ______ quickly or slowly depending on the tempo.
5. (cook) I often ______ while listening to jazz.
6. (cook) Last night I ______a dinner of pasta, salad, and garlic bread.
7. (cook) As I was ______ the spaghetti sauce, everyone came in to see what smelled so good.

8. (cook) It isn't easy to ignore someone who is _______ with fresh garlic.

9. (cook) That's why whenever I have _______ my famous sauce, the whole family and even some of the neighbors show up at the table.

10. (cook) I will always enjoy _______ for other people.

Exercise 2

1. (buy) My parents should _______ a new television because they _______ their current TV back in the 1980s.

2. (know) They do not even _______ how outdated their TV is. If I _______ of a way to make it break down, I would do it.

3. (be) That _______ the only way they would discuss getting a new TV. Unfortunately, old television sets _______ really reliable and well-made.

4. (agree) Both of my parents _______ that if something isn't broken, it shouldn't be replaced. Obviously, my siblings and I do not _______ with them.

5. (tell) My brother and I have _______ them all about the great features available on the new sets. We might as well have been _______ them about spaceships.

6. (sit) Our mom and dad will happily _______ through local broadcast-station shows and would never dream of subscribing to a cable or dish service. Once I house-_______ for my parents while they were on vacation and was extremely bored.

7. (have) Well, at least my parents are _______ fun together. Maybe *I* _______ the wrong attitude.

8. (get) Last year, I _______ a state-of-the-art TV. I may be _______ hundreds of stations now, but I'm still not satisfied.

9. (need) In fact, I may _______ companionship much more than my parents _______ a new TV.

10. (be) I _______ sure that my mom and dad _______ the most old-fashioned people I know, but they are also the happiest people I know.

Exercise 3

1. (take, suppose) My friend Brenda _______ a day off last week even though she was _______ to be working.

2. (do, earn) She _______ not feel sick exactly; she just felt that she had _______ a day of rest.

3. (call, tell, feel) So Brenda _______ her office and _______ her boss that she did not _______ well enough to work that day.

4. (think, be) She never _______ that she would get caught, but she _______ wrong.

5. (leave, drive, see) Just as Brenda was _______ the house to buy some lunch, her coworker _______ by and _______ her.

6. (feel, know, tell) She _______ such panic because she _______ that he would _______ their boss that she looked fine.

7. (try, go) Brenda _______ to explain herself when she _______ back to the office the next day.

8. (be, undo) The damage had _______ done, however, and nothing could _______ it.

9. (wish, take) Now Brenda _______ that she could _______ back that day.

10. (use, call, do) She _______ to have a great relationship with her boss, but since the day she _______ in sick, he _______ not trust her anymore.

Exercise 4

1. (use, put) Many people ________ a direct deposit system that ________ their salary money directly into their bank accounts.
2. (do, do) With such a system, the employer ________ not have to issue paychecks, and employees ________ not have to cash or deposit them.
3. (transfer, spend) The employer's computer just ________ the money to the bank's computer, and the employee can ________ it as usual after that.
4. (be, like, choose) Direct deposit ________ almost always optional, but so many people ________ the system that most people ________ it.
5. (do, want) My roommate ________ not trust such systems; he ________ to have complete control over his cash.
6. (trust, be) He barely even ________ banks to keep his money safe for him, so he ________ definitely suspicious of direct deposit.
7. (imagine, make) I can ________ him as a pioneer in an old Western movie sleeping on a mattress stuffed with all of the money he has ever ________.
8. (talk, ask, worry) I was ________ to my roommate about money the other day, and I ________ him why he always ________ about it so much.
9. (look, say, live, understand) He just ________ at me and ________ , "If you had ever ________ without money, you would ________."
10. (wonder, be) I ________ about my roommate's past experiences and hope that he ________ never without money again.

Exercise 5

1. (lie, fall) I was _______ out in the sun last Sunday, and I _______ asleep.
2. (be, do) That _______ the worst thing I could have _______.
3. (wear, shield) I was _______ a pair of big dark sunglasses, which _______ my eyes from the light.
4. (lie, wake, realize, happen) I must have _______ there for over an hour before I _______ up and _______ what had _______.
5. (feel, start) At first I _______ fine, but then my skin _______ to feel really tight and thin.
6. (pass, turn, begin) As the minutes _______, my skin _______ bright red, and the pain _______.
7. (describe, experience) I can't even _______ how much pain I _______.
8. (be, feel, see) Almost worse than the pain _______ the embarrassment I _______ as I _______ my face in the mirror.
9. (look, tape, be, protect, wear) Around my eyes, it _______ as if someone had _______ the shape of white glasses to my face, but that _______ just the skin that had been _______ by the sunglasses I was _______.
10. (have, feel) The people at work _______ a big laugh the next day at my expense, but then they just _______ sorry for me.

PROGRESS TEST

This test covers everything you've learned in the Sentence Structure section so far. One sentence in each pair is correct. The other is incorrect. Read both sentences carefully before you decide. Then write the letter of the incorrect sentence in the blank. Try to name the error and correct it if you can.

1. ____ **A.** Darryl use to teach preschool.
   B. Now he tutors in the writing center.
2. ____ **A.** I visited the credit union office the other day.
   B. Because I needed to skip one of my loan payments.
3. ____ **A.** When I returned the radio was playing.
   B. I forgot that I had left it on to scare away burglars.
4. ____ **A.** My classmates and I were suppose to go into the library.
   B. We gathered on the library lawn and talked instead.
5. ____ **A.** She will have already painted the room by the time I arrive.
   B. She will probably used a fan to dry the paint quickly.
6. ____ **A.** We tried everything to open the old lock.
   B. Even a little handsaw that we found in a drawer.
7. ____ **A.** We had to wait for the bus so we played a guessing game.
   B. The bus pulled up to the curb while we were in the middle of a clue.
8. ____ **A.** I was able to swim across the pool without stopping.
   B. Without needing to take a breath either.
9. ____ **A.** They have seen many movies together.
   B. Last week they seen the newest thriller.
10. ____ **A.** Our new car is huge our old car was tiny by comparison.
    B. The new car holds seven people and has twelve cup holders.

Maintaining Subject/Verb Agreement

As we have seen, the subject and verb in a sentence work together, so they must always agree. Different subjects need different forms of verbs. When the correct verb follows a subject, we call it subject/verb agreement.

The following sentences illustrate the rule that *s* verbs follow most singular subjects but not plural subjects.

One turtle walks.	Three turtles walk.
The baby cries.	The babies cry.
A democracy listens to the people.	Democracies listen to the people.
One child plays.	Many children play.

The following sentences show how forms of the verb *be* (*is, am, are, was, were*) and helping verbs (*be, have,* and *do*) are made to agree with their subjects.

This puzzle is difficult.	These puzzles are difficult.
I am amazed.	You are amazed.
He was sleeping.	They were sleeping.
That class has been canceled.	Those classes have been canceled.
She does not want to participate.	They do not want to participate.

The following words are always singular and take an *s* verb or the irregular equivalent (*is, was, has, does*):

one	anybody	each
anyone	everybody	
everyone	nobody	
no one	somebody	
someone		

Someone feeds my dog in the morning.

Everybody was at the party.

Each does her own homework.

Remember that prepositional phrases often come between subjects and verbs. You should ignore these interrupting phrases, or you may mistake the wrong word for the subject and use a verb form that doesn't agree.

Someone from the apartments feeds my dog in the morning. (*Someone* is the subject, not *apartments.*)

Everybody on the list of celebrities was at the party. (*Everybody* is the subject, not *celebrities.*)

Each of the twins does her own homework. (*Each* is the subject, not *twins.*)

However, the words *some, any, all, none,* and *most* are exceptions to this rule of ignoring prepositional phrases. These words can be singular or plural, depending on the words that follow them in prepositional phrases.

Some of the *pie* is gone.
Some of the *cookies* are gone.

Is any of the *paper* still in the supply cabinet?
Are any of the *pencils* still in the supply cabinet?

All of her *work* has been published.
All of her *poems* have been published.

None of the *jewelry* is missing.
None of the *clothes* are missing.

On July 4th, most of the *country* celebrates.
On July 4th, most of the *citizens* celebrate.

When a sentence has more than one subject joined by *and,* the subject is plural:

The teacher *and* the tutors eat lunch at noon.
A glazed donut *and* an onion bagel were sitting on the plate.

However, when two subjects are joined by *or,* then the subject *closest* to the verb determines the verb form:

Either the teacher *or* the *tutors* eat lunch at noon.

Either the tutors *or* the *teacher* eats lunch at noon.

A glazed donut *or* an onion *bagel* was sitting on the plate.

In most sentences, the subject comes before the verb. However, in some cases, the subject follows the verb, and subject/verb agreement needs special attention. Study the following examples:

Over the building flies a solitary flag. (flag flies)

Over the building fly several flags. (flags fly)

There is a good reason for my actions. (reason is)

There are good reasons for my actions. (reasons are)

EXERCISES

Underline the correct verbs in parentheses to maintain subject/verb agreement in the following sentences. Remember to ignore prepositional phrases, unless the subjects are *some, any, all, none,* or *most.* Check your answers ten at a time.

Exercise 1

1. Do you know why the skin on our fingertips (wrinkle, wrinkles) after a long shower or bath?
2. The explanation (is, are) simple.
3. All of our skin (absorb, absorbs) water.
4. The bottoms of our hands and feet (absorb, absorbs) the most water.
5. They (soak, soaks) up more water because they (has, have) the thickest layers of skin on our bodies.
6. This thick skin on our fingers (swell, swells) and (expand, expands) from the excess water.
7. Wrinkles (result, results) from the expansion of the skin covering the small surface of our fingertips.
8. The same thing (doesn't, don't) happen as quickly in sea water, however.
9. The salts and other minerals in the sea water (block, blocks) it from being absorbed.

10. So next time you (take, takes) a long bath, you will understand why your fingers and toes (get, gets) so wrinkled.

Source: Discover, October 2002

Exercise 2

1. A group of scientists (is, are) looking into the sensation that we (call, calls) déjà vu.
2. Déjà vu (is, are) the feeling that we (is, are) repeating an exact experience that (has, have) happened before.
3. Part of the odd sensation (is, are) that we (is, are) aware of the illogical part of déjà vu while it (is, are) happening.
4. One theory of Sigmund Freud's (was, were) that déjà vu (take, takes) place when a real experience (connect, connects) us with our unconscious thoughts.
5. Another of the psychiatrists studying déjà vu (believe, believes) that our previous experiences (is, are) stored like holographic images.
6. And déjà vu (happen, happens) when a new experience closely matches the 3-D memory of an old one.
7. The most recent theory (hypothesize, hypothesizes) that two different parts of the brain (control, controls) memory and familiarity.
8. One part (give, gives) us access to individual clear memories.
9. The other part (is, are) responsible for vague feelings of familiarity.
10. Experts in the field of psychiatry now (think, thinks) that the brain (produce, produces) déjà vu when this familiar feeling (activate, activates) during a brand-new experience.

Source: Scientific American, September 2002

Exercise 3

1. Tony Schwartz (collect, collects) sounds.

2. He (has, have) been recording ordinary sounds since he was a young man and (is, are) saving them for future generations.
3. In his collection (is, are) everything from the "ka-ching" of an old cash register bell to the voice of an elevator man calling out the merchandise available on the different floors of an old department store.
4. His assortment of sounds (include, includes) the various noises his dog made during its first year of life.
5. Schwartz's talent at recording sounds (has, have) helped him get many jobs over the years.
6. One of these jobs (was, were) recording the voices of child actors for advertisers in the 1950s and 1960s.
7. Schwartz's love of sounds (stem, stems) from a brief period of blindness that he went through as a teenager.
8. Now Schwartz (stay, stays) close to his home in Manhattan.
9. In his own neighborhood (is, are) enough sounds to keep him busy.
10. One of his most unusual recordings (was, were) of the burial of a little boy's pet turtle.

Source: People, October 4, 1999

Exercise 4

1. There (is, are) new risks for kids in this technological age; these risks primarily (involve, involves) their wrists.
2. Many adults already (suffer, suffers) from carpal tunnel syndrome.
3. And now children (is, are) also coming down with similar conditions, called repetitive stress injuries (RSIs).
4. From the use of computers and video games (come, comes) unnatural body positions that (lead, leads) to health problems.
5. The child's wrists, neck, and back (start, starts) to hurt or feel numb after he or she (work, works) or (play, plays) on the computer for a long time.

6. The problem (start, starts) with computer furniture.
7. The chairs, desks, and screens (is, are) usually not at the proper height to be used comfortably by children.
8. Straining and repetition often (cause, causes) reduced circulation and even nerve damage.
9. Often RSI damage to the wrists (is, are) irreversible.
10. Experts in the field of RSI (warn, warns) parents to teach children how to avoid these injuries.

Source: U.S. News & World Report, July 5, 1999

Exercise 5

1. Everyone in my drawing class (is, are) supposed to finish a drawing a week.
2. But each of us (has, have) a different way of beginning.
3. One of my classmates always (start, starts) by humming and rocking back and forth in front of his easel.
4. Another one just (put, puts) dots in the places where she (want, wants) her figures to go.
5. Jennifer, my best friend, (like, likes) to draw really light circles wherever the faces will be.
6. In the past, I (has, have) usually started by drawing a continuous line until it (look, looks) like something.
7. In other words, I (let, lets) the drawing tell me what it (want, wants) to be.
8. But Jennifer and my other classmates (has, have) taught me something.
9. It (help, helps) to have a plan; their drawings often (turn, turns) out better than mine.
10. Either they or I (am, are) right, but I don't know which it (is, are) yet.

PROOFREADING EXERCISE

Find and correct the ten subject/verb agreement errors in the following paragraph. (Some of the verbs may be written as part of a contraction—there's for there *is,* for example.)

I make friends easily. There's only a few people who can resist my charming personality once I gets started talking. For this reason, I have developed many casual friendships with the people I see regularly. But my friends at school is very different from my friends at work. At school, most of the single students sits around and talks after class. Sometimes, we go out for coffee and pleasantly discuss our futures. At work, however, there's too many pressures to relax and talk with my coworkers. I call my work friends on the phone before or after work, but we hardly ever has a chance to mingle on the job or even during our breaks. My friends at work loves to gossip. Whenever my coworkers call, either they or I starts to tell the latest tale, and we all has a good laugh. I have fun with both my classmates and my coworkers. They're just different kinds of fun.

SENTENCE WRITING

Write ten sentences in which you describe the clothes you are wearing. Use verbs in the present time. Then go back over your sentences—underline your subjects once, underline your verbs twice, and be sure they agree.

Avoiding Shifts in Time

People often worry about using different time frames in writing. Let common sense guide you. If you begin writing a paper in past time, don't shift back and forth to the present unnecessarily; and if you begin in the present, don't shift to the past without good reason. In the following paragraph, the writer starts in the present and then shifts to the past, then shifts again to the present:

> In the novel *To Kill a Mockingbird,* Jean Louise Finch is a little girl who lives in the South with her father, Atticus, and her brother, Jem. Everybody in town calls Jean Louise "Scout" as a nickname. When Atticus, a lawyer, chose to defend a black man against the charges of a white woman, some of their neighbors turned against him. Scout protected her father by appealing to the humanity of one member of the angry mob. In this chapter, five-year-old Scout turns out to be stronger than a group of adult men.

All the verbs should be in the present:

> In the novel *To Kill a Mockingbird,* Jean Louise Finch is a little girl who lives in the South with her father, Atticus, and her brother, Jem. Everybody in town calls Jean Louise "Scout" as a nickname. When Atticus, a lawyer, chooses to defend a black man against the charges of a white woman, some of their neighbors turn against him. Scout protects her father by appealing to the humanity of one member of the angry mob. In this chapter, five-year-old Scout turns out to be stronger than a group of adult men.

This sample paragraph discusses only the events that happen within the novel's plot, so it needs to maintain one time frame—the present, which we use to write about literature and repeated actions.

However, sometimes you will write about the present, the past, and even the future together. Then it may be necessary to use these different time frames within the same paragraph, each for its own reason. For example, if you were to give biographical information about Harper Lee, author of *To Kill a Mockingbird,* within a discussion of the novel and its influence, you might need to use all three time frames:

> Harper Lee grew up in Alabama, and she based elements in the book on experiences from her childhood. Like the character Atticus, Lee's father was a lawyer. She wrote the novel in his law offices. *To Kill a Mockingbird* is Harper Lee's most famous work, and it received the Pulitzer Prize for fiction in 1960. Lee's book turned forty years old in the year 2000. It will always remain one of the most moving and compassionate novels in American literature.

This paragraph uses past (*grew, based, was, wrote, received, turned*), present (*is*), and future (*will remain*) in the same paragraph without committing the error of shifting. Shifting occurs when the writer changes time frames *inconsistently* or *for no reason,* confusing the reader (as in the first example given).

PROOFREADING EXERCISES

Which of the following student paragraphs shift *unnecessarily* back and forth between time frames? In those that do, change the verbs to maintain one time frame, thus making the entire paragraph read smoothly. (First, read the paragraphs to determine whether unnecessary shifting takes place. One of the paragraphs is correct.)

1. There is an old joke that people told about being on the "see-food diet." When they are asked what the "see-food diet" means, the jokers replied, "Whenever I *see* food, I eat it." There is a kernel of truth in this old joke, according to scientists. When the human brain sees food, it sent out a chemical that gave people pleasure. That substance was called dopamine, and it is probably the way that the brain tempted the body to eat so that it doesn't starve. Unfortunately, there is so much food around most of us in our modern society that it makes people want food even when they didn't need it.

Source: Discover, September 2002

2. I watched a documentary on the Leaning Tower of Pisa last night. I was amazed to find out that the tower began leaning before it was even finished. Workers over several centuries adjusted their materials as they built the tower to compensate for its increasing angle. That's why the tower is actually shaped a little like a banana. I'm surprised that the famous landmark is still standing after everything people have done to it since it was finished. In the 1930s, for instance, Mussolini thought that it should be straightened. So he had workers drill holes in the foundation and pour tons of concrete beneath it. Others tried digging out the earth around the sunken part. But that just caused flooding because they went below the soil's water table. The narrator of the documentary said that every time anyone tries to correct the tower, it leans a little more to the south. Most recently, scientists have used special drilling techniques to extract enough soil deep beneath the tower to reverse its angle a little. This most recent correction may add as much as three hundred years to the life of the Leaning Tower of Pisa.

3. I really enjoyed my winter break this year. It was too short, of course, but I make the most of the time I had. My extended family had a reunion at my aunt's house in St. Louis. I didn't pack enough coats and sweaters, but the loving atmosphere keeps me warm. Once I'm back in the same room with my cousins, we goofed off just the way we used to when we were kids. One night my four closest cousins and I stay up after everyone else is in bed. We played board games and ate buttery popcorn and got the game pieces all greasy just like the old days. Overall, my trip to St. Louis with its late-night game marathon is the highlight of my winter vacation.

Recognizing Verbal Phrases

We know (from the discussion on p. 92) that a verb phrase is made up of a main verb and at least one helping verb. But sometimes certain forms of verbs are used not as real verbs but as some other part of a sentence. Verbs put to other uses are called *verbals.*

A verbal can be a subject:

> *Skiing* is my favorite Olympic sport. (*Skiing* is the subject, not the verb. The verb is *is.*)

A verbal can be a descriptive word:

> His *bruised* ankle healed very quickly. (*Bruised* describes the subject, ankle. *Healed* is the verb.)

A verbal can be an object:

> I like *to read* during the summer. (*To read* is the object. *Like* is the verb.)

Verbals link up with other words to form *verbal phrases.* To see the difference between a real verb phrase and a verbal phrase, look at these two sentences:

> I was bowling with my best friends. (*Bowling* is the main verb in a verb phrase. Along with the helping verb *was,* it shows the action of the sentence.)

I enjoyed *bowling* with my best friends. (Here the real verb is *enjoyed. Bowling* is not the verb; it is part of a verbal phrase—*bowling with my best friends*—which is what I enjoyed.)

Three Kinds of Verbals

1. *ing* verbs used without helping verbs (*running, thinking, baking . . .*)
2. verb forms that often end in *ed, en,* or *t* (*tossed, spoken, burnt . . .*)
3. verbs that follow *to* (*to walk, to eat, to cause . . .*)

Look at the following sentences using the previous examples in verbal phrases:

Running two miles a day is great exercise. (real verb = is)

She spent two hours *thinking of a title for her essay.* (real verb = spent)

We had such fun *baking those cherry vanilla cupcakes.* (real verb = had)

Tossed in a salad, artichoke hearts add zesty flavor. (real verb = add)

Spoken in Spanish, the dialogue sounds even more beautiful. (real verb = sounds)

The gourmet pizza, *burnt by a careless chef,* shrunk to half its normal size. (real verb = shrunk)

I like *to walk around the zoo by myself.* (real verb = like)

To eat exotic foods takes courage. (real verb = takes)

They actually wanted *to cause an argument.* (real verb = wanted)

EXERCISES

Each of the following sentences contains at least one verbal or verbal phrase. Double underline the real verbs or verb phrases and put brackets around the verbals and verbal phrases. Remember to locate the verbals first (*running, wounded, to sleep . . .*) and include any word(s) that go with them (*running a race, wounded in the fight, to sleep all night*). Real verbs will never be inside verbal phrases. Check your answers after the first set before going on to the next.

Exercise 1

1. Mixing light of different colors sometimes produces surprising results.
2. It is an entirely different process from mixing colored paints.
3. For example, mixing red and green paints produces a dark brown color.
4. But mixing red and green light produces yellow light.
5. Mixing paints is an example of a process called color subtraction.
6. Mixing colored light is an example of color addition.
7. White light is made up of colored light.
8. When looking at a rainbow, you are seeing sunlight.
9. The band of color in a rainbow is called a spectrum, containing seven basic colors—red, orange, yellow, green, blue, indigo, and violet.
10. Light of these colors can be recombined to form white light.

Source: A modified excerpt from *New Encyclopedia of Science Special Projects Book* (Funk and Wagnalls, 1986)

Exercise 2

1. Email has begun to be the most popular form of written communication.
2. In the beginning, people searched for a way to show emotion.
3. It was time to invent a new type of punctuation, now known as "emoticons."
4. Scott Fahlman proposed two of the first emoticons in the early 1980s to show when something was meant to be funny or not.
5. Called the "smiley" and the "frown," these combinations of colon, hyphen, and parentheses look like this :-) and :-(.
6. In an effort to document computer history, Mike Jones, Jeff Baird, and others worked hard to retrace the steps of the first uses of the smiley and the frown.
7. They found them used by Scott Fahlman in a posting to a computer bulletin board in 1982.

8. These and other emoticons have continued to help people express themselves online.
9. So when you finish typing your next joke in an email, don't forget to add a :-).
10. Frowning :-(is seen by some as questionable net etiquette and is consequently not as common.

Source: http://www.cs.cmu.edu/~sef/sefSmiley.htm

Exercise 3

1. The idea of home schooling children has become more popular recently.
2. Many parents have decided to teach kids themselves instead of sending them off to public or private school classrooms.
3. There are many different reasons to choose home schooling.
4. In Hollywood, for instance, child actors often are forced to drop out of traditional schools due to their schedules.
5. The home schooling option allows for one of their parents, or a special teacher, to continue to instruct them on the set.
6. Other parents simply want to be directly involved in their child's learning.
7. Many school districts have special independent study "schools," offering parents the structure and materials that they need to provide an appropriate curriculum on their own.
8. Children do all of their reading and writing at home, with their parents guiding them along the way.
9. The family meets with the independent study school's teacher regularly to go over the child's work and to clarify any points of confusion.
10. Many parents would like to have the time to home school their children.

Exercise 4

1. It's easy to give someone the bubonic plague these days—in tie form, that is.

2. A microscopic picture of the plague is just one of the "decorations" adorning the Infectious Awareables collection of ties sold by Roger Freeman.
3. Freeman was a dentist before becoming a tie salesman.
4. The diseased ties have started to become popular.
5. There are ties showing cholera, staph, ebola, and malaria, to name just a few.
6. Makers decided to label the ties with information about the conditions pictured on their surfaces and to donate five percent of their proceeds to research.
7. Freeman took over selling the stock of ties after being given a herpes tie as a present.
8. Freeman loves the disease patterns seen through a microscope.
9. Their vivid colors and abstract shapes make them perfect to use as tie designs; and they're also being used to decorate scarves and boxer shorts.
10. The Infectious Awareables ties are priced reasonably, selling for around forty dollars apiece.

Sources: Discover, October 2002; and *www.iawareables.com*

Exercise 5

1. John Steinbeck, author of *The Grapes of Wrath,* was the first native of California to receive the Nobel Prize for literature.
2. Calling his hometown of Salinas "Lettuceberg," Steinbeck's writing made the area famous.
3. At the time, not everyone liked the attention brought by his portrayals of life in *Cannery Row* and other works.
4. Steinbeck's father was the treasurer of Monterey County for ten years, working also for the Spreckels company.

5. John Steinbeck tried to find satisfaction in his birthplace, enrolling in and quitting his studies at Stanford University many times.
6. Finally, Steinbeck moved to New York, distancing himself from his California roots.
7. Steinbeck won the Nobel Prize in 1962, revealing the literary world's esteem for his work.
8. Not writing anything of the caliber of the Salinas stories while living in New York, Steinbeck did return to California before he died in 1968.
9. In 1972, the Salinas library changed its name, to be known thereafter as the John Steinbeck Library.
10. And the house Steinbeck was born in became a restaurant and then a full-fledged museum chronicling the life of Salinas' most celebrated citizen.

Source: California People (Peregrine Smith, 1982)

PARAGRAPH EXERCISE

Double underline the real verbs or verb phrases and put brackets around the verbals and verbal phrases in the following excerpt on the history of the toaster from *The Encyclopedia of Collectibles:*

Toast reached its central position on the breakfast table only after a marketing war between makers of bread and makers of cereals—and a great deal of inventiveness on the part of toaster designers. Electric toasters did not come on the market until several decades after Americans started to use electric lights. Some utility companies, in fact, discouraged efforts to introduce home appliances of any kind—they were too busy competing with gas companies for the lighting business.

In most cities in the late 19th Century, electricity was available in homes only at night, to power light bulbs; during the day the generators shut down. Not until 1903 was the superintendent of the power plant in Ontario, California, Earl Richardson, able to persuade his bosses to run the generators all day Tuesday—the traditional ironing day—to allow people to use the electric iron he had invented.

By 1910, however, a variety of irons, toasters, and other gadgets were in production. Early toasters consisted of heating elements with wire racks for the bread; like the coal stove racks they sought to replace, they often burned the toast—and the fingers that had to turn the slices over.

Burned fingers were the first problem inventors set out to solve.

SENTENCE WRITING

Write ten sentences that contain verbal phrases. Use the ten verbals listed here to begin your verbal phrases: *marching, diving, waxing, keeping, to ask, to sit, to understand, to look, closed, written.* The last two may seem particularly difficult to use as verbals. There are sample sentences listed in the Answers section at the back of the book. But first, try to write your own so that you can compare the two.

Correcting Misplaced or Dangling Modifiers

When we modify something, we change whatever it is by adding something to it. We might modify a car, for example, by adding special tires. In English, we call words, phrases, and clauses *modifiers* when they add information to part of a sentence. To do its job properly, a modifier should be in the right spot—as close to the word it describes as possible. If we put new tires on the roof of the car instead of where they belong, they would be misplaced. In the following sentence, the modifier is too far away from the word it modifies to make sense. It is a misplaced modifier:

Swinging from tree to tree, we watched the monkeys at the zoo.

Was it *we* who were swinging from tree to tree? That's what the sentence says because the modifying phrase *Swinging from tree to tree* is next to *we.* It should be next to *monkeys.*

At the zoo, we watched the monkeys swinging from tree to tree.

The next example has no word at all for the modifier to modify:

At the age of eight, my family finally bought a dog.

Obviously, the family was not eight when it bought a dog. Nor was the dog eight. The modifier *At the age of eight* is dangling there with no word to attach itself to, no word for it to modify. We can get rid of the dangling modifier by turning it into a dependent clause. (See p. 69 for a discussion of dependent clauses.)

When I was eight, my family finally bought a dog.

Here the clause has its own subject and verb—*I was*—and there's no chance of misunderstanding the sentence. Here's another dangling modifier:

After a two-hour nap, the train pulled into the station.

Did the train take a two-hour nap? Who did?

After a two-hour nap, I awoke just as the train pulled into the station.

EXERCISES

Carefully rephrase any of the following sentences that contain misplaced or dangling modifiers. Some sentences are correct.

Exercise 1

1. After looking out the window several times, my bus arrived.
2. He found his keys resting on top of his car.
3. I used a flashlight to fix the circuit breaker.
4. Before taking algebra, my counselor said that I should take pre-algebra.
5. I always carry my lunch in a small cooler.
6. Our tutor slipped and fell on a piece of chalk.

7. Asking five questions in a row, the audience members waited for the speaker's replies.
8. Now that I have a credit card, I can afford to buy a new television.
9. My mother sent me a picture of my new nephew as an attachment to an email.
10. Hoping to see the star of the play, we waited by the stage door.

Exercise 2

1. The blue rug needs to be replaced in the hallway.
2. I found a puppy sweeping up the alley.
3. Full of enthusiasm, the violinist's performance was thrilling.
4. Written in pink ink, I found the teacher's comments easy to read.
5. The library has increased the number of books in its collection.
6. With a smile on her face, we watched the teacher tell a funny story.
7. Sitting on my desk for two weeks, I finally paid the bills.
8. We filled out the survey with a no. 2 pencil.
9. Checking her answers carefully, Cheryl's homework was finished.
10. Before calling the doctor, my ankle started to feel better.

Exercise 3

1. Distracted by the crowd, the officer tried to write a report.
2. When I was twelve, I bought my first share of stock.
3. She kicked her mother in the store by accident.
4. The inspector found a few termites looking outside the house.
5. Mixing the paints together, we found the color we wanted.
6. Flying around in a circle above the tree, I saw the mother bird.
7. Hating the smell of gasoline, the new attendant will have to work inside.
8. The bicycles at that store are reasonably priced.
9. We bought a house with a swimming pool.
10. At the moment of impact, the airbags will inflate.

Exercise 4

1. Getting a headache from the fumes, the ferry finally made it across the river.
2. Full of empty calories, that carnival sold the best cotton candy I'd ever tasted.
3. Two months after moving, our old apartment is still empty.
4. She promised to return the library books in her email message.
5. The students took the notes sitting in small groups.
6. Before saying goodnight, the porch light burned out.
7. Decorated beautifully, our hostess showed us her favorite room.
8. Scampering along the baseboards of the cabin, I saw a tiny gray mouse.
9. Trying to open my car door with a hanger, I stared at the keys dangling from the ignition.
10. All along the highway, volunteers planted trees wearing special T-shirts.

Exercise 5

1. Feeling the excitement of the first day of school, my backpack was left behind.
2. Full of surprises, we saw the new movie that everyone is talking about.
3. My cousins and I always wrapped our gifts in our pajamas on the night before the holiday.
4. Practicing for an hour a day, his tennis has improved.
5. The price of gasoline fluctuates, rising and falling several times a year.
6. Sitting on the beach all day, I made a decision.
7. They discovered a new trail hiking in the nearby mountains.
8. She felt the pressure of trying to get good grades from her parents.
9. I enjoy traveling to new places with my friends and even my family.
10. Written in green ink, the teacher's comments seemed positive even when pointing out a problem.

PROOFREADING EXERCISE

Find and correct any misplaced or dangling modifiers in the following paragraphs.

A man in Edinburgh, Scotland, has invented a device, hoping to become famous and wealthy. The device is a variation on the center-mounted brake light used in the design of many new cars, located just above the trunk and visible from behind. Instead of just a solid red brake light, however, this invention displays words to other drivers written in bold, red-lighted letters.

With simplicity in mind, the vocabulary the inventor gave the machine is limited to three words: "Sorry," "Thanks," and "Help." After making an aggressive lane change, the machine could apologize for us. Or after being allowed to go ahead of someone, the device could offer thanks to the considerate person responsible. Of course, at the sight of the "Help" display, we could summon fellow citizens for assistance.

And there is no need to worry about operating the device while driving. With three easy-to-reach buttons, the messages can be activated without taking our eyes off the road.

SENTENCE WRITING

Write five sentences that contain misplaced or dangling modifiers; then revise those sentences to put the modifiers where they belong. Use the examples in the explanations as models.

Following Sentence Patterns

Sentences are built according to a few basic patterns. For proof, rearrange each of the following sets of words to form a complete statement (not a question):

apples a ate raccoon the

the crashing beach were waves the on

your in am partner I life

been she school has to walking

you wonderful in look green

There are only one or two possible combinations for each due to English sentence patterns. Either *A raccoon ate the apples,* or *The apples ate a raccoon,* and so on. But in each case, the verb or verb phrase makes its way to the middle of the statement.

To understand sentence patterns, you need to know that verbs can do three things.

1. Verbs can show actions:

The raccoon ate the apples.

The waves were crashing on the beach.

She has been walking to school.

2. Verbs can link subjects with descriptive words:

I am your partner in life.

You look wonderful in green.

3. Verbs can help other verbs form verb phrases:

The waves were crashing on the beach.

She has been walking to school.

Look at these sentences for more examples:

Mel grabbed a slice of pizza. (The verb *grabbed* shows Mel's action.)

His slice was the largest one in the box. (The verb *was* links *slice* with its description as *the largest one.*)

Mel had been craving pizza for a week. (The verbs *had* and *been* help the main verb *craving* in a verb phrase.)

Knowing what a verb does in a clause helps you gain an understanding of the three basic sentence patterns:

Subject + Action Verb + Object Pattern

Some action verbs must be followed by a person or an object that receives the action.

S AV Obj
Sylvia completed the difficult math test. (*Sylvia completed* makes no sense without being followed by the object that she completed—*test.*)

Subject + Action Verb (+ No Object) Pattern

At other times, the action verb itself completes the meaning and needs no object after it.

S AV
She celebrated at home with her family. (*She celebrated* makes sense alone. The two prepositional phrases—*at home* and *with her family*—are not needed to understand the meaning of the clause.)

Subject + Linking Verb + Description Pattern

A special kind of verb that does not show an action but links a subject with a description is called a *linking verb.* It acts like an equal sign in a clause. Learn to recognize the most common linking verbs: *is, am, are, was, were, seem, feel, appear, become, look.*

S LV Desc
Sylvia is very intelligent. (*Very intelligent* describes *Sylvia.*)

S LV Desc
Sylvia has become an excellent student. (*Sylvia* equals *an excellent student.*)

Note - We learned on page 92 that a verb phrase includes a main verb and its helping verbs. Helping verbs can be used in any of the sentence patterns.

S AV
Sylvia is going to Seattle for a vacation. (Here the verb *is* helps the main verb *going,* which is an action verb with no object followed by two prepositional phrases—*to Seattle* and *for a vacation.*)

The following chart outlines the patterns using short sentences that you could memorize:

Three Basic Sentence Patterns
S + AV + Obj
Kids trade candy.
S + AV
They play (with their friends) (on the playground). *not objects*
S + LV + Desc
They are fourth-graders.
They look happy.

These are the basic patterns for most of the clauses used in English sentences. Knowing them can help you control your sentences and improve your use of words.

EXERCISES

First, put parentheses around any prepositional phrases. Next, underline the subjects once and the verbs or verb phrases twice. Then mark the sentence patterns above the words. Remember that the patterns never mix together. For example, unlike an action verb, a linking verb will almost never be used alone (for example, "He seems."), nor will an action verb be followed by a description of the subject (for example, "She took tall."). And if there are two clauses, each one may have a different pattern. Check your answers after the first set of ten.

Exercise 1

1. Cakes can be plain or fancy.
2. Most grocery stores and almost all bakeries sell cakes.
3. They range in price depending on size, occasion, and amount of decoration.

4. A cake with a "Happy Birthday" inscription will usually cost thirty to fifty dollars.
5. Wedding cakes, however, are often very expensive.
6. An elaborate wedding cake may cost several hundred or even a thousand dollars.
7. The multi-layered traditional white wedding cake still seems the most popular kind.
8. These delicate structures need special care during transportation.
9. Some couples order two or more smaller cakes for the occasion.
10. People sometimes save a slice or section of their wedding cake as a memento.

Exercise 2

1. In 1998, Sotheby's auction house sold a piece of 60-year-old wedding cake for an amazing price.
2. It had belonged to the Duke and Duchess of Windsor.
3. On June 3, 1937, the famous couple married in France.
4. On the day of their wedding, they put a piece of cake in a pink box and tied a pink bow around it.
5. They identified its contents as "a piece of our wedding cake"; they initialed and dated the box, and they kept it as a memento for the rest of their lives.
6. This couple's relationship, which began in the 1930s, was one of the most famous love affairs in history.
7. The Duke of Windsor gave up the throne of England to be with Wallis Simpson, the woman that he loved.
8. Unfortunately, she was a divorced American woman and could not, therefore, marry the king of England, so he abdicated.
9. The pre-auction estimate for the box containing the piece of their wedding cake was five hundred to a thousand dollars.

10. When the gavel came down, the high bid by a couple from San Francisco was $29,900.

Sources: http://www.cnn.com/US/9802/21/windsor.auction; and Sotheby's Holdings, Inc. Annual Report 1998

Exercise 3

1. Tumbleweeds are nature's seed scatterers.
2. They grow to the size of a bush and then break off at ground level.
3. As the wind blows them across the open spaces, the tumbleweeds scatter their seeds.
4. But tumbleweeds can cause problems when they encounter structures.
5. For instance, thousands of tumbleweeds blew into one woman's yard in Colorado, buried her house, and trapped her.
6. She called for help, and firefighters worked for half an hour to cut a path to her door.
7. On another occasion, tumbleweeds caused a commotion in South Dakota.
8. Members of a family awoke in the middle of the night to the sound of someone ringing their doorbell frantically.
9. When they opened the door, they were very surprised.
10. The mysterious visitor was an 18-foot-high pile of tumbleweeds leaning against the doorbell.

Source: Current Science, September 13, 2002

Exercise 4

1. My sister Belinda is allergic to many things.
2. She gets hives from mold and pollen.
3. Of course, milk upsets her stomach.
4. Strawberries and raspberries are many people's favorite fruits.

5. But they give Belinda a rash on her face and arms.
6. The doctor has made a list of Belinda's allergies.
7. Soon she'll be receiving allergy shots.
8. The shots should reduce Belinda's sensitivity to these substances.
9. Everyone in my family is hoping for the best.
10. With luck, Belinda will feel better soon.

Exercise 5

1. Giuseppe Verdi's opera *A Masked Ball* is a classic, and performances of it are usually spectacular.
2. But two British men, Richard Jones and Anthony McDonald, staged a truly unique offering of Verdi's opera for the Bregenz Festival in Austria in the summer of 1999.
3. The most amazing part of the Austrian production was the stage, shaped like an open book.
4. The stage floated on a lake, and the audience watched the performance from seats on the shore.
5. This floating book was also huge; its surface covered more than eight thousand square feet.
6. Actors crossed a bridge to the stage and then walked great distances during the opera.
7. The size, shape, and location of the stage were unique enough.
8. Then Jones and McDonald stunned audiences with an eighty-foot prop next to the stage.
9. The prop was a human skeleton, and just one of its fingers was the same height as an actor on the stage.
10. During each performance, the towering skeleton moved and pushed one of the actors across the stage.

Source: People, October 4, 1999

PARAGRAPH EXERCISE

Label the sentence patterns in the following paragraphs. They are from a book by Paul Zelanski and Mary Pat Fisher titled, simply, *Color.* It helps to put parentheses around prepositional phrases first to isolate them from the words that make up the sentence patterns—the subjects, the verbs, and any objects after action verbs or any descriptive words after linking verbs (*is, was, were, seem, appear,* and so on).

Color is perhaps the most powerful tool at an artist's disposal. It affects our emotions beyond thought and can convey any mood, from delight to despair. It can be subtle or dramatic, capture attention or stimulate desire. Used more boldly and freely today than ever before, color bathes our vision with an infinite variety of sensations, from clear, brilliant hues to subtle, elusive mixtures. Color is the province of all artists, from painters and potters to product designers and computer artists.

SENTENCE WRITING

Write ten sentences describing the weather today and your feelings about it. Keep your sentences short and clear. Then go back and label the sentence patterns you have used.

Avoiding Clichés, Awkward Phrasing, and Wordiness

Clichés

A cliché is an expression that has been used so often it has lost its originality and effectiveness. Whoever first said "light as a feather" had thought of an original way to express lightness, but today that expression is worn out. Most of us use an occasional cliché in speaking, but clichés have no place in writing. The good writer thinks up fresh new ways to express ideas.

Here are a few clichés. Add some more to the list.

the bottom line
older but wiser
last but not least
in this day and age
different as night and day
out of this world
white as a ghost
sick as a dog
tried and true
at the top of their lungs
the thrill of victory
one in a million
busy as a bee
easier said than done
better late than never

Clichés lack freshness because the reader always knows what's coming next. Can you complete these expressions?

the agony of . . .
breathe a sigh of . . .
lend a helping . . .
odds and . . .
raining cats and . . .
as American as . . .
been there . . .
worth its weight . . .

Clichés are expressions too many people use. Try to avoid them in your writing.

Awkward Phrasing

Another problem—awkward phrasing—comes from writing sentence structures that *no one* else would use because they break basic sentence patterns, omit necessary words, or use words incorrectly. Like clichés, awkward sentences might *sound* acceptable when spoken, but as polished writing, they are usually unacceptable.

Awkward

There should be great efforts in terms of the communication between teachers and their students.

Corrected

Teachers and their students must communicate.

Awkward

During the experiment, the use of key principles was essential to ensure the success of it.

Corrected

The experiment was a success. *or* We performed the experiment carefully.

Awkward

My favorite was when the guy with the ball ran the wrong way all the way across the field in the movie.

Corrected

In my favorite part of the movie, the receiver ran across the field in the wrong direction.

Wordiness

Good writing is concise writing. Don't use ten words if you can say it better in five. "In today's society" isn't as effective as "today," and it's a cliché. "At this point in time" could be "presently" or "now."

Another kind of wordiness comes from saying something twice. There's no need to write "in the month of August" or "9 a.m. in the morning" or "my personal opinion." August *is* a month, 9 a.m. *is* morning, and anyone's opinion *is* personal. All you need to write is "in August," "9 a.m.," and "my opinion."

Still another kind of wordiness comes from using expressions that add nothing to the meaning of the sentence. "The point is that we can't afford it" says no more than "We can't afford it."

Here is a sample wordy sentence:

The construction company actually worked on that particular building for a period of six months.

And here it is after eliminating wordiness:

> The construction company worked on that building for six months.

Wordy Writing	Concise Writing
advance planning	planning
an unexpected surprise	a surprise
ask a question	ask
at a later date	later
basic fundamentals	fundamentals
but nevertheless	but (or nevertheless)
combine together	combine
completely empty	empty
down below	below
each and every	each (or every)
end result	result
fewer in number	fewer
free gift	gift
green in color	green
in order to	to
in spite of the fact that	although
just exactly	exactly
large in size	large
new innovation	innovation
on a regular basis	regularly
past history	history
rectangular in shape	rectangular
refer back	refer
repeat again	repeat
serious crisis	crisis
sufficient enough	sufficient (or enough)
there in person	there

two different kinds	two kinds
very unique	unique

EXERCISES

Exercise 1

Rewrite the following sentences to eliminate *clichés* and *awkward phrasing.* If a whole sentence is a cliché, eliminate it.

1. Inventing something new is as American as apple pie.
2. NASA recently had a bright idea that turned into a reality.
3. The thing that this is even made it into the Guinness Book of World Records.
4. Believe it or not, it is a solid made of 99.8% air.
5. It's strange but true!
6. The Guinness World Record for the stuff NASA invented is for the "least solid object in the world."
7. There is a name for the kind of stuff it is.
8. It's an aerogel, which is a substance as light as a feather but as strong as an ox, and it will be used to build airplanes and spaceships.
9. The new aerogel that NASA invented looks exactly like a frozen cloud.
10. It's hard to impress people with inventions in this day and age, but this new aerogel is one in a million.

Source: Current Science, August 30, 2002

Exercise 2

Rewrite the following sentences to eliminate *wordiness.* See how few words you can use without changing the meaning of the sentence.

1. There is one man in the world who has done something that nobody had ever done before he did it.
2. Irv Gordon put an incredible two million miles on his cherry red Volvo P1800 car.

3. Of course it goes without saying that Gordon's achievement was a new world record for the amount of miles an individual drove his own personal car.
4. Gordon has absolutely loved to drive his Volvo since the very first day he bought it in 1966.
5. He purchased his Volvo after he had to return another type of car that turned out to be a lemon and that broke down on the way home from the dealership.
6. Once Gordon had purchased his Volvo, he couldn't stop driving it around.
7. Within the first two days of owning the brand-new car, Gordon put 1,500 miles on its odometer.
8. The company named Volvo celebrated its 75th anniversary at the exact same time that Gordon's odometer was passing the two-million-mile mark.
9. Gordon sees no reason why he shouldn't try to drive his car for another million miles to reach the three-million-mile mark.
10. In spite of the fact that he and his Volvo are getting kind of old, Gordon is a retired science teacher and knows how to maintain his precious car.

Source: Car-Data.com

Exercise 3

Revise the sentences in the remaining exercises to eliminate any clichés, awkward phrasing, or wordiness.

1. After Irv Gordon celebrated his record-breaking accumulation of mileage on his '66 Volvo, he arranged for the transportation of his famous car to Europe so that he could begin putting even more miles on his car during an overseas vacation.
2. The Volvo company was continuing its 75th anniversary celebration in several European countries, and of course Gordon was invited to attend.

3. Unfortunately, Gordon suffered three unlucky mishaps during his European tour.
4. The first of his unfortunate misadventures happened in Sweden.
5. Gordon was taking a bite out of a piece of crayfish, and one of the fillings in his teeth came out.
6. Things went from bad to worse when he couldn't find a dentist for a period of about a week as he drove his car through Holland and Germany.
7. Once Gordon made it to England, a mechanic at a Volvo dealership helped him find a dentist just in the nick of time.
8. Strange as it may seem, Gordon was then injured when a hydraulic lift at the mechanic's shop smashed Gordon's toe and broke it.
9. Last but not least, after a dentist had fixed his tooth and doctors had treated his broken toe, Gordon was stung on the eyelid by a bee at a rugby match.
10. Gordon must have been quite a sight as he drove his celebrated Volvo onto the ship to take it home from their European vacation.

Source: Volvo Club of America (*http://www.vcoa.org/irv_o_meter.shtml*)

Exercise 4

1. I just got finished reading an article that explains that the ancient Egyptians used what we now call makeup in a lot of different ways, not just for beauty.
2. First of all, they used makeup to paint their faces in an effort to make themselves more attractive to other human beings.
3. Egyptians seemed to be just as hung up on staying young and gorgeous looking as we modern folks do.
4. And it was a big eye-opener to me that the Egyptian men put makeup on their eyes and lips just like the Egyptian women.

5. French scientists and beauty experts have been studying the leftover contents that remain inside ancient vessels found inside the buried tombs of kings and queens of the Nile as far back in time as 2700 B.C.
6. From these leftover remains of ancient makeup, scientists have been able to identify the ingredients that the Egyptians used in their makeup concoctions.
7. The list of ingredients that the scientists discovered includes goose fat, lettuce, animal blood, crushed beetles, cinnamon, and some other ingredients that did not naturally occur in nature.
8. That means that the Egyptians had to know enough about chemistry to make artificial ingredients in the same way that we make artificial ingredients in this day and age.
9. Last but not least, the Egyptians seemed to have used makeup for medicinal rather than only cosmetic purposes.
10. Two of the substances that the Egyptians made artificially were laurionite and phosgenite, and these two ingredients may have helped to cure the eye problems that many Egyptians had due to the fact that the Nile river often flooded the valley and contained bacteria that commonly infected people's eyes.

Source: Discover, September 1999

Exercise 5

1. I was as happy as a clam when I found out a few days ago that I will be getting a tax return of eight hundred dollars this year.
2. Before this, I used to do my own taxes myself.
3. I would wait for my W-2 forms to get here in the mail and then fill out the short form that lets me get the whole thing over with quick, even if I don't get a whole lot back from Uncle Sam.

4. Then my mom started giving me the old song and dance about that I'm getting old enough to do the right thing instead of taking the easy way out.
5. Well, that was all it took to make me wake up and smell the coffee.
6. I asked around at work to see if anyone knew a tax person to recommend, and my friend Jason said that he did, and he gave me her number.
7. I called the tax preparer that Jason used; her name was Helen.
8. After I went to see Helen, she explained to me that I should be the one to control the amount that gets taken out of my paycheck for taxes, not the other way around.
9. I never even had a clue that there was so much to know about being a "grownup," as my mom calls it.
10. And I bet I've just started to scratch the surface of what "real" grownups understand.

PROOFREADING EXERCISE

Revise the sentences in the following paragraph to eliminate any clichés, awkward phrasing, or wordiness.

In my family, I don't think that you could call anybody in it "normal." In fact, every single member of my family is a bit of an oddball. The oddest one of all has to be my Uncle Crank. His real name is actually Frank, but ever since I was growing up, Uncle Frank told us kids to call him Uncle "Crank." That's because of his arm. Frank has an arm that is out of the ordinary because it doesn't bend the right way at the elbow. So you can go right up to it and turn it like a crank on an old car in the silent films. He is as proud as a peacock about the trick his arm can do. He is unique, all right, but I wish the doctors had fixed his elbow so that Uncle "Crank" could have been just a normal Uncle Frank. That way he wouldn't have to call attention to how different he is all the time.

SENTENCE WRITING

Go back to the sentences you wrote for the Sentence Writing exercise on page 23 or page 104 and revise them to eliminate any clichés, awkward phrasing, or wordiness.

Correcting for Parallel Structure

Your writing will be clearer and more memorable if you use parallel structure. That is, when you write two pieces of information or any kind of list, put the items in similar form. Look at this sentence, for example:

> My favorite movies are comic, romantic, or the ones about outer space.

The sentence lacks parallel structure. The third item in the list doesn't match the other two. Now look at this sentence:

> My favorite movie categories are comedies, love stories, and sci-fi fantasies.

Here the items are parallel; they are all plural nouns. Or you could write the following:

> I like movies that make me laugh, that make me cry, and that make me think.

Again the sentence has parallel structure because all three items in the list are dependent clauses. Here are some more examples. Note how much easier it is to read the sentences with parallel structure.

Without Parallel Structure	With Parallel Structure
I like to hike, to ski, and going sailing.	I like to hike, to ski, and to sail. (all "to" verbs)
The office has run out of pens, paper, ink cartridges, and we need more toner, too.	The office needs more pens, paper, ink cartridges, and toner. (all nouns)
They decided that they needed a change, that they could afford a new house, and wanted to move to Arizona.	They decided that they needed a change, that they could afford a new house, and that they wanted to move to Arizona. (all dependent clauses)

The parts of an outline should always be parallel. Following are two brief outlines about food irradiation. The parts of the outline on the *left* are not parallel. The first subtopic (I.) is a question; the other (II.) is just a noun. And the supporting points (A., B., C.) are written as nouns, verbs, and even clauses. The parts of the outline on the *right* are parallel. Both subtopics (I. and II.) are plural nouns, and all details (A., B., C.) are action verbs followed by objects.

Not Parallel	Parallel
Food Irradiation	Food Irradiation
I. How is it good?	I. Benefits
A. Longer shelf life	A. Extends shelf life
B. Using fewer pesticides	B. Requires fewer pesticides
C. Kills bacteria	C. Kills bacteria
II. Concerns	II. Concerns
A. Nutritional value	A. Lowers nutritional value
B. Consumers are worried	B. Alarms consumers
C. Workers' safety	C. Endangers workers

Using parallel structure will make your writing more effective. Note the parallelism in these well-known quotations:

> A place for everything and everything in its place.
>
> *Isabella Mary Beeton*

> Ask not what your country can do for you; ask what you can do for your country.
>
> *John F. Kennedy*

We hold these truths to be self-evident, that all men are created equal, that they are endowed by their creator with certain unalienable rights, that among these are Life, Liberty, and the pursuit of Happiness.

Thomas Jefferson

EXERCISES

Rephrase the following sentences so that any pairs or lists contain parallel structure.

Exercise 1

1. I like coffee, and I sort of like tea.
2. I've heard that coffee is bad for you, but drinking tea is good.
3. It must not be the caffeine that's bad because coffee has caffeine and so does tea.
4. I heard one expert say that it's the other chemicals in the coffee and tea that make the difference in health benefits.
5. All teas are supposed to be healthy, but the healthiest is green tea supposedly.
6. Unfortunately, green tea is the only type of tea I don't like.
7. I love orange pekoe tea with tons of milk and a ton of sugar too.
8. I was really surprised to find out that all tea leaves come from the same plant.
9. I know that all coffee comes from coffee beans, but it shocked me to find out that green tea and orange pekoe are both made with leaves from the *Camellia sinensis* plant.
10. Maybe I'll give green tea another try since it could improve my health.

Exercise 2

1. Both men and, it turns out, some women also fought as soldiers in the Civil War.

2. The women disguised themselves as men, and they could fight as stubbornly as their male counterparts, and even were enlisting for the same reasons.
3. They signed up to be soldiers for excitement, wanting to get revenge for something done to relatives, not being able to bear being separated from their relatives, and for financial gain.
4. One Confederate soldier, Henry Clark, was captured by Union forces.
5. While examining Clark's wounds, the doctor discovered that Henry was a woman.
6. In fact, her real name was Mary Ann Clark, and a single mother of two children was her real identity.
7. The Union soldiers who captured Clark provided her with a dress, she was given her freedom, and then they made her swear to return to her life as a female in society.
8. After she left the Union camp, Clark got rid of the dress, she was able to rejoin her fellow Confederate soldiers as a woman, and a promotion to lieutenant was her reward.
9. Letters from soldiers on both sides of the war—from men and females—support the historical findings of the two writers of the book *They Fought Like Demons: Women Soldiers in the American Civil War.*
10. The coauthors of the book, Lauren Cook and DeAnne Blanton is the other author's name, have been able to prove that there were between 250 and 400 undercover female soldiers who fought in the Civil War.

Source: Smithsonian, October 2002

Exercise 3

1. Nearly anyone who has grown up in America during the last century remembers putting a baby tooth under a pillow and the result of a quarter or two in its place in the morning.

2. The tradition of leaving a tooth for the Tooth Fairy and its significance are hard to trace.
3. One person who is trying to understand the myth and collects everything to do with it is Dr. Rosemary Wells.
4. Dr. Wells runs the Tooth Fairy Museum in Deerfield, Illinois, and knows as much as anyone else about the elusive tooth taker.
5. Wells' interest in the legend of the Tooth Fairy started in the early 1970s when one of her dental students asked where it came from.
6. Since then Wells has gathered books, written essays, has an art collection, and receives gifts about the Tooth Fairy.
7. One of the most intriguing things about the story is that, unlike Santa Claus, the Tooth Fairy does not have any specific "look," and people don't think of the Tooth Fairy's gender.
8. Wells has discovered a few ancient rituals having to do with lost teeth, such as tossing the tooth into the air or that you should pitch it at a rat.
9. Both children in Europe and Mexican children have the story of the "Tooth Mouse" that comes to take away discarded baby teeth.
10. This story and the fairy stories brought over from England, Ireland, and Scotland probably melded together to form the legend of the Tooth Fairy.

Source: America's Strangest Museums (Citadel, 1996)

Exercise 4

1. I was washing my car two weeks ago, and that's when I noticed a few bees buzzing around the roof of my garage.
2. I didn't worry about it at the time, but it was something that I should have worried about.

3. As I drove into my driveway a week later, a whole swarm of bees flew up and down in front of my windshield.
4. The swarm wasn't that big, but the bees flying tightly together looked really frightening.
5. They flew in a pattern as if they were riding on a roller coaster or almost like waves.
6. I was glad that my wife and kids were away for the weekend.
7. There was nothing I could do but to wait in my car until they went away.
8. Finally, the bees flew straight up into the air and then disappeared.
9. Once inside my house, I opened the phone book and started to call a bee expert.
10. The bees had made a hive out of part of my garage roof, the expert said, but once I replace the lumber in that area, I should not be bothered with bees anymore.

Exercise 5

Make the following sentences into a list of clear suggestions using parallel structures. You may want to add transitions like *first* and *finally* to help make the steps clear.

1. Experts give the following tips to those who want to get the most out of a visit to the doctor.
2. Avoid getting frustrated in the waiting room or if you have to wait a long time in the exam room.
3. You should always answer the doctor's questions first then asking the doctor a few of your own might be a good idea.
4. It's smart to inquire about a referral to a specialist if you think you need one.
5. Finding out if there are other treatments besides the one the doctor first recommends can't hurt.

6. Ask about any tests that the doctor orders and you might wonder what the results mean, so you probably want to get in touch with the doctor after the results come back.
7. Prescriptions are often given hastily and with little explanation, so ask about side effects and optional medicines if one doesn't work.
8. Discussing these things should not make a good doctor nervous, but try not to be too aggressive in your approach.
9. Get prepared to wait in a long line at the pharmacy.
10. If you follow these suggestions when visiting a doctor, you will be more informed and also you can feel involved in your own treatment.

PROOFREADING EXERCISE

Proofread the following paragraph about Shirley Temple, the famous child star of the 1930s, and revise it to correct any errors in parallel structure.

Shirley Temple was born in 1928. In 1931, when she was just three years old, someone discovered her natural talent at a dance lesson, and she was asked to be in movies. She starred in many films that are still popular today. Among them are *Heidi, Rebecca of Sunnybrook Farm,* and *Curly Top* was one of her earliest. Directors loved Shirley's acting style and the fact that she was able to do a scene in only one take, but not everyone trusted Shirley Temple. Graham Greene was sued when he claimed that Shirley was about thirty years old and in reality was a dwarf. Little Shirley's parents helped with her career, and they also earned money for their efforts. In the early days, the studios paid her mother several hundred dollars a week to put fifty-six curlers in Shirley's hair each night. That way, her famous ringlets would always be perfect, and her hair looked the same each time. Shirley's father managed her money, so much money that at one point Shirley Temple was among the ten highest paid people in America. It was 1938, and she was only ten years old.

Source: California People (Peregrine Smith, 1982)

SENTENCE WRITING

Write ten sentences that use parallel structure in a list or a pair of objects, actions, locations, or ideas. You may choose your own subject or describe the process of shopping for your favorite CDs or DVDs.

Using Pronouns

Nouns name people, places, things, and ideas—such as *students, school, computers,* and *cyberspace.* Pronouns take the place of nouns to avoid repetition and to clarify meaning. Look at the following two sentences:

> Naomi's father worried that the children at the party were too loud, so Naomi's father told the children that the party would have to end if the children didn't calm down.
>
> Naomi's father worried that the children at the party were too loud, so *he* told *them* that *it* would have to end if *they* didn't calm down.

Nouns are needlessly repeated in the first sentence. The second sentence uses pronouns in their place. *He* replaces *father, they* and *them* replace *children,* and *it* takes the place of *party.*

Of the many kinds of pronouns, the following cause the most difficulty because they include two ways of identifying the same person (or people), but only one form is correct in a given situation:

Subject Group	**Object Group**
I	me
he	him
she	her
we	us
they	them

Use a pronoun from the Subject Group in two instances:

1. Before a verb as a subject:

   He is my cousin. (*He* is the subject of the verb *is.*)

   He is taller than *I.* (The sentence is not written out in full. It means "*He* is taller than *I* am." *I* is the subject of the verb *am.*)

Whenever you see *than* in a sentence, ask yourself whether a verb has been left off the end of the sentence. Add the verb, and then you'll automatically use the correct pronoun. In both speaking and writing, always add the verb. Instead of saying, "She's smarter than (I, me)," say, "She's smarter than I *am.*" Then you will use the correct pronoun.

2. After a linking verb (*is, am, are, was, were*) as a pronoun that renames the subject:

   The ones who should apologize are *they.* (*They* are *the ones who should apologize.*

   Therefore, the pronoun from the Subject Group is used.)

   The winner of the lottery was *she.* (*She* was *the winner of the lottery.*

   Therefore, the pronoun from the Subject Group is used.)

Modern usage allows some exceptions to this rule, however. For example, *It's me* or *It is her* (instead of the grammatically correct *It is I* and *It is she*) may be common in spoken English.

Use pronouns from the Object Group for all other purposes. In the following sentence, *me* is not the subject, nor does it rename the subject. It follows a preposition; therefore, it comes from the Object Group.

My boss went to lunch with Jenny and *me.*

A good way to tell whether to use a pronoun from the Subject Group or the Object Group is to leave out any extra name (and the word *and*). By leaving out *Jenny and,* you will say, *My boss went to lunch with me.* You would never say, *My boss went to lunch with I.*

My father and *I* play chess on Sundays. (*I* play chess on Sundays.)

She and her friends rented a video. (*She* rented a video.)

We saw Kevin and *them* last night. (We saw *them* last night.)

The teacher gave *us* students certificates. (Teacher gave *us* certificates.)

The coach asked Craig and *me* to wash the benches. (Coach asked *me* to wash the benches.)

Pronoun Agreement

Just as subjects and verbs must agree, pronouns should agree with the nouns they refer to. If the word referred to is singular, the pronoun should be singular. If the word referred to is plural, the pronoun should be plural.

Each classroom has its own chalkboard.

The pronoun *its* refers to the singular noun *classroom* and therefore is singular.

Both classrooms have their own chalkboards.

The pronoun *their* refers to the plural noun *classrooms* and therefore is plural.

The same rules that we use to maintain the agreement of subjects and verbs also apply to pronoun agreement. For instance, ignore any prepositional phrases that come between the noun and the pronoun that takes its place.

The *box* of chocolates has lost *its* label.

Boxes of chocolates often lose *their* labels.

A *player* with the best concentration usually beats *her or his* opponent.

Players with the best concentration usually beat *their* opponents.

When a pronoun refers to more than one word joined by *and*, the pronoun is plural:

The *teacher* and the *tutors* eat *their* lunches at noon.

The *salt* and *pepper* were in *their* usual spots on the table.

However, when a pronoun refers to more than one word joined by *or*, then the word closest to the pronoun determines its form:

Either the teacher or the *tutors* eat *their* lunches in the classroom.

Either the tutors or the *teacher* eats *her* lunch in the classroom.

Today many people try to avoid gender bias by writing sentences like the following:

If anyone wants help with the assignment, he or she can visit me in my office.

If anybody calls, tell him or her that I'll be back soon.

Somebody has left his or her pager in the classroom.

But those sentences are wordy and awkward. Therefore some people, especially in conversation, turn them into sentences that are *not* grammatically correct.

If anyone wants help with the assignment, they can visit me in my office.

If anybody calls, tell them that I'll be back soon.

Somebody has left their pager in the classroom.

Such ungrammatical sentences, however, are not necessary. It just takes a little thought to revise each sentence so that it avoids gender bias and is also grammatically correct:

Anyone who wants help with the assignment can visit me in my office.

Tell anybody who calls that I'll be back soon.

Somebody has left a pager in the classroom.

Probably the best way to avoid the awkward *he or she* and *him or her* is to make the words plural. Instead of, "Each actor was in his or her proper place on stage," write, "All the actors were in their proper places on stage," thus avoiding gender bias and still writing a grammatically correct sentence.

Pronoun Reference

A pronoun replaces a noun to avoid repetition, but sometimes the pronoun sounds as if it refers to the wrong word in a sentence, causing confusion. Be aware that when you write a sentence, *you* know what it means, but your reader may not. What does this sentence mean?

The students tried to use the school's computers to access the Internet, but they were too slow, so they decided to go home.

Who or what was too slow, and who or what decided to go home? We don't know whether the two pronouns (both *they*) refer to the students or to the computers. One way to correct such a faulty reference is to use singular and plural nouns:

The students tried to use a school computer to access the Internet, but it was too slow, so they decided to go home.

Here's another sentence with a faulty reference:

Calvin told his father that he needed a haircut.

Who needed the haircut—Calvin or his father? One way to correct such a faulty reference is to use a direct quotation:

> Calvin told his father, "You need a haircut."
>
> Calvin said, "Dad, I need a haircut."

Or you could always rephrase the sentence completely:

> Calvin noticed his father's hair was sticking out in odd places, so he told his father to get a haircut.

Another kind of faulty reference is a *which* clause that appears to refer to a specific word, but it doesn't really.

> I wasn't able to finish all the problems on the exam, which makes me worried.

The word *which* seems to replace *exam,* but it isn't the exam that makes me worried. The sentence should read

> I am worried because I wasn't able to finish all the problems on the exam.

The pronoun *it* causes its own reference problems. Look at this sentence, for example:

> When replacing the ink cartridge in my printer, it broke, and I had to call the technician to come and fix it.

Did the printer or the cartridge break? Here is one possible correction:

> The new ink cartridge broke when I was putting it in my printer, and I had to call the technician for help.

EXERCISES

Exercise 1

Underline the correct pronoun. Remember the trick of leaving out the extra name to help you decide which pronoun to use. Use the correct grammatical form even though an alternate form may be acceptable in conversation.

1. My mother and (I, me) went bowling last night.
2. I usually enjoy these trips to the bowling alley more than (she, her).
3. This time, however, both (she and I, her and me) enjoyed it.

4. Since my mother bowls less often than (I, me), she usually doesn't feel as comfortable as (I, me).
5. Every time (she and I, her and me) have been bowling before, I have chosen the lane and the weight of the ball she has used.
6. The one who made those choices this time was (she, her).
7. She may not bowl as often as (I, me), but she sure picked a winner of a ball.
8. The pins seemed to be waiting for (she, her) to knock them over.
9. I guess I am still more of a regular bowler than (she, her), but I have learned to appreciate my mother's instincts.
10. In the future, I will leave the decisions of which lane to bowl in and which ball to use up to (she, her).

Exercise 2

Underline the pronoun that agrees with the word the pronoun replaces. If the correct answer is *his or her/her or his,* revise the sentence to eliminate the need for this awkward expression. Check your answers as you go through the exercise.

1. I live a long way from the city center and don't own a car, so I use public transportation and rely on (its, their) stability.
2. Based on my experiences, I'd say the city's system of buses has (its, their) problems.
3. Each of the bus routes that I travel on my way to work falls behind (its, their) own schedule.
4. Many of the other passengers also transfer on (his or her, their) way to work.
5. One day last week, each of the passengers had to gather (his or her, their) belongings and leave the bus, even though it had not reached a scheduled stop.
6. Both the driver and the mechanic who came to fix the bus offered (his, their) apologies for making us late.

7. Once the bus was fixed, the passengers were allowed to bring (his or her, their) things back on board.
8. Everyone did (his or her, their) best to hide (his or her, their) annoyance from the driver because he had been so nice.
9. As every passenger stepped off the bus at the end of the line, the driver thanked (him or her, them) for (his or her, their) patience and understanding.
10. Sometimes it is the people within a system that makes (it, them) work after all.

Exercise 3

Underline the correct pronoun. Again, if the correct answer is *his or her/her or his,* revise the sentence to eliminate the need for this awkward expression.

1. A rental car agency must be very competitive in (its, their) pricing.
2. The one blamed for the accident was (she, her).
3. Each of the new employees has (his or her, their) own locker in the employee lounge.
4. The debate teams from each school will continue (its, their) tournament tomorrow.
5. Every member of the audience had (his or her, their) opinion of the play and expressed it in the volume of (his or her, their) applause.
6. When it comes to plants, no one knows more than (he, him).
7. The teacher gave my fellow students and (I, me) a few suggestions.
8. (You and he, You and him) are similar in many ways.
9. My mother is actually younger than (she, her).
10. All of the customers at the supermarket shopped for (his or her, their) groceries at different speeds.

Exercise 4

Most—but not all—of the sentences in the next two sets aren't clear because we don't know what word the pronoun refers to. Revise such sentences, making the meaning clear. Since there are more ways than one to rewrite each sentence, yours may be as good as the ones at the back of the book. Just ask yourself whether the meaning is clear.

1. As I was cooking my burrito in the microwave, it exploded.
2. The student told the librarian that she didn't understand her.
3. While we were putting the decorations on the tables, they blew away.
4. Our cat sleeps all the time, which is boring.
5. Samantha asked her friend why she wasn't invited to join the debate team.
6. I shuffled the cards and asked Josh to pick one.
7. He finished printing his book report, turned off the printer, and put it in his folder.
8. Max told his brother that his bike had a flat tire.
9. I bought my parking pass early, which gave me one less thing to worry about.
10. Irene's mom lets her take her cell phone to school even though it's against the rules.

Exercise 5

1. The Howells purchased new lawn chairs, but they were too fancy for them.
2. The teacher ordered a new textbook, and it arrived the next week.
3. I initialed the changes on the contract, put the top back on my pen, and handed it to the real estate agent.
4. When students join study groups, they help a lot.
5. As we placed the jars in pans of boiling water, they shattered.
6. Whenever I receive good news, I enjoy it.
7. Phone companies offer different prices for their handling of long-distance calls.
8. Dan's tutor asked him to rewrite his essay.

9. Many people visit amusement parks for their thrilling rides.
10. The committee members interviewed the applicants in their offices.

PROOFREADING EXERCISE

The following paragraph contains errors in the use of pronouns. Find and correct the errors.

My daughter and me drove up the coast to visit a little zoo I had heard about. It was a hundred miles and took about two hours. Once her and I arrived, we saw the petting zoo area and wanted to pet the baby animals, but they wouldn't let us. They said that it was the baby animals' resting time, so we couldn't pet them. Then we got to the farm animals. There was a prize-winning hog that was as big as a couch when it was lying down. My daughter liked the hog best of all, and as she and I drove home in the car, it was all she could talk about.

SENTENCE WRITING

Write ten sentences in which you describe similarities and/or differences between you and someone else in your family. Then check that your pronouns are grammatically correct, that they agree with the words they replace, and that references to specific nouns are clear.

Avoiding Shifts in Person

To understand what "person" means when using pronouns, imagine a conversation between two people about a third person. The first person speaks using "I, me, my. . ."; the second person would be called "you"; and when the two of them talked of a third person, they would say "he, she, they. . . ." You'll never forget the idea of "person" if you remember it as a three-part conversation.

First person—*I, me, my, we, us, our*

Second person—*you, your*

Third person—*he, him, his, she, her, hers, they, them, their, one, anyone*

You may use all three of these groups of pronouns in a paper, but don't shift from one group to another without a good reason.

Wrong: Few people know how to manage *their* time. *One* need not be an efficiency expert to realize that *one* could get a lot more done if *he* budgeted *his* time. Nor do *you* need to work very hard to get more organized.

Better: *Everyone* should know how to manage *his or her* time. *One* need not be an efficiency expert to realize that *a person* could get a lot more done if *one* budgeted *one's* time. Nor does *one* need to work very hard to get more organized. (Too many *one*'s in a paragraph make it sound overly formal, and they lead to the necessity of avoiding sexism by using *s/he* or *he or she,* etc. Sentences can be revised to avoid using either *you* or *one.*)

Best: Many of *us* don't know how to manage *our* time. *We* need not be efficiency experts to realize that *we* could get a lot more done if *we* budgeted *our* time. Nor do *we* need to work very hard to get more organized.

Often students write *you* in a paper when they don't really mean *you, the reader.*

You wouldn't believe how many times I saw that movie.

Such sentences are always improved by getting rid of the *you.*

I saw that movie many times.

PROOFREADING EXERCISES

Which of the following student paragraphs shift *unnecessarily* between first-, second-, and third-person pronouns? In those that do, revise the sentences to eliminate such shifting, thus making the entire paragraph read smoothly. (First, read the paragraphs to determine whether unnecessary shifting takes place. One of the paragraphs is correct.)

1. Americans have always had more than we actually need. Americans have gotten used to having as much food, water, and clothes as they want. Our restaurants throw away plates and plates of food every day. If you don't want something, you throw it in the trash. But a lot of people have started to think differently. Recycling doesn't just involve aluminum cans and plastic bottles. Americans can recycle food, water, and clothes if we think more creatively and responsibly than they've been doing in the past. You can change the society's view of recycling by just doing it.

2. Christopher Wolfe will always have a reason to be proud. When he was seven years old, Christopher discovered a new dinosaur, and scientists named it after him. They called it *Zuniceratops christopheri.* This unknown species of dinosaur had two horns, one over each eye. There have been other discoveries of dinosaurs with horns, but the one whose bones Christopher found lived twenty million years earlier than any others. Christopher's father, Douglas Wolfe, was with him when he spotted the fossil in the Arizona/New Mexico desert. Douglas, a paleontologist, knew right away that his son's find was genuine. However, the kids at school had a hard time believing Christopher when he came in the next school day and told his classmates that he had discovered a new dinosaur species.

Source: People, November 2, 1998

3. If I had a choice to live in the city or the country, I would choose the city. I would choose the city because you are surrounded by other people there, and it feels friendly. The country is too quiet. There is dirt everywhere, flies flying around in the sky, bugs—which I hate—crawling on the floor inside and out. The city is a place where the lights are always on. Yes, you deal with pollution, smog, and crowds, but it just feels like home to me. A city house can be any size, shape, and color. All the houses in the country look the same to me. No matter who you are, you have a white house and a big red barn. I have to admit that I have only been to the country a couple of times to visit my relatives, but the city would have to be the place for me.

REVIEW OF SENTENCE STRUCTURE ERRORS

One sentence in each pair contains an error. Read both sentences carefully before you decide. Then write the letter of the *incorrect* sentence in the blank. Try to name the error and correct it if you can. You may find any of these errors:

awk	awkward phrasing
cliché	overused expression
dm	dangling modifier
frag	fragment
mm	misplaced modifier
pro	incorrect pronoun
pro agr	pronoun agreement error
pro ref	pronoun reference error
ro	run-on sentence
shift	shift in time or person
s/v agr	subject/verb agreement error
wordy	wordiness
//	not parallel

1. _____ **A.** I prefer dill pickles to sweet pickles.

   B. Dill pickles have a snappy flavor that sweet pickles just don't have.

2. _____ **A.** My biggest problem in school is following directions.

   B. The bottom line is that I don't like being forced into things.

3. _____ **A.** My classmates and I have a new plan for our group project.

   B. We all think that it was going to be really effective.

4. _____ **A.** My architecture class took a field trip.

   B. One of the tour guides gave my friend and I a map of the area.

5. _____ **A.** Students who study hard and the ones who don't miss class usually do well.

   B. Most teachers reward good attendance and neat, careful work.

6. _____ **A.** Everyone in the room had a surprised look on their faces.

B. The president of the college came in for a visit.

7. ______ **A.** Each of my classes challenge me in a different way.

B. I am taking three classes this semester, and I like them all.

8. ______ **A.** She buys houses that are run-down, need paint, and old.

B. Then she fixes them up and sells them.

9. ______ **A.** Our dog had puppies in the kitchen.

B. There are seven of them they're all adorable.

10. ______ **A.** The point of my essay is that real poverty is unimaginable to most people.

B. Volunteers helped the victims in the poorest areas of town recover from the earthquake and start new lives.

11. ______ **A.** My teacher and I talked after class.

B. Me and him agreed that I needed a tutor.

12. ______ **A.** After taking so long to explain the assignment on Friday.

B. The teacher ran out of time and had to start over again on Monday.

13. ______ **A.** Pencils and pens seem to have a life of their own sometimes.

B. They escape from backpacks and purses, never being seen again.

14. ______ **A.** Some people will never admit when they are wrong.

B. You can even show them the facts, and they won't admit it.

15. ______ **A.** After resting on the couch, the television didn't seem very loud at all.

B. I started to feel sleepy and dozed off for a few minutes.

PROOFREADING EXERCISE

Can you find and correct the sentence structure errors in the following essay?

Mother Tells All

The most memorable lessons I have learned about myself have come from my own children. A mother is always on display she has nowhere to hide. And children are like parrots. Whatever they hear her say will be repeated again. If I change my mind about anything, you can be sure they will repeat back every word I uttered out of my mouth.

For example, last summer I told my kids that I was going to go to an exercise class and lose about forty pounds. Well, I lost some of the weight, and I did go to that exercise class. But as soon as I lost weight, I felt empty like a balloon losing air. I felt that I did not want to lose any more weight or do exercise anymore. I thought that my children would accept what I had decided.

When I stopped, the first thing one of my sons said was, "Mom, you need to go back to exercise class." Then they all started telling me what to eat all the time and I felt horrible about it. I had given up these things because I wanted to, but my words were still being repeated to me like an alarm clock going off without stopping. Finally, my kids ran out of steam and got bored with the idea of my losing weight. Once in a while, one of them still make a joke about my "attempt" to lose weight it hurts me that they don't understand.

The lesson that I have learned from this experience is that, if I am not planning on finishing something, I won't tell my children about it. They will never let me forget.

PART 3

Punctuation and Capital Letters

Period, Question Mark, Exclamation Point, Semicolon, Colon, Dash

Every mark of punctuation should help the reader. Here are the rules for six marks of punctuation. The first three you have known for a long time and probably have no trouble with. The one about semicolons you learned when you studied independent clauses (p. 84). The ones about the colon and the dash may be less familiar.

Put a period (.) at the end of a sentence and after most abbreviations.

> The students elected Ms. Daniels to represent the class.
>
> Sept. Mon. in. sq. ft. lbs.

Put a question mark (?) after a direct question but not after an indirect one.

> Will we be able to use our notes during the test? (direct)
>
> I wonder if we will be able to use our notes during the test. (indirect)

Put an exclamation point (!) after an expression that shows strong emotion. This mark is used mostly in dialogue or informal correspondence.

> I can't believe I did so well on my first exam!

Put a semicolon (;) between two independent clauses in a sentence unless they are joined by one of the connecting words *for, and, nor, but, or, yet, so.*

My mother cosigned for a loan; now I have my own car.

Some careers go in and out of fashion; however, people will always need teachers.

To be sure that you are using a semicolon correctly, see if a period and capital letter can be used in its place. If they can, you are putting the semicolon in the right spot.

My mother cosigned for a loan. Now I have my own car.

Some careers go in and out of fashion. However, people will always need teachers.

Put a colon (:) after a complete statement that introduces one of the following elements: a name, a list, a quotation, or an explanation.

The company announced its Employee of the Month: Lee Jones. (The sentence before the colon introduces the name that follows it.)

That truck comes in the following colors: red, black, blue, and silver. (The complete statement before the colon introduces the list that follows it.)

That truck comes in red, black, blue, and silver. (Here the list is simply part of the sentence. There is no complete statement used to introduce the list and set it off from the rest of the sentence.)

Thoreau had this to say about time: "Time is but the stream I go a-fishin in." (The writer introduces the quotation with a complete statement. Therefore, a colon comes between them.)

Thoreau said, "Time is but the stream I go a-fishin in." (Here the writer leads directly into the quotation; therefore, no colon—just a comma—comes between them.)

Use dashes (—) to isolate inserted information, to signal an abrupt change of thought, or to emphasize what follows.

Lee Jones—March's Employee of the Month—received his own special parking space.

I found out today—or was it yesterday?—that I have inherited a fortune.

We have exciting news for you—we're moving!

EXERCISES

Add to these sentences the necessary punctuation (periods, question marks, exclamation points, semicolons, colons, and dashes). The commas used within the sentences are correct and do not need to be changed. Check your answers after the first set.

Exercise 1

1. Have you ever heard someone describe a beer-gone-bad as "skunky"
2. The comparison is obvious the beer smells like skunk spray
3. Now scientists at the University of North Carolina at Chapel Hill can explain this phenomenon
4. The ingredients in beer have one main enemy light
5. A beer that gets too much light undergoes a chemical change the result is a smell that is very similar to that of a skunk
6. That is why beer usually comes in colored bottles
7. Consumers like the colored beer bottles however, dark bottles are more expensive
8. Therefore, beer makers would like to use clear bottles they would cost less and be easier to recycle
9. New discoveries about the chemical changes in beer due to light might allow makers to avoid the problem in the future
10. Then beers could be sold in clear bottles they would be less expensive they would be more environmentally friendly, and they would never smell "skunky" again

Source: National Geographic, October 2002

Exercise 2

1. Wasn't the company's holiday party nice this year
2. At first, I wasn't sure that I wanted to go now I'm glad I did
3. The music especially the harp music made everyone so calm and contented

4. The twinkling lights in the trees on the patio gave off a beautiful light
5. Even the cubicles around our desks looked festive
6. The boss announced our new Employee of the Year Ted Haynes
7. With so many of us doing the same job, there is a lot a competition however, all that was put aside for the party
8. The boss's husband is nicer than I thought he would be I enjoyed meeting him
9. I talked with coworkers that I haven't had any fun with in a long time even Charlie
10. I hope that everyone will still be in a holiday spirit once we get back to work on Monday

Exercise 3

1. Have you ever heard of Dare Wright
2. She was a photographer who created some of the most interesting children's books of the 1950s, 60s, and 70s
3. Wright's main series of books began when she published *The Lonely Doll* in 1957 it was the story of Edith the lonely doll and two teddy bears who came to live with her
4. The way that Dare Wright illustrated her books was unique she photographed the doll and two bears as if they were real people living in an apartment of their own in New York City
5. One of the bears who came to live with Edith was strict, bossy, and older than Edith that was Mr. Bear
6. The other bear was carefree, daring, and younger than Edith that was Little Bear
7. Dare Wright's stories were edgy and often involved Edith and Little Bear getting into real trouble in one book they even get kidnapped at knifepoint by a bear called Big Bad Bill

8. Wright's black-and-white photographs give the books an artistic look that makes them highly prized by book collectors today
9. Most of Dare Wright's books are out of print however, a few of the *Lonely Doll* books have recently been reissued some even colorized
10. It's been nearly fifty years since Dare Wright started her *Lonely Doll* series however, they are still being appreciated by children and adults alike

Exercise 4

1. Nancy Cartwright is a well-known actress on television however, we never see her when she is acting
2. Cartwright is famous for playing one part the voice of Bart Simpson
3. Besides her career as the most mischievous Simpson, Cartwright is married and has children of her own a boy and a girl
4. Wouldn't it be strange if your mother had Bart Simpson's voice
5. Cartwright admits that she made her own share of trouble in school
6. But the similarities between her and her famous character end there
7. Bart is perpetually ten years old Cartwright is in her forties
8. Bart is a boy Cartwright is obviously a woman
9. It's no surprise that Cartwright is very popular with her children's friends
10. When they yell for her to "Do Bart Do Bart" she declines with Bart's favorite saying "No way, man"

Source: People, December 14, 1998

Exercise 5

1. Other nations have given America gifts that have become part of our national landscape for example, France gave us the Statue of Liberty
2. In 1912, Japan sent the United States three thousand cherry trees as a goodwill gesture

3. The Japanese wanted to share their own tradition of Sakura Matsuri that is the spring celebration of the beauty of the cherry blossoms
4. During cherry blossom time, there are picnics and field trips wherever the cherry trees are blooming in Japan
5. Of the three thousand cherry trees that Japan sent to America, only one hundred and twenty five remain they bloom in Washington, DC, every spring
6. Thanks to the National Park Service, the lost Japanese trees have been replaced with ones grown in America however, the original gift trees are the most prized of all
7. New technology has allowed scientists to take clippings from the original Japanese cherry trees and grow new ones consequently, the gift will live on
8. Every spring in Washington, DC, thousands of people come to join in the Japanese enjoyment of cherry blossom time in America it's called the Cherry Blossom Festival
9. And beginning in 2001, the first five hundred offspring of the gift trees will be planted they will continue to grow next to the originals
10. The Statue of Liberty stands in New York Harbor the cherry trees bloom in the capital both were gifts from other nations that add to the beauty of our own

Source: U.S. News & World Report, April 5, 1999

PROOFREADING EXERCISE

Can you find the punctuation errors in this student paragraph? They all involve periods, question marks, exclamation points, semicolons, colons, and dashes. Any commas used within the sentences are correct and should not be changed.

The ingredients you will need for a lemon meringue pie are: lemon juice, eggs, sugar, cornstarch, flour, butter, water, and salt. First, you combine flour, salt, butter, and water for the crust and bake until lightly brown then you mix and cook the lemon juice, egg yolks, sugar, cornstarch, butter, and water for the filling. Once the filling is poured into the cooked crust; you whip the meringue. Meringue is made of egg whites and sugar! Pile the meringue on top of the lemon filling; place the pie in the hot oven for a few minutes, and you'll have the best lemon meringue pie you've ever tasted.

SENTENCE WRITING

Write ten sentences of your own that use periods, question marks, exclamation points, semicolons, colons, and dashes correctly. Imitate the examples used in the explanations if necessary. Write about a success you had at school, at home, or at work and explain how you felt as a result.

Comma Rules 1, 2, and 3

Commas and other pieces of punctuation guide the reader through your sentence structures in the same way that signs guide drivers on the highway. Imagine what effects misplaced or incorrect road signs would have. Yet students often randomly place commas in their sentences. Try not to use a comma unless you know there is a need for it. Memorize this rhyme about comma use: *When in doubt, leave it out.*

Among all of the comma rules, six are most important. Learn these six rules, and your writing will be easier to read. You have already studied the first rule on pages 84–85.

1. **Put a comma before *for, and, nor, but, or, yet, so* (remember these seven words as the *fanboys*) when they connect two independent clauses.**

   The neighbors recently bought a minivan, and now they take short trips every weekend.

   We wrote our paragraphs in class today, but the teacher forgot to collect them.

   Karen was recently promoted, so she has moved to a better office.

If you use a comma alone between two independent clauses, the result is an error called a *comma splice.*

The cake looked delicious, it tasted good too. (comma splice)

The cake looked delicious, and it tasted good too. (correct)

Before using a comma, be sure such words do connect two independent clauses. The following sentence is merely one independent clause with one subject and two verbs. Therefore, no comma should be used.

The cake looked delicious and tasted good too.

2. **Use a comma to separate three or more items in a series.**

   Students in literature classes are reading novels, stories, poems, and plays.

   Today I did my laundry, washed my car, and cleaned my room.

Occasionally, writers leave out the comma before the *and* connecting the last two items in a series, but it is more common to use it to separate all of the items equally.

Some words work together and don't need commas between them even though they do make up a kind of series.

The team members wanted to wear their brand new green uniforms.

The bright white sunlight made the room glow.

To see whether a comma is needed between words in a series, ask yourself whether *and* could be used naturally between them. It would sound all right to say *novels and stories and poems and plays;* therefore, commas are used. But it would not sound right to say *brand and new and green uniforms* or *bright and white sunlight;* therefore, no commas are used.

If an address or date is used in a sentence, put a comma after every item, including the last.

My father was born on August 19, 1941, in Mesa, Arizona, and grew up there.

Shelby lived in St. Louis, Missouri, for two years.

When only the month and year are used in a date, no commas are needed.

My aunt graduated from Yale in May 1985.

3. **Put a comma after an introductory expression (a word, a phrase, or a dependent clause) or before a tag comment or question at the end.**

Finally, he was able to get through to his insurance company.

During her last performance, the actress fell and broke her foot.

Once I have finished my homework, I will call you.

He said he needed to ruminate, whatever that means.

The new chairs aren't very comfortable, are they?

EXERCISES

Add commas to the following sentences according to the first three comma rules. Some sentences may not need any commas, and some may need more than one. Any other punctuation already in the sentences is correct. Check your answers after the first set.

Exercise 1

1. During the past few weeks I have fallen behind schedule on several projects.
2. I'm not sure how the time got away from me but it did.
3. When I first received my assignments to prepare a speech create a photo collage and write a response to a newspaper article I thought I could find the time to finish them all.
4. I took out my student planner and began to map out my work days and due dates.
5. That was a good idea wasn't it?
6. However my planning got all messed up when my car started acting strangely.
7. Unfortunately I spent last Tuesday sitting in a car repair shop lobby instead of gathering the facts for my speech.

8. As soon as my car was fixed I rushed over to pick up the pictures for my collage but the photo place had already closed.
9. I decided to write the newspaper response but couldn't find an article of the right length or on the right topic to fulfill the assignment.
10. Now I've fallen so far behind on the speech the collage and the newspaper response that I don't think I will finish any of them in time.

Exercise 2

1. Most people don't know how coffee is decaffeinated do you?
2. I just discovered that there are three methods used to decaffeinate coffee but one of them is the most popular.
3. The most popular method is called water processing and it draws the caffeine from the coffee beans into a water solution that removes most of the caffeine.
4. After going through the water processing method the coffee may be a little less flavorful but at least the process is "natural."
5. To decaffeinate coffee another way manufacturers add a chemical solution to the beans and then steam them to remove the leftover chemicals.
6. Compared to the water processing method the chemical method is more "scientific" and removes more of the caffeine.
7. Finally there is the method that infuses coffee beans with carbon dioxide gas to get rid of the caffeine.
8. Since carbon dioxide is safe plentiful and nontoxic this process is also popular.
9. The carbon dioxide method may be the most expensive of the three ways to decaffeinate coffee but it also removes the most caffeine.
10. Whenever I drink a cup of decaf in the future I'll wonder which method was used to remove the caffeine.

Source: Scientific American, October 2002

Exercise 3

1. When I was in high school I was lucky to have a great English teacher.
2. Her name was Mrs. Kern and she always tried to make us learn more than one thing at a time.
3. If we read a story in her class we had to do research about the writer too.
4. We read a short play chose parts to memorize and gave a performance of the play in front of class.
5. One of my favorite of Mrs. Kern's assignments was the complaint letter that she asked us to write.
6. She was trying to teach us how to follow directions how to explain something clearly and how to think about what she called our "tone of voice" when we wrote.
7. We had to write a real letter of complaint about a product a service or an experience that was unsatisfactory to us.
8. Then we sent out two copies of our letters one to the company we were complaining to and one to Mrs. Kern's school address.
9. If we explained our complaint well and if the tone of the letter was appropriate we would receive a response from the company Mrs. Kern assured us.
10. When the big envelope from my company arrived I learned that she was absolutely right for in it was a letter of apology a bumper sticker and a coupon for a lifetime discount at the company's stores.

Exercise 4

1. When the government issued the Susan B. Anthony dollar coin it met with some disapproval.
2. People didn't dislike the person on the coin but they did dislike the size and color of the coin.

3. It was nearly the same size as a quarter had a rough edge like a quarter's and was the same color as a quarter.
4. It differed from a quarter in that it was faceted around the edge was lighter in weight and was worth four times as much.
5. Due to these problems the Susan B. Anthony dollar has been replaced by a new dollar coin.
6. Like the Anthony dollar the new coin holds the image of a famous American woman.
7. She was the young Native American guide and interpreter for the Lewis and Clark expedition and her name was Sacagawea.
8. The story of Sacagawea's life tells of hardship suffering and illness but it also tells of incredible knowledge courage and strength.
9. While the men on the famous expedition had only themselves to worry about Sacagawea assisted the men and made the treacherous journey from North Dakota to the Pacific with her baby strapped to her back.
10. Although the same size as the previous dollar coin the Sacagawea dollar has a smooth, wide edge and it is gold.

Source: U.S. News & World Report, May 17, 1999

Exercise 5

1. People used to think that emeralds had magical powers.
2. They were supposed to cure disease lengthen life and protect innocence.
3. Part of their appeal comes from how rare they are for emeralds are even rarer than diamonds.
4. Geologists have been mystified by emeralds because they are produced through a unique process—the blending of chromium vanadium and beryllium.
5. These are substances that almost never meet nor do they often combine—except in emeralds.

6. In South Africa Pakistan and Brazil emeralds were created by intrusions of granite millions to billions of years ago.
7. These areas are known for their beautiful gems but emeralds from Colombia are larger greener and more sparkling.
8. Scientists believe that the difference lies in the makeup of the sedimentary rock in Colombia.
9. Instead of the granite found in other emerald-rich countries the predominant substance in Colombia is black shale.
10. Even though these lustrous green gems can now be synthesized a real emerald always contains a trapped bubble of fluid and this minuscule natural imperfection is known in the gem business as a "garden."

Source: Discover, May 1999

PROOFREADING EXERCISE

Apply the first three comma rules to the following paragraph:

When Niels Rattenborg studied the brains of mallard ducks he made an interesting discovery. Rattenborg wondered how ducks protected themselves as they slept. The ducks slept in rows and these rows were the secret to their defense. To his surprise Rattenborg found that the two ducks on the ends of the row did something special with the sides of their heads facing away from the row. Instinctively the ducks on the edge kept one eye open and one half of their brains awake as they slept. The rest of the ducks slept with both eyes closed and both sides of their brains inactive. The two guard ducks were able to frame the ducks in the middle watch for danger and sleep almost as soundly as their neighbors.

Source: Discover, May 1999

SENTENCE WRITING

Combine the following sets of sentences in different ways using all of the first three comma rules. You may need to reorder the details and change the phrasing. Sample responses are provided in the Answers section.

I enjoy skiing in the winter.
I like hiking in the summer better.

Tutors will not "fix" a student's writing.
They will explain how to clarify ideas.
They will explain how to add stronger details.
They will explain how to improve organization.

Mark and Mary don't know what to do.
They are getting married.
Mark's last name is Perry.
Mary doesn't want to be called Mary Perry.
She might keep her own last name instead.

Comma Rules 4, 5, and 6

The next three comma rules all involve using pairs of commas to enclose what we like to call "scoopable" elements. Scoopable elements are certain words, phrases, and clauses that can be taken out of the middle of a sentence without affecting its meaning. Notice that the comma (,) is shaped somewhat like the tip of an ice cream scoop? Let this similarity help you remember to use commas to enclose *scoopable* elements. Two commas are used, one before and one after, to show where scoopable elements begin and where they end.

4. **Put commas around the name of a person spoken to.**

   Did you know, Danielle, that you left your backpack at the library?

   We regret to inform you, Mr. Davis, that your policy has been canceled.

5. **Put commas around expressions that interrupt the flow of the sentence (such as *however, moreover, therefore, of course, by the way, on the other hand, I believe, I think*).**

   I know, of course, that I have missed the deadline.

   They will try, therefore, to use the rest of their time wisely.

   Today's exam, I think, was only a practice test.

Read the previous examples *aloud,* and you'll hear how these expressions surrounded by commas interrupt the flow of the sentence. Sometimes such expressions flow smoothly into the sentence and don't need commas around them.

   Of course he checked to see if there were any rooms available.

   We therefore decided to stay out of it.

   I think you made the right decision.

Remember that when a word like *however* comes between two independent clauses, that word needs a semicolon before it. It may also have a comma after it, especially if there seems to be a pause between the word and the rest of the sentence. (See p. 84)

   The bus was late; *however,* we still made it to the museum before it closed.

   I am improving my study habits; *furthermore,* I am getting better grades.

   She was interested in journalism; *therefore,* she took a job at a local newspaper.

   I spent hours studying for the test; *finally,* I felt prepared.

Thus, you've seen a word like *however* or *therefore* used in three ways:

1. as a "scoopable" word that interrupts the flow of the sentence (needs commas around it)
2. as a word that flows into the sentence (no commas needed)
3. as a connecting word between two independent clauses (semicolon before and often a comma after)

6. **Put commas around additional information that is not needed in a sentence.**

Certain additional information is "scoopable" and should be surrounded by commas whenever the meaning would be clear without it. Look at the following sentence:

Maxine Taylor, who organized the fund-raiser, will introduce the candidates.

The clause *who organized the fund-raiser* is not needed in the sentence. Without it, we still know exactly who the sentence is about and what she is going to do: "Maxine Taylor will introduce the candidates." Therefore, the additional information is surrounded by commas to show that it is scoopable. Now read the following sentence:

The woman who organized the fund-raiser will introduce the candidates.

The clause *who organized the fund-raiser* is necessary in this sentence. Without it, the sentence would read as follows: "The woman will introduce the candidates." The reader would have no idea *which woman.* The clause *who organized the fundraiser* cannot be left out because it identifies which woman. Therefore, the clause is not scoopable, and no commas are used around it. Here is another sample sentence:

Hamlet, Shakespeare's famous play, has been made into a movie many times.

The additional information *Shakespeare's famous play* is scoopable. It could be left out, and we would still understand the meaning of the sentence: "*Hamlet* has been made into a movie many times." Therefore, the commas surround the scoopable information to show that it could be taken out. Here is the same sentence with the information reversed:

Shakespeare's famous play *Hamlet* has been made into a movie many times.

Here the title of the play is necessary. Without it, the sentence would read as follows: "Shakespeare's famous play has been made into a movie many times." The reader would have no idea which of Shakespeare's famous plays has been made into a movie many times. Therefore, the title is not scoopable, and commas should not be used around it.

The trick in deciding whether additional information is scoopable or not is to remember, "If I can scoop it out and still understand the sentence, I'll put commas around it."

EXERCISES

Surround any "scoopable" elements with commas according to Comma Rules 4, 5, and 6. Any commas already in the sentences follow Comma Rules 1, 2, and 3. Some sentences may be correct. Check your answers after the first set.

Exercise 1

1. This year's company picnic I think was better than last year's.
2. I think this year's company picnic was better than last year's.
3. We certainly had better weather this year.
4. Certainly we had better weather this year.
5. The person who brought the huge umbrellas for everyone to sit under was the star of the day.
6. Mr. Saunders who brought the huge umbrellas for everyone to sit under was the star of the day.
7. Marcus and Jonathan who catered the party did a great job; there was a variety of food, and it was all delicious.
8. The people who catered the party did a great job; there was a variety of food, and it was all delicious.
9. The desserts I have to say were better last year.
10. I have to say the desserts were better last year.

Exercise 2

1. We trust of course that people who get their driver's licenses know how to drive.
2. Of course we trust that people who get their driver's licenses know how to drive.
3. The people who test drivers for their licenses make the streets safer for all of us.
4. Mr. Kraft who tests drivers for their licenses makes the streets safer for all of us.
5. We may therefore understand when we fail the driving test ourselves.
6. Therefore we may understand when we fail the driving test ourselves.
7. The driver's seat we know is a place of tremendous responsibility.
8. We know that the driver's seat is a place of tremendous responsibility.

9. We believe that no one should take that responsibility lightly.
10. No one we believe should take that responsibility lightly.

Exercise 3

1. The writing teacher Ms. Gonzales has published several of her own short stories.
2. The Ms. Gonzales who teaches writing is not the Ms. Gonzales who teaches history.
3. My daughter's friend Harry doesn't get along with her best friend Jenny.
4. My daughter's best friend Jenny doesn't get along with one of her other friends Harry.
5. The tiger which is a beautiful and powerful animal symbolizes freedom.
6. The tiger that was born in September is already on display at the zoo.
7. The students who helped set up the chairs were allowed to sit in the front row.
8. Kim and Teresa who helped set up the chairs were allowed to sit in the front row.
9. My car which had a tracking device was easy to find when it was stolen.
10. A car that has a tracking device is easier to find if it's stolen.

Exercise 4

1. Arthur S. Heineman a California architect designed and built the world's first motel in the mid-1920s.
2. He chose the perfect location the city San Luis Obispo which was mid-way between Los Angeles and San Francisco.
3. Heineman an insightful man of business understood the need for inexpensive drive-in accommodations on long motor vehicle trips.
4. Hotels which required reservations and offered only high-priced rooms within one large structure just didn't fulfill the needs of motorists.

5. Heineman envisioned his "Motor Hotel" or Mo-Tel as a place where the parking spaces for the cars were right next to separate bungalow-style apartments for the passengers.
6. Heineman's idea was so new that when he put up his "Motel" sign several residents of the area told him to fire the sign's painter who couldn't even spell the word *hotel.*
7. Heineman had the sign painter place a hyphen between *Mo* and *Tel* to inform the public of a new kind of resting place.
8. Heineman's Milestone Mo-Tel the world's first motel opened in San Luis Obispo in 1925.
9. Before Heineman's company the Milestone Interstate Corporation could successfully trademark the name "Mo-Tel," other builders adopted the style and made *motel* a generic term.
10. Much of the original Milestone Mo-Tel building now called the Motel Inn still stands on the road between L.A. and San Francisco.

Source: Westways, May/June 2000

Exercise 5

1. Frozen "TV" dinners which were first sold by Swanson & Sons in 1954 had only one original variety—turkey on cornbread with sweet potatoes, peas, and gravy.
2. The company sold its original three-part dinner trays for ninety-nine cents a piece.
3. Campbell Soup Company seeing the success of the TV dinner concept bought the Swanson brand in 1955.
4. The need for frozen foods began after women started to hold jobs of their own during WWII, so Swanson offered frozen chicken and frozen meat pies.
5. These women's families who had been used to complete home-cooked meals needed a fast alternative.

6. Clarke Swanson who inherited his father's business brought the TV dinner concept to life.
7. He interviewed women who were shopping at supermarkets and asked them questions about packages and preferences.
8. Clarke Swanson is the one responsible for the eye-catching package that the first TV dinners came in.
9. The front of the package looked like a TV screen surrounded by the image of a wooden TV cabinet complete with knobs and the featured meal on the screen.
10. The frozen TV dinner which was born in the 1950s lives on as a billion-dollar industry today.

Source: Frozen Food Age, March 1994

PROOFREADING EXERCISE

Surround any "scoopable" elements in the following paragraph with commas according to Comma Rules 4, 5, and 6.

Do you know Ryan that there is a one-unit library class that begins next week? It's called Library 1 Introduction to the Library and we have to sign up for it before Friday. The librarians who teach it will give us an orientation and a series of assignment sheets. Then as we finish the assignments at our own pace we will turn them in to the librarians for credit. Ms. Kim the librarian that I spoke with said that we will learn really valuable library skills. These skills such as finding books or articles in our library and using the Internet to access other databases are the ones universities will expect us to know. I therefore plan to take this class, and you I hope will take it with me.

SENTENCE WRITING

Combine the following sets of sentences in different ways according to Comma Rules 4, 5, and 6. Try to combine each set in a way that needs commas and in a way that doesn't need commas. In other words, try to make an element "scoopable" in one sentence and not "scoopable" in another. You may reorder the details and change the phrasing as you wish. Sample responses are provided in the Answers section.

Chili tastes best when it's spicy.
Chili can be made with beans.
Chili can be made with meat.

I believe.
The Hudsons have a new dog.
The dog barks all night.

My roommate won a $100 lottery prize.
His name is Kevin.
He acts as if he has won a million dollars.

Review of the Comma

Six Comma Rules

1. Put a comma before *for, and, nor, but, or, yet, so* when they connect two independent clauses.
2. Put a comma between three or more items in a series.
3. Put a comma after an introductory expression or before a tag comment or question.
4. Put commas around the name of a person spoken to.
5. Put commas around words like *however* or *therefore* when they interrupt a sentence.
6. Put commas around unnecessary additional ("scoopable") information.

COMMA REVIEW EXERCISE

Add the missing commas, and identify which one of the six comma rules applies in the brackets at the *end* of each sentence. Each of the six sentences illustrates a different rule.

I'm writing you this reminder Tracy to be sure that you don't forget our plans to visit the zoo this Saturday. [ ] I know we're sisters but lately you have let our plans slip your mind. [ ] When we were supposed to go to the flea market last week you forgot all about it. [ ] I'm taking this opportunity therefore to refresh your memory. [ ] I can't wait to see the polar bears the gorillas the giraffes and the elephants. [ ] And I have made special plans for a behind-the-scenes tour of several of the exhibits by Max Bronson the zoo's public relations officer. [ ] See you Saturday!

SENTENCE WRITING

Write at least one sentence of your own to demonstrate each of the six comma rules.

Quotation Marks and Underlining/*Italics*

Put quotation marks around a direct quotation (the exact words of a speaker) but not around an indirect quotation.

The officer said, "Please show me your driver's license." (a direct quotation)

The officer asked to see my driver's license. (an indirect quotation)

If the speaker says more than one sentence, quotation marks are used before and after the entire speech.

She said, "One of your brake lights is out. You need to take care of the problem right away."

If the quotation begins the sentence, the words telling who is speaking are set off with a comma unless the quotation ends with a question mark or an exclamation point.

"I didn't even know it was broken," I said.

"Do you have any questions?" she asked.

"You mean I can go!" I shouted.

"Yes, consider this just a warning," she said.

Notice that each of the previous quotations begins with a capital letter. But when a quotation is interrupted by an identifying phrase, the second part doesn't begin with a capital letter unless the second part is a new sentence.

"If you knew how much time I spent on the essay," the student said, "you would give me an A."

"A chef might work on a meal for days," the teacher replied. "That doesn't mean the results will taste good."

Put quotation marks around the titles of short stories, poems, songs, essays, TV program episodes, or other short works.

I couldn't sleep after I read "The Lottery," a short story by Shirley Jackson.

My favorite Woodie Guthrie song is "This Land Is Your Land."

We had to read George Orwell's essay "A Hanging" for my speech class.

Jerry Seinfeld's troubles in "The Puffy Shirt" episode are some of the funniest moments in TV history.

Underline titles of longer works such as books, newspapers, magazines, plays, record albums or CDs, movies, or the titles of TV or radio series.

The Color Purple is a novel by Alice Walker.

I read about the latest discovery of dinosaur footprints in Newsweek.

Gone with the Wind was re-released in movie theaters in 1998.

My mother listens to The Writer's Almanac on the radio every morning.

You may choose to *italicize* instead of underlining if your word processor gives you the option. Just be consistent throughout any paper in which you use underlining or italics.

The Color Purple is a novel by Alice Walker.

I read about the latest discovery of dinosaur footprints in *Newsweek.*

Gone with the Wind was re-released in movie theaters in 1998.

My mother listens to *The Writer's Almanac* on the radio every morning.

EXERCISES

Correctly punctuate quotations and titles in the following sentences by adding quotation marks or underlining (*italics*). Check your answers often.

Exercise 1

1. Do you need any help? my sister asked.
2. In her book Gift from the Sea, Anne Morrow Lindbergh writes, The beach is not the place to work; to read, write or think. . . . One should lie empty, open, choiceless as a beach—waiting for a gift from the sea.
3. Sir Laurence Olivier had this to say about Shakespeare's most famous work: Hamlet is pound for pound . . . the greatest play ever written.
4. In 1999, singer Weird Al Yankovic released a parody of The Phantom Menace; it was sung to the tune of American Pie.
5. Civility costs nothing and buys everything, observed Lady Mary Wortley Montagu (1689–1762).
6. Forrest Gump made many sayings famous, but Life is like a box of chocolates is the most memorable.
7. My teacher wrote Good Work! at the top of my essay.

8. The first time a contestant won a million dollars on the television quiz show Who Wants To Be a Millionaire? was in November 1999.
9. Karen asked, Where will you be at noon?
10. My family subscribes to Newsweek, and we all enjoy reading it.

Exercise 2

1. Have you read the book Who Moved My Cheese?
2. Anton Chekhov once said, Any idiot can face a crisis--it's this day-to-day living that wears you out.
3. I gulped when my counselor asked, How many math classes have you had?
4. Let's start that again! shouted the dance teacher.
5. Last night we watched the Beatles' movie A Hard Day's Night on DVD.
6. Paul McCartney's song Yesterday still makes my mom cry whenever she hears it.
7. Abraham Lincoln stated, I like to see a man proud of the place in which he lives. I like to see a man live so that his place will be proud of him.
8. Time is the only incorruptible judge is just one translation of Creon's line from the Greek play Oedipus Rex.
9. Don't you hate it when your dentist asks How are you? as soon as he or she starts working on your teeth?
10. My favorite essay that we've read this semester has to be I Want a Wife by Judy Brady.

Exercise 3

1. Marks is a poem by Linda Pastan.
2. I'll never understand what No news is good news means.
3. Can you help me find an article on spontaneous human combustion? the student asked.

4. Whatever happened to The Book of Lists?
5. O Pioneers is the title of Willa Cather's most famous novel.
6. Let's begin, the relaxation expert said, by closing our eyes and imagining ourselves in an empty theater.
7. Television series like 1900 House and Frontier House have made PBS a real competitor for reality-TV-hungry audiences.
8. I can't keep this a secret anymore, my neighbor told me. Your son has a tatoo that he hasn't shown you yet.
9. A few days after Emily Dickinson's eight-year-old nephew Gilbert died of typhoid fever, the Amherst Record included a beautiful tribute to him entitled Death of a Promising Boy.
10. I was shocked when my high school English teacher told us, Most of Shakespeare's stories came from other sources; he just dramatized them better than anyone else did.

Exercise 4

1. George Sterling described San Francisco as the cool, grey city of love.
2. One of the most famous actresses of the early twentieth century was Mary Pickford; movie producer Samuel Goldwyn had this to say about working with her: It took longer to make Mary's contracts than it did her pictures.
3. Goldwyn himself was no easier to get along with: He would not acknowledge rejection, according to one biographer. He could not be insulted. He could not be deterred. He could not be withstood.
4. When someone suggested that Walt Disney run for mayor of Los Angeles following the success of Disneyland, Disney declined, saying, I'm already king.
5. Disney knew what it meant to succeed; having dropped out of high school and having moved to Los Angeles with less than fifty dollars in

his pocket, he empathized with Mickey Mouse, a character he described as a little fellow doing the best he could.

6. Mark Twain said of California, It's a great place to live, but I wouldn't want to visit there.
7. There is a French expression *L'amour est aveugle; l'amitié ferme les yeux,* which translates as follows: Love is blind; friendship closes its eyes.
8. Let's keep our voices down, the librarian said as we left the study room.
9. Box-Car Bertha, renowned woman of the rails, suggested that Nobody can hurt you but yourself. Every experience you have makes you all the more fit for life.
10. Pain is inevitable, said M. Kathleen Casey, Suffering is optional.

Exercise 5

1. In Booker T. Washington's autobiography Up from Slavery, he describes his early dream of going to school.
2. I had no schooling whatever while I was a slave, he explains.
3. He continues, I remember on several occasions I went as far as the schoolhouse door with one of my young mistresses to carry her books.
4. Washington was incredibly attracted by what he saw from the doorway: several dozen boys and girls engaged in study.
5. The picture, he adds, made a deep impression upon me.
6. Washington cherished this glimpse of boys and girls engaged in study.
7. It contrasted directly with his own situation: My life had its beginning in the midst of the most miserable, desolate, and discouraging surroundings.
8. I was born, he says, in a typical log cabin, about fourteen by sixteen feet square.
9. He explains, In this cabin I lived with my mother and a brother and sister till after the Civil War, when we were all declared free.

10. As a slave at the door of his young mistress's schoolhouse, Booker T. Washington remembers, I had the feeling that to get into a schoolhouse and study in this way would be about the same as getting into paradise.

Source: Great Americans in Their Own Words (Mallard Press, 1990)

PARAGRAPH EXERCISE

Correctly punctuate quotations and titles in the following paragraph by adding quotation marks or underlining (*italics*).

I've been reading the book How Children Fail by John Holt. I checked it out to use in a research paper I'm doing on education in America. Holt's book was published in the early 1960s, but his experiences and advice are still relevant today. In one of his chapters, Fear and Failure, Holt describes intelligent children this way: Intelligent children act as if they thought the universe made some sense. They check their answers and their thoughts against common sense, while other children, not expecting answers to make sense, not knowing what is sense, see no point in checking, no way of checking. Holt and others stress the child's self-confidence as one key to success.

SENTENCE WRITING

Write ten sentences that list and discuss your favorite songs, TV shows, characters' expressions, movies, books, and so on. Be sure to punctuate quotations and titles correctly. Refer to the rules at the beginning of this section if necessary.

Capital Letters

1. Capitalize the first word of every sentence.

Peaches taste best when they are cold.

A piece of fruit is an amazing object.

2. Capitalize the first word of every direct quotation.

She said, "I've never worked so hard before."

"I have finished most of my homework," she said, "but I still have a lot to do." (The *but* is not capitalized because it does not begin a new sentence.)

"I love my speech class," she said. "Maybe I'll change my major." (*Maybe* is capitalized because it begins a new sentence.)

3. Capitalize the first, last, and every important word in a title. Don't capitalize prepositions (such as *in, of, at, with*), short connecting words (such as *and, but, or*), the *to* in front of a verb, or *a, an,* or *the.*

I saw a copy of Darwin's *The Origin of Species* at a yard sale.

The class enjoyed the essay "How to Write a Rotten Poem with Almost No Effort."

Shakespeare in Love is a film based on Shakespeare's writing of the play *Romeo and Juliet.*

4. Capitalize specific names of people, places, languages, races, and nationalities.

Rev. Jesse Jackson	China	Cesar Chavez
Ireland	Spanish	Japanese
Ryan White	Philadelphia	Colorado Blvd.

5. Capitalize names of months, days of the week, and special days, but not the seasons.

March	Fourth of July	spring
Tuesday	Easter	winter
Valentine's Day	Labor Day	fall

6. Capitalize a title of relationship if it takes the place of the person's name. If *my* (or *your, her, his, our, their*) is in front of the word, a capital is not used.

I think Mom wrote to him.	*but*	I think my mom wrote to him.
We visited Aunt Sophie.	*but*	We visited our aunt.
They spoke with Grandpa.	*but*	They spoke with their grandpa.

7. Capitalize names of particular people or things, but not general terms.

I admire Professor Washborne.	*but*	I admire my professor.
We saw the famous Potomac River.	*but*	We saw the famous river.
Are you from the South?	*but*	Is your house south of the mountains?
I will take Philosophy 4 and English 100.	*but*	I will take philosophy and English.
She graduated from Sutter High School.	*but*	She graduated from high school.
They live at 119 Forest St.	*but*	They live on a beautiful street.
We enjoyed the Monterey Bay Aquarium.	*but*	We enjoyed the aquarium.

EXERCISES

Add all of the necessary capital letters to the sentences that follow. Check your answers after the first set.

Exercise 1

1. hidden beneath the church of st. martin-in-the-fields in london is a great little place to have lunch.
2. it's called the café in the crypt, and you enter it down a small staircase just off trafalgar square.
3. the café is literally in a crypt, the church's resting place for the departed.
4. the food is served cafeteria style: soups, stews, sandwiches, and salads.
5. you grab a tray at the end of the counter and load it up with food as you slide it toward the cash register.
6. although the café is dark, the vaulted ceilings make it comfortable, and you can just make out the messages carved into the flat tombstones that cover the floor beneath your table.
7. one of london's newspapers ranked the café in the crypt high on its list of the "50 best places to meet in london."

8. the café in the crypt can even be reserved for private parties.
9. the café has its own gallery, called—what else?—the gallery in the crypt.
10. so if you're ever in london visiting historic trafalgar square, don't forget to look for that little stairway and grab a bite at the café in the crypt.

Source: www.stmartin-in-the-fields.org

Exercise 2

1. now that dvds are more popular than vhs tapes, i am updating my movie library.
2. my friends say that i shouldn't waste my money on repeat titles.
3. but my friend jake is on my side because he and i are usually the ones who watch movies together.
4. even though I have good vhs copies of famous films such as *chinatown, jaws,* and *blade runner,* the dvd versions offer behind-the-scenes footage and original trailers that vhs tapes don't include.
5. of course, i'm aware that another technology will replace dvds before too long.
6. then i guess i'll just have to commit to that new format.
7. there are always collectors who want the old stuff.
8. in fact, i know someone who has a collection of video discs and 8-track cassette tapes.
9. i may be leaning that way myself.
10. i haven't disposed of my vhs duplicates yet, and i've been buying old record albums at thrift stores.

Exercise 3

1. when my art teacher asked the class to do research on frida kahlo, i knew that the name sounded familiar.
2. then i remembered that the actress selma hayek starred in the movie *frida,* which was about this mexican-born artist's life.

3. frida kahlo's paintings are all very colorful and seem extremely personal.
4. she painted mostly self portraits, and each one makes a unique statement.
5. one of these portraits is called *my grandparents, my parents, and i.*
6. kahlo gave another one the title *the two fridas.*
7. but my favorite of kahlo's works is *self-portrait on the borderline between mexico and the united states.*
8. in an article i read in *smithsonian* magazine, kahlo's mother explains that after frida was severely injured in a bus accident, she started painting.
9. kahlo's mother set up a mirror near her daughter's bed so that frida could use herself as a model.
10. in the *smithsonian* article from the november 2002 issue, kahlo is quoted as saying, "i never painted dreams. i painted my own reality."

Exercise 4

1. sir laurence olivier was one of the most famous british actors of the twentieth century.
2. he was well known for playing the leading roles in shakespeare's plays.
3. he performed in london, on such stages as the old vic theatre and st. james's theatre, and for several years, he was director of the national theatre.
4. of course, olivier also played to audiences in cities around the world, such as new york, los angeles, moscow, and berlin.
5. among olivier's most celebrated roles were henry V, othello, richard III, and king lear.
6. though we can no longer see him on stage, we can still watch the film versions of his classic performances.
7. olivier also directed many plays and some of his own films.
8. he directed the 1948 black-and-white film version of *hamlet* and received the academy award for best actor for his performance in the title role.

9. one of olivier's most treasured memories was of a single live performance of *hamlet* in elsinore, denmark; it was scheduled to have been played outside but had to be moved inside at the last minute, causing all the actors to be especially brilliant under pressure.
10. american audiences might remember sir laurence olivier best for his portrayal of the tempestuous heathcliff in the movie *wuthering heights,* but he was a shakespearean actor at heart.

Source: Laurence Olivier on Acting (Simon, 1986)

Exercise 5

1. my mom and dad love old movie musicals.
2. that makes it easy to shop for them at christmas and other gift-giving occasions.
3. for mom's birthday last year, i gave her the video of gilbert and sullivan's comic opera *the pirates of penzance.*
4. it isn't even that old; it has kevin kline in it as the character called the pirate king.
5. i watched the movie with her, and i enjoyed the story of a band of pirates who are too nice for their own good.
6. actually, it is funnier than i thought it would be, and kevin kline sings and dances really well!
7. dad likes musicals, too, and i bought him tickets to see the revival of *chicago* on stage a few years ago.
8. he loves all those big production numbers and the bob fosse choreography.
9. thanks to baz luhrmann and others, movie musicals are making a comeback.
10. *moulin rouge* and the film version of *chicago* are just two recent examples.

REVIEW OF PUNCTUATION AND CAPITAL LETTERS

Punctuate these sentences. They include all the rules for punctuation and capitalization you have learned. Compare your answers carefully with those at the back of the book. Sentences may require several pieces of punctuation or capital letters.

1. the hollywood walk of fame is a famous landmark in southern california
2. have you ever seen woody allens early films such as bananas or take the money and run
3. theyve remodeled their house and now theyre ready to sell it
4. how much will the final exam affect our grades the nervous student asked
5. we have reviewed your policy mr martin and will be sending you a refund soon
6. the two students who earn the most points for their speeches will face each other in a debate
7. ms thomas the new english 4b teacher recently received a national poetry award
8. even though i am enjoying my french class i believe i should have taken spanish first
9. you always remember valentines day and our anniversary but you forget my birthday
10. the most memorable saying from the original toy story movie is when buzz lightyear exclaims to infinity and beyond
11. my sister subscribes to architectural digest magazine and my whole family loves to look through it when shes finished reading it
12. finding low air fares takes time patience and luck
13. my friend is reading the novel thousand pieces of gold in her english class
14. i wonder how much my art history textbook will cost
15. bill gates founder of microsoft is one of the richest people in the world

COMPREHENSIVE TEST

In these sentences you'll find all the errors that have been discussed in the entire text. Try to name the error in the blank before each sentence, and then correct the error if you can. You may find any of the following errors:

apos	apostrophe
awk	awkward phrasing
c	comma needed
cap	capitalization
cliché	overused expression
cs	comma splice
dm	dangling modifier
frag	fragment
mm	misplaced modifier
p	punctuation
pro	incorrect pronoun
pro agr	pronoun agreement
pro ref	pronoun reference
ro	run-on sentence
shift	shift in time or person
sp	misspelled word
s/v agr	subject/verb agreement
wordy	wordiness
ww	wrong word
//	not parallel

A perfect—or almost perfect—score will mean you've mastered the first part of the text.

1. ______ When you step inside the alarm panel will beep.
2. ______ People should avoid driving over potholes because you never know what's at the bottom of them.
3. ______ My cell phone was ringing, and at the same time, her doorbell started to ring.

4. ______ Either the pastry chef or her assistants has made the pie crusts.
5. ______ Someones' bicycle has been parked on the corner of our block for two days.
6. ______ The twins spent there allowance on new computer games.
7. ______ There are one or two things that I'd like to find out before we go ahead and apply for that loan.
8. ______ My favorite season is Fall, but my kids like Summer best of all.
9. ______ The company president gave my coworker and I a bonus for finding the lost files.
10. ______ The absolute worst part of an outdoor camping trip is the complete lack of running water.
11. ______ The lawn needs mowing and the weeds need pulling.
12. ______ I consider myself smart, however, I know that my mom is smarter.
13. ______ On her computer, my sister enlarged a precious family photograph.
14. ______ If I had the instruction sheet to put the bookcase together.
15. ______ Each of the trees were lightly dusted with snow.
16. ______ After a 10-minute break, my manager asked me to restock the shelves.
17. ______ The test was more difficult then I expected; I'm sure I didn't do well.
18. ______ We students inquired to the newspaper about the story.
19. ______ I returned the DVD back to the store; it had been overdue for two days.
20. ______ Everyone in town put their flags out in support of the rescue crews.

PART 4

Writing

Aside from the basics of word choice, spelling, sentence structure, and punctuation, what else do you need to understand to write better? Just as sentences are built according to accepted patterns, so are other "structures" of English—paragraphs and essays, for example.

Think of writing as including levels of structures, beginning small with words connecting to form phrases, clauses, and sentences. Then sentences connect to form paragraphs and essays. Each level has its own set of "blueprints." To communicate clearly in writing, you must choose and spell your words correctly. Sentences must have a subject, a verb, and a complete thought. Paragraphs must be indented and should contain a main idea supported with sufficient detail. Each of your essays should explore a valuable topic in several coherent paragraphs, usually including an introduction, a body, and a conclusion.

Not everyone approaches writing as structure, however. You can write better without thinking about structure at all. A good place to start might be to write what you care about and care about what you write. You can make an amazing amount of progress by simply being *genuine*, being who you are naturally. No one has to tell you to be yourself when you speak, but you might need encouragement to be yourself in your writing.

Writing is almost never done without a reason. The reason may come from an experience, such as receiving an unfair parking ticket, or from a requirement in a class. And when you are asked to write, you often receive guidance in the form of an assignment: tell a story to prove a point, paint a picture with your words, summarize an article, compare two subjects, share what you know about something, explain why you agree with or disagree with an idea.

Learning to write well is important, one of the most important things you will do in your education. Confidence is the key. The Writing sections will help you build confidence, whether you are expressing your own ideas or summarizing and responding to the ideas of others. Like the Sentence Structure sections, the Writing sections are best taken in order. However, each one discusses an aspect of writing that you can review on its own at any time.

What Is the Least You Should Know about Writing?

"Unlike medicine or the other sciences," William Zinsser points out, "writing has no new discoveries to spring on us. We're in no danger of reading in our morning newspaper that a breakthrough has been made in how to write [clearly]. . . . We may be given new technologies like the word processor to ease the burdens of composition, but on the whole we know what we need to know."

One thing we know is that we learn to write by *writing*—not by reading long discussions about writing. Therefore the explanations and instructions in this section are as brief as they can be, followed by samples from student and professional writers.

Understanding the basic structures and learning the essential skills covered in this section will help you become a better writer.

Basic Structures

I. The Paragraph
II. The Essay

Writing Skills

III. Writing in Your Own Voice
IV. Finding a Topic
V. Organizing Ideas
VI. Supporting with Details
VII. Revising Your Papers
VIII. Presenting Your Work
IX. Writing about What You Read

Basic Structures

I. The Paragraph

A paragraph is unlike any other structure in English. Visually, it has its own profile: the first line is indented about five spaces, and sentences continue to fill the space between both margins until the paragraph ends (which may be in the middle of the line):

     ____
____
____
____
____
___________________________________.

As a beginning writer, you might forget to indent your paragraphs, or you may break off in the middle of a line within a paragraph, especially when writing in class. You must remember to indent whenever you begin a new paragraph and fill the space between the margins until it ends. (*Note:* In business writing, paragraphs are not indented but double-spaced in between.)

Defining a Paragraph

A typical paragraph centers on one idea, usually phrased in a topic sentence from which all the other sentences in the paragraph radiate. The topic sentence does not need to begin the paragraph, but it most often does, and the other sentences support it with specific details. (For more on topic sentences and organizing paragraphs, see p. 226.) Paragraphs usually contain several sentences, though no set number is required. A paragraph can stand alone, but more commonly paragraphs are part of a larger composition, an essay. There are different kinds of paragraphs, based on the jobs they are supposed to do.

Types of Paragraphs

Sample Paragraphs in an Essay

Introductory paragraphs begin essays. They provide background information about the essay's topic and usually include the thesis statement or main idea of the essay. (See p. 224 for information on how to write a thesis statement.) Here is the introductory paragraph of a student essay entitled "Really Understanding":

> I was so excited when my parents told me that I could join them in America. Four years earlier, they left China to open a Chinese fast food restaurant in Los Angeles. After my parents asked me to help them in the restaurant, I started to worry about my English because I knew only a few words that I learned in China. They told me not to worry, that I would quickly grasp the language once I heard it every day. Soon after I joined them, I made a big mistake because of my lack of English skills and my conceit. From this experience, I learned the importance of really understanding.

In this opening paragraph, the student leads up to the main idea—"the importance of really understanding"—with background information about her family's restaurant and "a big mistake" that she made.

Body paragraphs are those in the middle of essays. Each body paragraph contains a topic sentence and presents detailed information about one subtopic or idea that relates directly to the essay's thesis. (See p. 226 for more information on organizing body paragraphs.) Here are the body paragraphs of the same essay:

> My mistake happened during my second week at the restaurant. Usually my mom and I stayed in front, dishing out the food and keeping

the tables clean, and my father cooked in the kitchen. If I needed any help or if someone asked a question in English, my mom took care of it. However, that day my mom was sick, so she stayed home. My father and I went to work. He went straight to the kitchen, and I wiped those six square tables. By noon, my father had put big steaming trays of food on the counter. There was orange chicken, chicken with mushrooms, sweet and sour pork, kong bao chicken, and B.B.Q. pork. People came in, ordering their favorite foods.

After I took care of the lunch rush, it was 2:00, but my favorite customer had not arrived. He was an old, kind, educated man who came in almost every day at 12:00. Why hadn't he come for the last two days? Was he sick? I looked at his favorite dish and started to worry about him. As I was wondering, he walked through the door. I smiled to see him. He ordered "the usual"—chicken with mushrooms and steamed rice—and sat down at the table in the left corner. I wanted to ask him why he came late to show that I cared about him, but more customers came in, and I had to serve them. They ordered all the chicken with mushrooms left in the tray, so I called to my father to cook more. The old man finished his food and walked toward me. He looked at that tray of newly cooked chicken with mushrooms for a second, and then he asked me something. I only understood the word *yesterday.* Since he had not been in yesterday, I guessed that he said "Were you open yesterday?" I quickly answered, "Oh, yes!" He looked at me, and I could see that he didn't believe my answer, so I said "Yes" again. He just turned and walked away.

I did not understand what had happened. Two days passed, and he did not return. I thought about what he could have asked me and stared at the chicken and mushrooms for a minute. Suddenly, I realized what must have happened. He had come in two hours later than usual, at 2:00 that day, but the dish had been cooked at 12:00. Fast food cooked two hours earlier would not taste as fresh as if it were just prepared. He must have asked me "Was this *cooked* yesterday?" How could I have answered "Yes" not once but twice? He must have felt so bad about us. "He will never come back," I told myself.

Notice that each of the three body paragraphs discusses a single stage of the experience that taught her the value of really understanding.

Concluding paragraphs are the final paragraphs in essays. They bring the discussion to a close and share the writer's final thoughts on the subject. (See p. 226 for more about concluding paragraphs.) Here is the conclusion of the sample essay:

Four years have passed since then, and my favorite customer has not come back. It still bothers me. Why didn't I ask him to say the question again? If I had not been so conceited, I would have risked looking foolish for a moment. Now I am so repentant. I will never answer a question or do anything before I really understand what it means.

In this concluding paragraph, the student describes the effects of her experience—the regret and the lesson she learned.

Sample of a Paragraph Alone

Single-paragraph writing assignments may be given in class or as homework. They test the beginning writer's understanding of the unique structure of a paragraph. They may ask the writer to answer a single question, perhaps following a reading, or to provide details about a limited topic. Look at this student paragraph, the result of a homework assignment asking students to report on a technological development in the news:

> I just read that soon there will be self-serve pet washing machines shaped like clothes washing machines. These machines will be located inside pet laundromats called Lavacans. The article states that a dirty dog or cat can be placed in one of these machines, which are controlled by computers, and then about forty nozzles will spray water and air onto the pet's fur. The makers of Lavacans say that the pets enjoy the massaging feeling of the spray. The three-cycle process of washing, rinsing, and drying takes about half an hour to complete. According to the article, these machines have already become popular in other countries, Spain for example, where the Lavacan originated. Pet laundromats seem to be a good idea, as long as the pets are safe and happy.
>
> *Source: Current Science,* September 27, 2002

These shorter writing assignments help students practice presenting information within the limited structure of a paragraph.

The assignments in the upcoming Writing Skills section will sometimes ask you to write paragraphs. Remember that you may review the previous pages as often as you wish until you understand the unique structure of the paragraph.

II. The Essay

Like the paragraph, an essay has its own profile, usually including a title and several paragraphs.

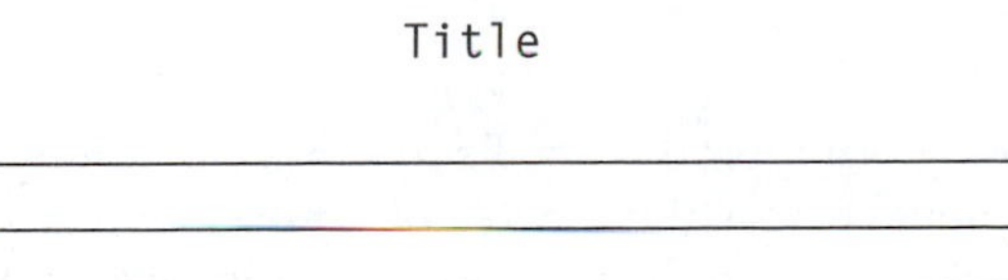

While the paragraph is the single building block of text used in almost all forms of writing (in essays, magazine articles, letters, novels, newspaper stories, and so on), an essay is a larger, more complex structure.

The Five-Paragraph Essay and Beyond

The student essay analyzed on pages 209–210 illustrates the different kinds of paragraphs within essays. Many people like to include five paragraphs in an essay: an introductory paragraph, three body paragraphs, and a concluding paragraph. Three is a comfortable number of body paragraphs—it is not two, which makes an essay seem like a comparison even when it isn't; and it is not four, which may be too many subtopics for the beginning writer to organize clearly.

However, an essay can contain any number of paragraphs. As you become more comfortable with the flow of your ideas and gain confidence in your ability to express yourself, you are free to create essays of many different shapes and sizes. As in all things, learning about writing begins with structure and then expands to include all possibilities.

Defining an Essay

There is no such thing as a typical essay. Essays may be serious or humorous, but the best of them are thought-provoking and—of course—informative. Try looking up the word *essay* in a dictionary right now. Some words that are used to define what an essay is might need to be explained themselves:

> An essay is *prose* (meaning it is written in the ordinary language of sentences and paragraphs).

An essay is *nonfiction* (meaning it deals with real people, factual information, actual opinions and events).

An essay is a *composition* (meaning it is created in parts that make up the whole, several paragraphs that explore a single topic).

An essay is *personal* (meaning it shares the writer's unique perspective, even if only in the choice of topic, method of analysis, and details).

An essay is *analytical* and *instructive* (meaning it examines the workings of a subject and shares the results with the reader).

A Sample Essay

For an example of a piece of writing that fits the previous definition, read the following essay by Cynthia Cavnar about the experience of receiving, losing, finding, and finally appreciating an odd family heirloom—an ancestor's umbilical cord.

Harmonious Cord

They say that every cloud has a silver lining and I have to agree: the loss of a car was a small price to pay for the recovery of the ancestral umbilical cord.

The problem with a 100-year-old umbilical cord is that it looks like a hardened bit of old string. Misplace it in the trunk of your automobile, already littered with the debris of years of hard driving, and it's gone forever. Or so we thought.

This curious relic came to us from my husband's side of the family, the Japanese side. The Japanese have a long tradition of saving the umbilical cords of their children as mementos of the happy occasion of birth. My ancestors, Irish and plainspoken, found the actual child memento enough. Nevertheless, when my mother-in-law sent along the umbilical cord of her father, Kutaro, I suppressed my first instinct—to wonder why our friends inherit stocks and bonds while we inherit mummified body parts—and graciously assumed responsibility for protecting the venerable item. In other words, after showing the cord to my delighted husband and children, I quietly put it away in a drawer.

But children never forget, and one day our fourth-grader decided he wanted to take the heirloom to school for cultural heritage day. "I don't think this is what the teacher had in mind," I told him, but he prevailed, and needless to say, his presentation was a crowd-pleaser—these were 10-year-olds, after all.

The cord gave me the creeps, though, and so for the drive home from school, I consigned it, in its box, to the trunk. Unfortunately, it worked its way free and into some uncharted abyss. Although we searched from time to time over the next few years, we never found it. We began to think of the car as a very large reliquary.

Then a pickup truck blew through a stop sign, totaling our vehicle. I walked away with hardly a scratch and wondered, at that moment, if Kutaro hadn't somehow extended a measure of paternal protection. I thought with remorse of my neglect of family duty and the fact that the search for the ancestral remains was undoubtedly over.

But what did I know of salvage yards, or the sensitive souls who run them? The proprietor at mine was a friendly fellow who seemed to perceive my dejection. He helped me clear out the car and then watched quietly as I continued to root through an obviously empty trunk. "Was there something else?" he asked delicately. Well, why not? "There's an old umbilical cord loose in there, and we've never been able to find it," I said without elaboration. I must have sounded deranged. And then, here's the wonderful thing. He didn't laugh, or ask questions, or slowly back away. He just turned to the trunk and, half a minute later, emerged with the prize. "This is it," he said with the serene assurance of an expert witness schooled in the lore of the ancient cord. I still don't know how he did it.

I now take my role as Keeper of the Cord more seriously. I bought a little silver box, placed the relic inside, and put it on the mantel. My husband is pleased. Our guests are puzzled but polite. As for me, I still think about the guy from the salvage yard. He may live on the Midwestern plains but deep inside him burns the spirit of the East. Perhaps, in some small way, I, too, have been enlightened.

Now that you have learned more about the basic structures of the paragraph and the essay, you are ready to practice the skills necessary to write them.

Writing Skills

III. Writing in Your Own Voice

All writing "speaks" on paper, and the person "listening" is the reader. Some beginning writers forget that writing and reading are two-way methods of communication, just like spoken conversations between two people. When you write, your reader listens; when you read, you also listen.

When speaking, you express a personality in your choice of phrases, your movements, your tone of voice. Family and friends probably recognize your voice messages on their answering machines without your having to identify yourself. Would they also be able to recognize your writing? They would if you extended your "voice" into your writing.

Writing should not sound like talking, necessarily, but it should have a "personality" that comes from the way you decide to approach a topic, to develop it with details, to say it your way.

The beginning of this book discusses the difference between spoken English (following looser patterns of speaking) and Standard Written English (following accepted patterns of writing). Don't think that the only way to add "voice" to your writing is to use the patterns of spoken English. Remember that Standard Written English does not have to be dull or sound "academic." Look at this example of Standard Written English that has a distinct voice, part of the book *Babies Remember Birth,* by David Chamberlain:

> What do you see when you look at a newborn baby, bright-eyed, gazing straight at you? Is there really a person there? Silently frowning or beet-red with rage, can this baby think and feel? For its small size, a newborn makes a powerful, compelling noise, but is it actually saying anything?
>
> Until recently, there were many theories about newborns but few known facts. For uncounted centuries, infants have been separated from the rest of us by a veil of ignorance. As close as we have been to them, we did not know how amazing they are. Common wisdom about babies was based on the obvious limitations of their size, weight, and muscle power.
>
> Consequently, babies were described as sometimes adorable but incapable, subhuman, prehuman, dull, and senseless, and treated as such. . . . The truth is, much of what we have traditionally believed about babies is false. We have misunderstood and underestimated their abilities. They are not simple beings but complex and ageless—small creatures with unexpectedly large thoughts.

Chamberlain's excerpt illustrates Standard Written English at its best—from its solid sentence structures to its precise use of words. But more important, Chamberlain's clear voice speaks to us and involves us in his fascination with the world of babies. You can involve your reader, too, by writing in your own voice.

Writing does not need to be about something personal to have a voice. Here is an example of a student writing about computer hackers:

> Some mischievous hackers are only out to play a joke. One of the first examples was a group who created the famous "Cookie Monster" program at Massachusetts Institute of Technology. Several hackers programmed MIT's computer to display the word "cookie" all over the screens of its users. In order for users to clear this problem, they had to "feed" the Cookie Monster by entering the word "cookie" or lose all the data on their screens.

Notice that both professional and student writers tell stories (narration) and paint pictures (description) in their writing. Narration and description require practice, but once you master them, you will gain a stronger voice and will be able to add interest and clarity to even the most challenging academic writing assignments.

Narration

Narrative writing tells the reader a story, and since most of us like to tell stories, it is a good place to begin writing in your own voice. An effective narration allows readers to experience an event with the writer. Since we all see the world differently and feel unique emotions, the purpose of narration is to take readers with us through our experiences. As a result, the writer gains a better understanding of what happened, and readers get to live other lives momentarily. Listen to the "voice" of this student writer telling stories from his life as "a bus person":

Catching the Bus

I'm going to tell you what I go through before and after I get onto a bus. I'm also going to describe what really goes on inside of a bus. I can do this because I'm a bus person. A bus person is someone who never bothered to learn how to drive a car or just can't afford one. I fit in the "can't afford a car" category and another one—the one where a person has been riding the bus since he was in his mother's womb. I've been through every kind of bus episode, all beginning with the following.

Every morning before leaving home, I look out the window to see if it's going to be cold or hot. Whether it's cold or not, I always put on a coat or a sweater. My destination is the school that I attend. There are usually five or more people waiting at each bus stop at every other corner along the way. What's funny is how the same people always fight to be closest to the curb, hoping that the bus door will open right in front of their faces. They do this to try to gain a seat that more than likely is already occupied by another passenger.

Some days, the bus driver won't stop but will just pass everyone by. It isn't that the driver is trying to ignore us; it's that the bus is already crowded with passengers. The only way to avoid this misfortune is to wake up before dawn and catch an earlier bus. Once I get on the bus, I still have to locate a vacant seat or at least look for a place to stand. I usually go straight to the back of the bus to avoid the pushing and shoving that goes on in the front, along with confrontations that will occur—most definitely.

It's like a circus in there; there's always a show to watch. I'll find a person who talks to himself or a person who tries to include everyone in his or her uncertain topic of conversation. Anyone who has ever ridden a bus can verify that there's always a loud bunch whose discussion everyone else sitting or standing can hear. In addition to the noisy crowd, there are the to-themselves people who are either reading a book or sitting next to a window just looking out at no particular place. These people get bored looking out the window, so they start daydreaming with their eyes on another passenger. This can lead to problems between passengers, confrontations often involving foul-mouthed language that children on the bus are forced to overhear. This is a situation that could be avoided if the daydreamer had kept his eyes to himself.

I've come across other less drastic scenarios. I've seen the mom with four or five children ages six and below getting on the bus. I feel sorry for that woman because she has to struggle all day with those kids and then get each one of them on the bus. The way she does this is by holding the youngest, the baby, in her left arm and holding the folded-up stroller in her right arm. This, all while trying to put her flattened dollars and change into the bus's slot machine, followed by her looking for a place to sit as well as trying to stop the baby from crying. This can be the worst part of riding the bus for some people.

There are also the dilemmas of whether a person should offer his or her seat to a pregnant woman, a woman carrying her newborn baby, a senior citizen, or a disabled person. What's interesting to me is how men are often the ones who have to debate with their conscience about whether to give up their seats for these "damsels in distress." It isn't even a question with me. I'll give up my butt's comfort whenever I'm placed in that kind of a situation, but that's only because I'm a lot nicer than some other people. It can be sad sometimes when people are just so rude that they don't offer their seat to someone who's obviously had a really long day. The way to tell if a person has had a really long day is by the tired, frustrated look on his or her face. Another scenario is when an elderly woman is trying to get on the bus with like nine grocery bags that all weigh about three or more pounds each. Usually someone will always help the old lady. But what can be really disappointing is when she has to get back off the bus and walk home carrying all those heavy groceries. Yet she can be lucky at times and have someone help her the rest of the way home, or she may bump into someone she knows on the street.

I hope the reader, especially a person who has never had to ride a bus before, has gotten some kind of visual picture of what can sometimes go on inside a bus. Maybe the reader will look at the people waiting for the bus a little differently. It'll be good in a way because not all of us bus riders are rude, cruel people, but then again don't push us. A little bit of advice when bus riding—don't stare at people. We really hate that.

Description

Descriptive writing paints word pictures with details that appeal to the reader's five senses—sight, sound, touch, taste, and smell. The writer of description often uses comparisons to help readers picture one thing by imagining something else, just as the writer of "Catching the Bus" compares riding a bus to being at the circus: "there's always a show to watch." In the following paragraph, a student uses vivid details to bring the place she loves best to life:

> Fort Baker is located across the bay from San Francisco, almost under the Golden Gate Bridge. When I lived there as a child, nature was all I saw. Deer came onto our porch and nibbled the plants; raccoons dumped the trash cans over; skunks sprayed my brother because he poked them with a stick, and little field mice jumped out of the bread drawer at my sister when she opened it. Behind the house was a small forest of strong green trees; the dirt actually felt soft, and tall grassy plants with bright yellow flowers grew all around. I don't know the plants' real name, but my friend and I called it "sour grass." When we chewed the stems, we got a mouth full of sour juice that made our faces crinkle and our eyes water.

Here is another example, the description of a museum devoted to the Salem witch trials, from the book *America's Strangest Museums* by Sandra Gurvis. As we read Gurvis's description, we can visualize the museum's location and feel the eeriness of its displays.

The Salem Witch Museum

> On the surface, Salem, Massachusetts, seems like an ordinary little town, replete with shopping malls, frozen yogurt shops, and fancy restaurants. But look a little closer and, along with historic homes, a quaint commons, and other points of interest befitting one of America's oldest settlements, you'll find symbols of witches on everything from street signs to T-shirts. For a real spook-out, among other sights, there's the Salem Witch Museum.
>
> Housed in an eerie stone church in historic Washington Square, the museum offers a half-hour multisensory presentation with (appropriately) thirteen diorama stage settings. Each scene is lit up and narrated in the three-story nave, or center, of the church. "Along with depicting the full course and aftermath of the Salem witch trials, we try to provide an idea of what life was like in 1692," explains Patty MacLeod. There's a circle with the names of the executed in the nave; informational signs are scattered throughout. . . .
>
> What exactly happened in the town of Salem over three hundred years ago? The apparently simple facts belie the complexity of events: More than two hundred people were accused of witchcraft, and of the

> twenty-three convicted, nineteen were hanged. Those who "confessed" were spared, while others who maintained their innocence went to their deaths. According to legend, two dogs were also hanged on Gallows Hill as witches (apparently they didn't confess either). . . .
>
> "What many people today don't understand was that in the 1600s, everyone was very superstitious, believing in magic and the devil," MacLeod continues. . . . Eventually cooler heads prevailed, and by the early 1700s legal procedures against witches were declared unlawful by the governor of Massachusetts. But thanks to the Salem Witch Museum and others, it looks like "witchcraft" has settled in for a spell.

You may have noticed that all of the examples in this section use both narration and description. In fact, most effective writing—even a good resume or biology lab report—calls for clear storytelling and the creation of vivid word pictures for the reader.

Writing Assignments

The following two assignments will help you develop your voice as a writer. For now, don't worry about topic sentences or thesis statements or any of the things we'll consider later. Narration and description have their own logical structures. A story has a beginning, a middle, and an end. And we describe things from top to bottom, side to side, and so on.

Assignment 1

NARRATION: FAMOUS SAYINGS

The following is a list of well-known expressions. No doubt you have had an experience that proves at least one of these to be true. Write a short essay that tells a story from your own life that relates to one of these sayings. (See if you can tell which of the sayings fits the experience narrated in the article "Harmonious Cord" on p. 213.) You might want to identify the expression you have chosen in your introductory paragraph. Then tell the beginning, middle, and end of the story. Be sure to use vivid details to bring the story to life. Finish with a brief concluding paragraph in which you share your final thoughts on the experience.

All that glitters is not gold.

A friend in need is a friend indeed.

Experience is the best teacher.

If at first you don't succeed . . . try, try again.

Absence makes the heart grow fonder.

When you have your health, you have everything.

Assignment 2

DESCRIPTION: A VALUABLE OBJECT

Describe an object that means a lot to you. It could be a gift that you received, an object you purchased for yourself, an heirloom in your family, or a memento from your childhood. Your goal is to make the reader visualize the object. Try to use details and comparisons that appeal to the reader's senses in some way. Look back at the examples for inspiration. Be sure the reader knows—from your choice of details—what the object means to you.

IV. Finding a Topic

You will most often be given a topic to write about, perhaps based on a reading assignment. However, when the assignment of a paper calls for you to choose your own topic without any further assistance, try to go immediately to your interests.

Look to Your Interests

If the topic of your paper is something you know about and—more important—something you *care* about, then the whole process of writing will be smoother and more enjoyable for you. If you ski, if you are a musician, or even if you just enjoy watching a lot of television, bring that knowledge and enthusiasm into your papers.

Take a moment to think about and jot down a few of your interests now (no matter how unrelated to school they may seem), and then save the list for use later when deciding what to write about. One student's list of interests might look like this:

buying and selling on eBay
playing video games with friends
boogie boarding in summer
collecting baseball cards

Another student's list might be very different:

playing the violin
going to concerts
watching old musicals on video
drawing caricatures of my friends

While still another student might list the following interests:

going to the horse races
reading for my book club
traveling in the summer
buying lottery tickets

These students have listed several worthy topics for papers. And because they are personal interests, the students have the details needed to support them. With a general topic to start with, you can use several ways to gather the details you will need to support it in a paragraph or an essay.

Focused Free Writing (or Brainstorming)

Free writing is a good way to begin. When you are assigned a paper, try writing for ten minutes putting down all your thoughts on one subject—traveling in the summer, for example. Don't stop to think about organization, sentence structures, capitalization, or spelling—just let details flow onto the page. Free writing will help you see what material you have and will help you figure out what aspects of the subject to write about.

Here is an example:

When my friends and I went to Sea World in San Diego last summer, we saw an amazing bird show. The birds weren't in cages or tied to perches. Instead they flew freely down out of the sky and out of windows in a phony town that surrounded the stage. And they didn't just have parrots and cockatoos like all the other bird shows I've ever seen before. In those shows the birds just did tricks for treats. But Sea world's show had eagles and falcons and really tall cranes with feathers that looked like ladies' hats on their heads. It was really amazing.

Now the result of this free writing session is certainly not ready to be typed and turned in as a paragraph. But what did become clear in it was that the student could probably compare the two types of bird shows she has seen—the species of birds used and how they were presented.

Clustering

Clustering is another way of thinking a topic through on paper before you begin to write. A cluster is more visual than free writing. You could cluster the topic of "flea markets," for instance, by putting it in a circle in the center of a piece of paper and then drawing lines to new circles as ideas or details occur to you. The idea is to free your mind from the limits of sentences and paragraphs to generate pure details and ideas. When you are finished clustering, you can see where you want to go with a topic.

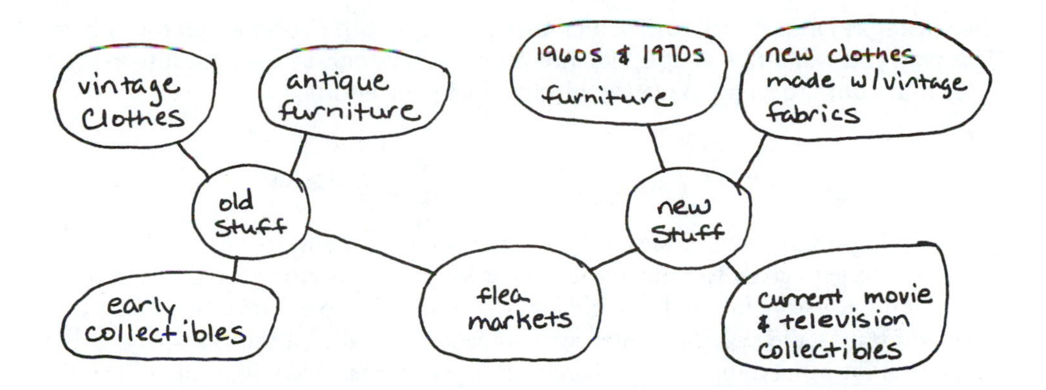

This cluster shows that the student has found two main categories of merchandise at flea markets. This cluster might lead to another where the student chooses one subcategory—early collectibles, for instance—and thinks of more details about them.

Talking with Other Students

It may help to talk to others when deciding on a topic. Many teachers break their classes up into groups at the beginning of an assignment. Talking with other students helps you realize that you see things just a little differently. Value the difference—it will help your written voice that we discussed earlier emerge.

Assignment 3

LIST YOUR INTERESTS

Make a list of four or five of your own interests. Be sure that they are as specific as the examples listed on p. 221. Keep the list for later assignments.

Assignment 4

DO SOME FREE WRITING

Choose one of your interests, and do some focused free writing about it. Write for ten minutes with that topic in mind but without stopping. Don't worry about anything such as spelling or sentence structures while you are free writing. The results are meant to help you find out what you have to say about the topic *before* you start to write a paper about it. Save the results for a later assignment.

Assignment 5

TRY CLUSTERING IDEAS

Choose another of your interests. Put it in the center of a piece of paper, and draw a cluster of details and ideas relating to it following the sample shown above. Take the cluster as far as it will go. Then choose one aspect to cluster again on its own. This way you will arrive at specific, interesting details and ideas—not just the first ones that come to mind. Save the results of all your efforts.

V. Organizing Ideas

The most important thing to keep in mind, no matter what you are writing, is the idea you want to get across to your reader. Whether you are writing a paragraph or an essay, you must have in mind a single idea that you want to express. In a paragraph, such an idea is called a topic sentence; in an essay it's called a thesis statement, but they mean the same thing—an idea you want to get across. We will begin with a discussion of thesis statements.

Thesis Statements

Let's choose one of the students' interests listed on p. 221 as a general topic. "Buying and selling on eBay" by itself doesn't make any point. What about it? What does it do for you? What point about buying and selling on eBay would you like to present to your reader? You might write

> Buying and selling on eBay is fun and educational.

But this is a vague statement, not worth developing. You might move into more specific territory and write

> I have learned about business and geography by buying and selling items on eBay.

Now you have said something specific. *When you write in one sentence the point you want to present to your reader, you have written a thesis statement.*

All good writers have a thesis in mind when they begin to write, or the thesis may well evolve as they write. Whether they are writing essays, novels, poems, or plays, they eventually have in mind an idea they want to present to the reader. They may develop it in various ways, but behind whatever they write is their ruling thought, their reason for writing, their thesis.

For any writing assignment, after you have done some free writing or clustering to explore your topic, the next step is to write a thesis statement. As you write your thesis statement, keep two things in mind:

1. A thesis statement must be a sentence *with a subject and a verb* (not merely a topic).
2. A thesis statement must be *an idea that you can explain or defend* (not simply a statement of fact).

Exercise 1

THESIS OR FACT?

Which of the following are merely topics or facts, and which are thesis statements that you could explain or defend? In front of each one that could be a thesis statement, write THESIS. In front of each one that is just a fact, write FACT. Check your answers with those at the back of the book.

1. _____ I have a friend who never lets me drive her car.
2. _____ Most people do not drink enough water.
3. _____ I am a college student because my parents want me to be.
4. _____ The word *happiness* is difficult to define.
5. _____ My life changed for the better when I got divorced.
6. _____ Most Americans see several movies a month.
7. _____ I woke up to find graffiti on my fence again.
8. _____ People should be allowed to use cell phones in cars.
9. _____ I would rather read a science fiction story than a love story.
10. _____ Prequels are more of a fad than a step forward in moviemaking.

Assignment 6

WRITE A THESIS STATEMENT

Use your free writing or clustering results from Assignments 4 and 5 (p. 223) and write at least one thesis statement based on one of your interests. Be sure that the thesis you write is phrased as a complete thought that can be defended or explained in an essay.

Organizing an Essay

Once you have written a good thesis and explored your topic through discussion with others or by free writing and clustering, you are ready to organize your essay.

First you need an introductory paragraph. It should catch your reader's interest, provide necessary background information, and either include or suggest your thesis statement. (See p. 209 and p. 216 for two examples of student writers' introductory paragraphs.) In your introductory paragraph, you may also list supporting points, but a more effective way is to let them unfold paragraph by paragraph rather than to give them all away in the beginning of the essay. Even if your supporting points don't appear in your introduction, your reader will easily spot them later if your paper is clearly organized.

Your second paragraph will present your first supporting point—everything about it and nothing more.

Your next paragraph will be about your second supporting point—all about it and nothing more.

Each additional paragraph will develop another supporting point.

Finally, you'll need a concluding paragraph. In a short paper, it isn't necessary to restate all your points. Your conclusion may be brief; even a single sentence to round out the paper may do the job. Remember that the main purpose of a concluding paragraph is to bring the paper to a close by sharing your final thoughts on the subject. (See p. 210 and p. 214 for two examples of concluding paragraphs.)

Learning to write a brief organized essay of this kind will help you to distinguish between the parts of an essay. Then when you're ready to write a longer paper, you'll be able to organize it clearly and elaborate on its design and content.

Topic Sentences

A topic sentence does for a paragraph what a thesis statement does for an essay—it states the main idea. Like thesis statements, topic sentences must be phrased as complete thoughts to be proven or developed through the presentation of details. But the topic sentence introduces an idea or subtopic that is the right size to cover in a paragraph. The topic sentence doesn't have to be the first sentence in a paragraph. It may come at the end or even in the middle, but putting it first is most common.

Each body paragraph should contain only one main idea, and no detail or example should be in a paragraph if it doesn't support the topic sentence or help to transition from one paragraph to another. (See p. 209, p. 215, and p. 216 for more examples of effective body paragraphs within essays and of paragraphs alone.)

Organizing Body Paragraphs (or Single Paragraphs)

A single paragraph or a body paragraph within an essay is organized in the same way as an entire essay only on a smaller scale. Here's the way you learned to organize an essay:

Thesis: stated or suggested in introductory paragraph
First supporting paragraph
Second supporting paragraph
Additional supporting paragraphs
Concluding paragraph

And here's the way to organize a paragraph:

Topic sentence
First supporting detail or example
Second supporting detail or example
Additional supporting details or examples
Concluding or transitional sentence

You should have several details to support each topic sentence. If you find that you have little to say after writing the topic sentence, ask yourself what details or examples will make your reader believe that the topic sentence is true for you.

Transitional Expressions

Transitional expressions within a paragraph and between paragraphs in an essay help the reader move from one detail or example to the next and from one supporting point to the next. When first learning to organize an essay, you might start each supporting paragraph in a paper with a transitional expression. Later, if they sound too repetitious, take these individual words out and replace them with more detailed prepositional phrases or dependent clauses, thereby improving your sentence variety.

There are transitions to show addition:

Also
Furthermore
Another (example, point, step, etc. . . .)
In addition

There are transitions to show sequence:

First	One reason	One example
Second	Another reason	Another example
Finally	Most important	In conclusion

There are transitions to show comparison or contrast:

Similarly	In the same way	In comparison
However	On the other hand	In contrast

Exercise 2

ADDING TRANSITIONAL EXPRESSIONS

Place the appropriate transitional expressions into the blanks in the following paragraph to make it read smoothly. Check your answers with those in the back of the book.

First Finally However In conclusion Next

I have been planning to take a cruise with my husband and maybe my kids for several years now. _________, I haven't decided what kind of cruise to go on yet. _________, there are the romantic couple cruises to the Caribbean. But then

I might worry about my children while we're away. _________, there are the breathtaking sights of Alaskan cruises. I've seen pictures of cruise ships passing right next to glaciers, although that seems a little dangerous. _________, there are the family cruises that cater to everyone's desire for adventure and fun. While the kids play one of the numerous supervised activities, the adults can relax and enjoy each other's company. _________, I think I've talked myself into a cruise for the whole family this summer!

Assignment 7

DO YOU WANT TO LIVE TO BE 100?

People are living longer these days. Research shows that more and more people will live to be 100 as medical improvements continue to lengthen our life expectancies. Do you want to live to be 100? Why or why not? Write a long paragraph or a short essay in which you answer this question. Your answer will be your main idea, and the reasons and details that support it should be based on your own experiences. Try free writing, clustering, or discussing the subject with others to find out how you feel about the topic before you begin to write.

VI. Supporting with Details

Now you're ready to support your main ideas with subtopics and specific details. That is, you'll think of ways to convince your reader that what you say in your thesis is true. How could you convince your reader that buying and selling on eBay has taught you about business and geography? You might write

> I have learned a great deal about business and geography by buying and selling items on eBay. (because)

1. I must be honest in my dealings with other buyers and sellers.
2. I have to keep good records and be very organized.
3. I learn about places I have never heard of before by shipping packages all over the world.

Note - Sometimes if you imagine a *because* at the end of your thesis statement, it will help you write your reasons or subtopics clearly and in parallel form.

Types of Support

The subtopics developing a thesis and the details presented in a paragraph are not always *reasons.* Supporting points may take many forms based on the purpose of the essay or paragraph. They may be

examples (in an illustration)
steps (in a how-to or process paper)
types or kinds (in a classification)
meanings (in a definition)
similarities and/or differences (in a comparison/contrast)
causes or effects (in a cause-and-effect analysis).

Whatever they are, supporting points should develop the main idea expressed in the thesis or topic sentence and prove it to be true.

Here is the final draft of a student essay about a challenging assignment. Notice how the body paragraphs map out the stages of the assignment. And all of the details within the body paragraphs bring the experience to life.

Drawing a Blank

On the day my drawing class started to learn about self-portraits last year, each of us had to bring a mirror to class. In backpacks and purses were make-up mirrors, dressing table mirrors—large and small mirrors of every shape and kind. I was nervous about drawing a self-portrait, so I brought only a tiny plastic pocket mirror. That way if I didn't do a good job, it would be my mirror's fault. I should have known I could do it if I tried.

I had never done well on human figure drawing. First our teacher, Ms. Newman, demonstrated the proportion of a human figure; she explained that a human body measures about seven times a human head. She used a tiny piece of chalk to draw on the board while she was talking. Then she showed how to sketch the face, from eyebrows to eyes, nose, mouth, and ears. After her lecture, she told us to begin drawing our self-portraits.

We all set up our mirrors. The ceiling danced with

the reflections they made as we got to work. I looked down at my little square of scratched-up plastic and started to draw gingerly on my paper. I tried to put the eyes, nose, and mouth I had seen on the paper. When I finished, I wondered, "Who the heck is this?" The drawing didn't look anything like me. I was frustrated and sank down in my chair. After a minute, I told myself, "Try again." I drew another one, and it was a little better. But I could not really call it a self-portrait because it didn't look exactly like me.

I asked Ms. Newman for help. She glanced at my previous attempts and said, "A good self-portrait doesn't just look like you, it also shows your personality and your feelings." She did not see any of these in my other drawings. So I tried again. I borrowed my friend's big glass mirror and stared into it; I was not only looking at my face, but also deep inside my face. This time, I freely sketched the shape of my face. Then I roughly placed my eyebrows, eyes, nose, mouth, and ears. I looked into the mirror again and drew the expression I saw there.

When my portrait was finished, I wondered at the amazing work I had done. Even though it did not perfectly look like me, it really showed my personality and emotions through the contrast of light and dark. When Ms. Newman saw it, she applauded. Not only did I get an A on this project, it also became one of the strongest pieces in my portfolio. I realized that few things can be done successfully the first time. If I had given up after my first try, I would never have captured the real me.

(Note: See p. 231 for a rough draft of the above essay, before its final revisions.)

Learning to support your main ideas with vivid details is perhaps the most important thing you can accomplish in this course. Many writing problems are not really *writing* problems but *thinking* problems. Whether you're writing a term paper or merely an answer to a test question, if you take enough time to think, you'll be able to write a clear thesis statement and support it with paragraphs loaded with meaningful details.

Assignment 8

WRITE AN ESSAY ON ONE OF YOUR INTERESTS

Return to the thesis statement you wrote about one of your interests for Assignment 6 on p. 225. Now write a short essay to support it. You can explain the allure of your interest, its drawbacks or its benefits (such as the one about eBay teaching the student about business and geography). Don't forget to use any free writing or clustering you may have done on the topic beforehand.

Assignment 9

A MISTAKE

Like the student writer of the essay "Really Understanding" (p. 209), we all make mistakes. And these mistakes often affect other people. Write an essay about a mistake you have made or a mistake someone else made that had an effect on you.

VII. Revising Your Papers

Great writers don't just sit down and write a final draft. They write and revise. You may have heard the expression, "Easy writing makes hard reading." True, it is *easier* to turn in a piece of writing the first time it lands on paper. But you and your reader will probably be disappointed by the results. Try to think of revision as an opportunity instead of a chore, as a necessity instead of a choice.

Whenever possible, you should write the paper several days before the first draft is due. Let it sit for a while. When you reread it, you'll see ways to improve the organization or to add more details to a weak paragraph. After revising the paper, put it away for another day, and try again to improve it. Save all of your drafts along the way to see the progress that you've made or possibly to return to an area left out in later drafts but that fits in again after revision.

Don't call any paper finished until you have worked it through several times. Revising is one of the best ways to improve your writing.

Take a look at an early draft of the student essay you read on page 229 on the assignment to draw a self-portrait. Notice that the student has revised her rough draft by crossing out some parts, correcting word forms, and adding new phrasing or reminders for later improvement.

Drawing a Blank

~~If at First You Don't Succeed . . . Try, Try Again~~

On the day ~~that~~ my drawing class started to learn
about self-portraits last year, each of us had to bring a

mirror to class. [In backpacks and purses] ~~There~~ were make-up mirrors, dressing table mirrors—large and small mirrors of every shape and kind. I was nervous about drawing a self[-]portrait, so I brought [only] a tiny plastic pocket mirror. That way if I didn't do a good job, it would be my mirror's fault. [*Add a thesis*]

I had never done well on human figure drawing. ~~Anyway~~ [First], our teacher[, Ms. Newman,] ~~showed us how to do~~ [demonstrated] the proportion of a human figure; ~~something like~~ [she explained that] a human body measures about seven times a human head. She used a tiny piece of chalk to draw on the board while she was talking. Then she ~~also~~ showed how to sketch ~~out~~ the face, from eyebrows to eyes, nose, mouth[,] and ears. After ~~all that~~ [her lecture], she ~~led~~ [told] us to ~~start out~~ [begin] drawing~~s~~ [our self-portraits].

~~Everyone in the class~~ [We all] set up ~~their~~ [our] mirrors[.] ~~and t~~[T]he ceiling danced with ~~all of~~ the reflections they made [as we got to work.] ~~Then we started to draw.~~ I looked down at my little square [of] scratched-up ~~mirror~~ [plastic] and started to draw gingerly on my ~~drawing~~ paper. ~~I looked at my face, eyebrows, eyes, nose, mouth, and ears~~. I tried to put ~~what~~ [the eyes, nose, and mouth] I had seen on the paper. ~~Then~~ [When] I finished, I ~~was like~~ [wondered,] "Who the heck is this?" The drawing ~~was totally bad. Nothing looked~~ [didn't look anything] like me. I was ~~so~~ frustrated and sank down in my chair. After a minute, I told myself, "Try again[."] ~~the next one will be better."~~ I drew another one, and it was a little better. ~~It looked a little like me. Nevertheless,~~ [But] I could not really ~~say that~~ [call] it ~~was~~ a self-portrait because it did not look exactly like me.

I asked ~~my teacher to come over and help me out.~~ [Ms. Newman for help.] She ~~saw~~ [glanced at] my previous ~~drawings~~ [attempts] and said, "A good self-portrait doesn't just look like you, it also shows your personality and ~~characteristics~~ [your feelings]." ~~From my drawing,~~ ~~s~~[S]he did not see

in my other drawings.
any of these. So I tried again. I borrowed my friend's big glass mirror and stared into it; I was not only looking at my face, but also deep inside my face. This time, I freely sketched ~~out~~ the shape of my face. ~~shape first.~~ Then, I roughly placed my eyebrows, eyes, nose, mouth, and ears. ~~And~~ I looked ~~at~~ into the mirror ~~, seeing my reflection closely. I~~ again and drew ~~what I felt to be like in the mirror.~~ the expression I saw there.

When my ~~drawing~~ portrait was finished, I wondered at ~~what an~~ the amazing work I had done. Even though it did not perfectly look like me, it really showed my ~~characteristics~~ personality and emotions through the contrast of light and dark. When ~~my teacher~~ Ms. Newman saw it, she applauded. ~~my drawing and she really liked it.~~ Not only did I get an A ~~in~~ on this project; it also became one of the strongest pieces in my portfolio. I ~~recognized~~ realized that ~~nothing could~~ few things can be done successfully the first time. If I ~~gave~~ had given up after my first try, I would never have ~~known I could have done such a great job. Now I know I will succeed no matter how many times I must try.~~ captured the real me.

Can you see why each change was made? Analyzing the reasons for the changes will help you improve your own revision skills.

Assignment 10

A TRADITION

Cynthia Cavnar writes about her husband's family tradition of saving the umbilical cords of relatives and passing them down as heirlooms ("Harmonious Cord" p. 213). Write about a tradition you or someone in your family has. How did the tradition come about? What are the reasons for maintaining the tradition? Are there any particular objects involved?

Write a rough draft of the paper and then set it aside. When you finish writing about the tradition, reread your paper to see what improvements you can make to your rough draft. Use the following checklist to help guide you through this or any other revision.

Revision Checklist

Here's a checklist of revision questions. If the answer to any of these questions is no, revise that part of your paper until you're satisfied that the answer is yes.

1. Does the introductory paragraph introduce the topic clearly and suggest or include a thesis statement that the paper will explain or defend?
2. Does each of the other paragraphs support the thesis statement?
3. Does each body paragraph contain a clear topic sentence and focus on only one supporting point?
4. Do the body paragraphs contain enough details, and are transitional expressions well used?
5. Do the final thoughts expressed in the concluding paragraph bring the paper to a smooth close?
6. Does your (the writer's) voice come through?
7. Do the sentences read smoothly and appear to be correct?
8. Are words well-chosen and are spelling and punctuation consistent and correct?

Exchanging Papers

This checklist could also be used when you exchange papers with another student in your class. Since you both have written a response to the same assignment, you will understand what the other writer went through and learn from the differences between the two papers.

Proofreading Aloud

Finally, read your finished paper *aloud.* If you read it silently, you will see what you *think* is there, but you are sure to miss some errors. Read your paper aloud slowly, pointing to each word as you read it to catch omissions and errors in spelling and punctuation. Reading a paper to yourself this way may take fifteen minutes to half an hour, but it will be time well spent. There are even word processing programs that will "speak" your text in a computer's voice. Using your computer to read your paper to you can be fun as well as helpful. If you don't like the way something sounds, don't be afraid to change it! Make it a rule to read each of your papers *aloud* before handing it in.

Here are four additional writing assignments to help you practice the skills of writing and revising.

Assignment 11

"HEY, MAN, GIVE ME SOME SPACE!"

Some people need almost no "personal space" and feel comfortable even when in crowded situations. Others need lots of physical space around them to be happy. How much "personal space" do you need? Make sure you answer the question, offer the reasons for your answer, and give a few examples in your discussion. Organize your results into the structure of a brief essay.

Assignment 12

WHAT IS HOME?

"Home is where the heart is" is just one of many old sayings that try to define the meaning of the word *home.* It is an abstract word—like *love*—that means different things to different people. How do you define the word *home?* Is it the building you live in or another place altogether? Do you consider yourself "home*less*"—if so, why? Write a brief essay in which you help the reader understand what you mean by "home." Be sure to use plenty of details to bring your definition to life.

Assignment 13

THE BEST ADVICE

What was the best advice you ever received? What prompted the advice? Who gave it to you, and why was it so valuable? Organize your responses to these questions into the structure of a brief essay.

Assignment 14

"LOVE IS BLIND; FRIENDSHIP CLOSES ITS EYES"

"Love is blind; friendship closes its eyes" is a quotation from Exercise 4 on p. 197. Write a short essay in which you react to this quotation and support your reaction or explanation with examples from your own experiences.

VIII. Presenting Your Work

Part of the success of a paper could depend on how it looks. The same paper written sloppily or typed neatly might even receive different grades. It is human nature to respond positively when a paper has been presented with care. Here are some general guidelines to follow.

Paper Formats

Your paper should be typed or written on a computer, double-spaced, or copied neatly in ink on 8 1/2-by-11-inch paper on one side only. A one-inch margin should be left around the text on all sides for your instructor's comments. The beginning of each paragraph should be indented five spaces.

Most instructors have a particular format for presenting your name and the course material on your papers. Always follow such instructions carefully.

Titles

Finally, spend some time thinking of a good title. Just as you're more likely to read a magazine article with an interesting title, so your readers will be more eager to read your paper if you give it a good title. Which of these titles from student papers would make you want to read further?

An Embarrassing Experience
Falling into The Gap
Hunting: The Best Sport of All?
Super Salad?
Buying Clothes Can Be Depressing
Got Elk?

Remember these three rules about titles:

1. Only the first letter of the important words in a title should be capitalized.

   A Night at the Races

2. Don't put quotation marks around your own titles unless they include a quotation or title of an article, short story, or poem within them.

   "To Be or Not to Be" Is Not for Me

3. Don't underline (or *italicize*) your own titles unless they include the title of a book, play, movie, or magazine within them.

   Still Stuck on *Titanic*

A wise person once said, "Haste is the assassin of elegance." Instead of rushing to finish a paper and turn it in, take the time to give your writing the polish it deserves.

IX. Writing about What You Read

Reading and writing are related skills. The more you read, the better you will write. When you are asked to prepare for a writing assignment by reading a newspaper story, a magazine article, a professional essay, or part of a book, there are many ways to respond in writing. Among them, you may be asked to write your reaction to a reading assignment or a summary of a reading assignment.

Writing a Reaction

Reading assignments become writing assignments when your teacher asks you to share your opinion about the subject matter or to relate the topic to your own experiences. In a paragraph, you would have enough space to offer only the most immediate impressions about the topic. However, in an essay you could share your personal reactions, as well as your opinions on the value of the writer's ideas and support. Of course, the first step is always to read the selection carefully, looking up unfamiliar words in a dictionary.

Sample Reaction Paragraph

Here is a sample paragraph-length response following the class's reading of an essay called "What Is Intelligence?" by Isaac Asimov. In the essay, Asimov explains that there are other kinds of intelligence besides just knowledge of theories and facts. This student shares Asimov's ideas about intelligence, and she uses her own experiences to support her statements.

> I totally agree with Isaac Asimov. Intelligence doesn't only belong to Nobel Prize winners. I define "intelligence" as being able to value that special skill that a person has been born with. Not everyone is a math genius or a brain surgeon. For example, ask a brain surgeon to rotate the engine in your car. It isn't going to happen. To be able to take that certain skill that you've inherited and push it to its farthest limits I would call "intelligence." Isaac Asimov's definition is similar to mine. He believes that academic questions are only correctly answered by academicians. He gives the example of a farmer. A farming test would only be correctly answered by a farmer. Not everyone has the same talent; we are all different. When I attend my math classes, I must always pay attention. If I don't, I end up struggling with what I missed. On the other hand, when I'm in my singing class, I really do not have to struggle because the musical notes come to me with ease. This is just one example of how skills and talents differ from each other. I would rather sing a song than do math any day. We are all made differently. Some people are athletic, and some people are brainy. Some people can sing, and some can cook. It really doesn't matter what other people can do. If they have a talent—that's a form of intelligence.

If this had been an essay-length response, the student would have included more details about her own and other people's types of intelligence. And she may have wanted to quote and discuss Asimov's most important points.

Assignment 15

WRITE A REACTION PARAGRAPH

The following is an excerpt from *Talking with Your Child about a Troubled World* by Lynn S. Dumas, in which she discusses ways to help children deal with disasters that they might see on the news or that might affect them personally. Write a paragraph in which you respond thoughtfully to Dumas' advice and to the details she uses to support it.

How to Talk with Your Child about Disasters

Encourage empathy. As awful as they are, disasters can offer us a chance to teach children that while the world can be troubling, it is also a place where people care about one another and, in times of distress, help each other out. Keep in mind, though, that this lesson can't be taught with words alone; actions do speak louder here. So if you and your child are watching a newscast about an earthquake in Mexico, you might say, "Isn't this terrible? I bet those people will need lots of food and clothing and toys. Why don't we call the Red Cross and see what we can send? Then, maybe you can pick out one or two of your toys and sweaters and we can send them to the children in Mexico." Not only does such action encourage empathy, but it gives them a sense of power. They learn that they have the ability to make a difference in someone else's life.

Stress the positives. So many negatives surround disasters that it's important to offer children a little balance by pointing out the positives. Of course, survivors will always say, "Aren't we lucky that we survived," and that's important to note. But you can go a step further; you can stress that not only do people weather a disaster but they rebuild after one. . . . You can point out to your nine-year-old, "You know, this flood was pretty awful. But look at how we learned to help each other, and to help our neighbors since it happened. Not only that, but we've made lots of new friends [give examples]. Also, we've learned how to share our feelings a little more. We know that we can cry in front of each other and that no one will make fun of us. Sometimes even bad events can make good things happen. And that's nice to know."

Before starting your reaction paragraph, *read the selection again carefully.* Be sure to use a dictionary to look up any words you don't know. You can also use the free writing and clustering techniques explained on page 222. Or your instructor may want you to discuss the reading in groups.

Coming to Your Own Conclusions

Often you will be asked to come to your own conclusions based on a reading that simply reports information. In other words, you have to think about and write about what it all means.

Read the following article, in which writer David Owen offers a prize of one million dollars to any reader who can help him increase his popularity:

Popularity

When I was a child, I wanted to be a cowboy, a soldier, or 007. As I grew older, though, I adopted a more down-to-earth ambition: to become the most popular writer in the history of the world. And yet, in spite of my ambition, I have made little progress. Although I have been a professional writer for twenty-five years, the majority of the people on the planet have never heard of me, or, if they have, the person they have heard of is actually someone else. I would not say that I'm the least popular writer in the history of the world, but I still have a hell of a long way to go. So I have decided, in the years of writing that remain to me, to give away, with every piece of writing that I produce from here on out, the sum of one million dollars.

One million dollars! To win this fabulous money, you have only to continue reading this story and provide the correct answer to a few questions concerning my writing and me. The questions are not difficult—or, at least, they won't seem difficult if you have spent the past two and a half decades studying my writing (and me).

Here is the first question: Why have so few of the books I have written reached the top (or bottom) of the *Times* best-seller list? Is it because (a) my books haven't really been all that good; (b) most people prefer to read trash, which my books definitely are not; (c) stupid editors, inadequately trained publicists, imbecilic reviewers, and cretinous readers have repeatedly and totally missed the point of my writing and also failed to do their jobs, which even a child could do better than they do; or (d) I've just had bad luck?

The answer is (d) I've just had bad luck. Did you pick it? If so, great. If not, goodbye, go look at the cartoons, better luck next time! (Yes, that's right, there will be many more chances to make a million dollars, even with short pieces like this—so don't give up!)

The second question: Why have I never written a novel, especially when you consider that writers who do write novels seem to be on easy street when it comes to increasing their popularity? Is it because (a) I can't make things up, but can only tell the truth, no matter how painful; (b) I am too much of a gentleman to humiliate my wife and our children by writing fictionalized accounts of their lives and their (to me) annoying behavior; (c) all the good plots have already been taken; or (d) I just don't feel like it?

The answer is (c) all the good plots have already been taken. Young man dreams of becoming a popular writer, young man "comes of age," young man writes a popular book about coming of age—a universe of plots, all hopelessly used. Birth order is so, so important, not only within families but also in the history of the human race. When William

Shakespeare and others were producing their enduringly popular writing, virtually all possible plots were still available. Well. "Regretting, though sometimes popular, is not the same as writing," they say. Farewell incorrect answerers! Your day may yet come.

There are only a few of you left, and I am not surprised. If I were now as popular a writer as it has long been my ambition to become, even people in foreign countries would be familiar with me and my work, having watched me talking in their own languages on television talk shows in their own countries, and they would have been able to answer the preceding questions even if I had phrased them as fill-in-the-blanks. But let's face it—I am nowhere near that popular yet.

So, for the final question, I am going to ask you lucky few to write a brief essay about me and my popularity, and especially about how the former (me) might increase the latter (my popularity). A word to the wise: outline your ideas before you begin writing. This is not a race. I am far more interested in quality than in quantity, although I am also very interested in quantity. Take some time in your essay to dwell on the aspects of me and my writing that are currently fairly popular and that, with minor tweaking, could become popular on a global scale within a short time. Two other points: I have never felt comfortable writing descriptions of sex organs, and I have no interest in doing the kind of writing that involves climbing Mt. Everest. Also, please concentrate on types of extremely popular writing that don't take all that long to produce.

You may begin.

Assignment 16

WHAT ARE YOUR CONCLUSIONS?

Now that you've read David Owens' discussion of his own "Popularity," why do you think he presented it in the form of a contest to win one million dollars? Try to think of three (or more) ways that he uses the contest format to get his ideas across. Then write an essay in which you share your conclusions and support them with references to Owens' article.

Writing 100-Word Summaries

One of the best ways to learn to read carefully and to write concisely is to write 100-word summaries. Writing 100 words sounds easy, but actually it isn't. Writing 200- or 300- or 500-word summaries isn't too difficult, but condensing all the main ideas of an essay or article into 100 words is a time-consuming task—not to be undertaken in the last hour before class.

A summary presents only the main ideas of a reading, *without including any reactions to it.* A summary tests your ability to read, understand, and *rephrase* the ideas contained in an essay, article, or book.

If you work at writing summaries conscientiously, you'll improve both your reading and your writing. You'll improve your reading by learning to spot main ideas and your writing by learning to construct a concise, clear, smooth paragraph. Furthermore, your skills will carry over into your reading and writing for other courses.

Sample 100-Word Summary

First, read the following excerpt from the book *Eccentrics: A Study of Sanity and Strangeness,* by Dr. David Weeks and Jamie James. It will be followed by a student's 100-word summary.

Franz Anton Mesmer

Today medicine is closely associated with chemistry, but in the past there were healers who looked to physics for the causes of illness, and for cures. Franz Anton Mesmer (1734–1815) thought he found a link between health and magnetism, and like other eccentric scientists, once he had found the connection, he devoted his lifetime to . . . his great discovery. . . .

Mesmer brought current theories of astronomy and Newton's law of gravitation into his biological model of animal magnetism. His theory assumed that there was an ethereal fluid present in all living things, similar to the *chi* of Chinese medicine. . . . Good health, he concluded, results when this inner magnetic fluid is in balance with the magnetic fluid that fills the universe. If the equilibrium got out of whack, order could be restored by pulling the fluids back into alignment with magnets.

At first Mesmer simply fitted small magnets onto various parts of his patients' bodies. . . . Soon he progressed to group healing at his lavishly appointed clinic, where patients sat around a tub filled with water and iron powder, and held tight to iron bars. . . .

Mesmer was widely criticized by the medical establishment, and he didn't help his case by the increasing theatricality of his performances. Before long, the group treatments resembled séances . . . which he presided over wearing a lilac cloak and waving an iron wand. He finally abandoned the use of magnets and began channeling the cosmic fluid through his own body and, via the iron wand, into his patients.

While Mesmer's theory of animal magnetism was, of course, without any foundation in fact, he did make a lasting contribution to science with the invention of hypnotism, which used to be known as mesmerism. . . . [H]is hypnotic technique is still in use today in legitimate medicine, with a multitude of practical applications.

Here is a student's 100-word summary of the article:

> Franz Anton Mesmer lived in the mid-1700s. He was an eccentric, someone who got stuck on an idea and built his life around it. Mesmer believed that people became sick when their magnetic juices were unbalanced. He felt that he could cure them by putting their juices in balance again. At first, he treated patients with magnets but eventually started zapping them with his magic wand. Mesmer made quite a production out of these curing sessions. Even though many scientists didn't take him seriously at the time, Mesmer actually invented hypnosis. Maybe other big ideas were considered crazy at first.

Assignment 17

WRITE A 100-WORD SUMMARY

Your aim in writing your summary should be to give someone who has not read the article a clear idea of it. First, read the following excerpt from the book *The Films of Elvis Presley* by Susan Doll and then follow the instructions given after it.

Elvis on Celluloid

No actor has been less appreciated than Elvis Presley; no group of films has been more belittled than Elvis's musical comedies. In countless Presley biographies and career overviews and in most rock 'n' roll histories and analyses,

Elvis's films have been written off as mindless, unrealistic, formulaic, and trite. Yet, no Presley picture ever lost money, and through the benefit of cable television and video, audiences still enjoy his 31 features and two concert films, as well as the many documentaries and TV shows and miniseries about his life. This contradiction points to the narrowness of the standard view concerning Elvis's Hollywood career while simultaneously calling for a reevaluation of his films by placing them in context.

Much of the rationale for the usual negative view of Presley's films derives from Elvis himself. Elvis became disillusioned with his film career when he was prevented from reaching his goal. From the moment he took his screen test with producer Hal Wallis in April 1956, the young singer had wanted to be a serious actor. Interviews with Elvis from this early period indicate his desire to work hard, learn from the veteran performers who costarred in his films, and become a dramatic actor—just as singers Frank Sinatra and Bing Crosby had done before him....

Elvis quickly became disappointed with what he termed the "Presley Travelogues," complaining about their unrealistic storylines and repetitive nature. He also found the tendency for his character to burst into song at any time to be particularly offensive. Friends, relatives, and acquaintances have all testified to his bitterness at having been thrust into so many musical comedies.

A good way to begin the summary of an article is to figure out the thesis statement, the main idea the author wants to get across to the reader. Write that idea down now *before reading further.*

How honest are you with yourself? Did you write that thesis statement? If you didn't, *write it now* before you read further.

You probably wrote something like this:

> Elvis Presley's film career disappointed many people but none more than Elvis himself.

Using that main idea as your first sentence, summarize the article by choosing the most important points. *Be sure to put them in your own words.* Your rough draft may be 150 words or more.

Now cut it down by including only essential points and by getting rid of wordiness. Keep within the 100-word limit. You may have a few words less but not one word more. (And every word counts—even *a, an,* and *the.*) By forcing yourself to keep within 100 words, you'll get to the kernel of the author's thought and understand the article better.

When you have written the best summary you can, then and only then compare it with the summary on page 325. If you look at the model sooner, you'll cheat yourself of the opportunity to learn to write summaries because, once you read the model, it will be almost impossible not to make yours similar. So do your own thinking and writing, and then compare.

Summary Checklist

Even though your summary is different from the model, it may be just as good. If you're not sure how yours compares, answer these questions:

1. Did you include the same main ideas?
2. Did you leave out all unnecessary words and examples?
3. Did you rephrase the writer's ideas, not just recopy them?
4. Does the summary read smoothly?
5. Would someone who had not read the article get a clear idea of it from your summary?

Assignment 18

WRITE A REACTION OR A 100-WORD SUMMARY

Respond to Sharon Begley's article "Are We Getting Smarter?" in any of the three ways we've discussed—in a reaction paragraph, an essay, or a 100-word summary. If you plan to respond with an essay, briefly summarize Begley's main ideas about the so-called "Flynn effect" in your introductory paragraph. Then write about your reactions to the article's information in your body paragraphs. Save your final thoughts for your concluding paragraph.

Are We Getting Smarter?

1. *The cops have put Tony, Uncle Junior, Silvio, Paulie Walnuts, and Livia in a lineup, standing in spots numbered 1 through 6 from left to right. There's one empty space. Livia is the third person from the left. Tony is to Uncle Junior's immediate left. If Paulie Walnuts stands in space 6 with no one beside him, where is Silvio?*

2. *Seven years ago Jack was three times as old as Jill. If Jack is now five years older than Jill, how old is he?*

   (a) 12 $\frac{1}{2}$ (b) 13 (c) 13 $\frac{1}{2}$ (d) 14 $\frac{1}{2}$ (e) 15

While generations of schoolchildren, military recruits, job applicants and Mensa wannabes have wrestled with IQ questions like these, some smart scientists who study intelligence have been stumped by an even more exasperating puzzle: why have IQ scores been rising? And not rising a little, by a point here and there, but soaring—27 points in Britain since 1942, 24 points in the United States since 1918, 22 points in Argentina since 1964, with comparable gains throughout Western Europe, Canada, Japan, China, Israel, Australia and New Zealand. The rise is so sharp that the average child today is as bright as the near genius of yesteryear. "This shatters our belief about the rigidity of IQ," says psychologist Ulrich Neisser of Cornell University. "It's powerful evidence that you can indeed change it."

There's just one little problem. Leaving aside for now the very real question of whether IQ is truly a proxy for intelligence, scientists can't explain what has made IQ scores take off. Neither nature nor nurture—genes nor environment—answers the question, for different reasons. A slew of data, from twin studies to adoption research, suggests that genes account for some 75 percent of the difference between individuals' IQs by late adolescence. That leaves precious little room for environment to play a role. But explaining the IQ rise by "smarter" genes makes no sense, because the genes in a population do not change quickly enough to explain the IQ chasm between the Greatest Generation and Gen Y. That would seem to make environment the leading suspect, but then you're back to that 800-pound gorilla in the corner: psychologists who study intelligence mostly agree that hereditary factors explain the lion's share of IQ differences.

"It's been a paradox," says William Dickens of the Brookings Institution. "The high heritability of IQ suggests that environment is feeble, but IQ gains over time suggest that environment is overwhelmingly powerful." To untangle the mystery, Dickens teamed up with James Flynn, who in 1987 discovered the IQ rise, now called the Flynn effect. In a study being published this week [April 2001] in *Psychological Review,* the duo offer an explanation that not only might resolve the paradox but may also shed light on the forces that shape intelligence. "People's IQs are affected by both environment and genes, but . . . their environments are matched to their IQs," the researchers conclude. In other words, genes do indeed have an important effect: they cause people to seek out certain environments, certain life experiences. If you have a biological edge in intelligence, for instance, you will likely enjoy school, books, puzzles, asking questions and thinking abstractly. All of which tend to amplify your innate brainpower. "Higher IQ leads one into better environments, causing still higher IQ," say Dickens and Flynn. Thanks to that multiplier effect, you will likely study even more, haunt the library, pester adults with questions, and choose bright peers as friends, boosting your intelligence yet again.

The dance between genes and environment starts young. A naturally verbal toddler will likely elicit hour after hour of reading from her parents, for instance. That will amplify her cognitive gifts even if her "verbal IQ genes" are only the slightest bit smarter than other kids'. "A modest genetic advantage turns into a huge performance advantage," says Dickens.

But if you start out with a slight deficit in IQ, you may get frustrated by reading and cogitating, stumble in school and grow to hate learning, reinforcing your genetic bent. A modest genetic difference again gets pumped up.

As far as scientists can tell, experiences that boost the intelligence of someone born with an IQ edge have just about the same positive effect on people of average intelligence. In other words, whether you seek out an IQ boosting environment or whether *it* finds *you* makes no difference. In either case, experiences and the social and technological surround should work their magic. This effect may account for the IQ rise over the decades. Crowded computer screens, videogames, fast-foodery place mats and cereal boxes (full of hidden-word games and mazes) might be training young brains in the pattern analysis that IQ tests assess. Smaller families, which offer children more individual attention and indulge their passion for "why's," might boost a generation's IQ. Jobs that demand more brainpower, more free time (at least some of which is spent reading, doing crossword puzzles, traveling to stimulating places) and technological gadgets that challenge our gray matter could also lift all IQ boats. "Leisure and even ordinary conversation are more cognitively demanding today," says Flynn, an American expatriate teaching at the University of Otago in New Zealand. Teen multitaskers—simultaneously IM'ing, downloading and channel-surfing—may be exercising their memory (a component of intelligence) and training their attention to switch focus in the blink of an eye.

All these expressions of social and technological change have one key characteristic: they are enduring. In contrast, a temporary IQ-boosting change—like an early-childhood enrichment program, or parents who provide intellectual stimulation only in their children's prekindergarten years—can have the staying power of a mayfly. "The kids get this great [intervention], but then they go back to their old environment," says psychologist Robert Sternberg of Yale University. "Of course they usually regress." Even 18 years of parental influence fades. All parents can do is hope that love of learning they imbue in their child takes hold, causing him to seek out the experiences and people that will keep stimulating his intelligence.

Those who believe in the power of genes and those who believe in the power of environment, says Dickens, "are both right." Genes working though environment account for the lion's share of individual differences in IQ, but only because genes lead you to certain life experiences, which collectively form your "environment." It is that environment which directly fosters IQ differences. "People often have a fatalistic sense that IQ is fixed," says psychologist John Gabrieli of Stanford University. "The Flynn effect shows that it can be enhanced by good environment. It doesn't have to be some fixed capacity you're born with."

Oh: Silvio stands in space 4. And Jack is 14 ½.

Answers

SPELLING

WORDS OFTEN CONFUSED, SET 1 (PP. 9–14)

Exercise 1

1. It's
2. do
3. A, effect
4. a, affect
5. already, knew, effect
6. due
7. a, it's
8. its
9. effect
10. advise, choose

Exercise 2

1. know
2. accepted
3. complemented
4. break
5. due
6. advice
7. Conscious
8. fill
9. chose
10. course

Exercise 3

1. know, hear
2. It's, except, it's
3. Its, are
4. an
5. a, it's
6. its, knew
7. an
8. a, feel, have, an
9. conscience, due, its
10. break, already

Exercise 4

1. already, do
2. clothes, choose
3. have, its
4. course, dessert
5. Due
6. feel, conscious
7. advice
8. have, complimented
9. course, do
10. except

Exercise 5

1. an, choose
2. course, it's
3. advice, an
4. effect
5. its, due
6. cloths, no, coarse
7. break
8. all ready, feel, it's
9. compliments
10. clothes

Proofreading Exercise

I'm enjoying all of my classes this semester ~~accept~~ *except* my speech class. ~~Its~~ *It's* not a bad class. The teacher is knowledgeable and supportive. My classmates and I have a good attitude, and we all ~~complement~~ *compliment* each other when we ~~due~~ *do* a good job. It's just that I don't ~~no~~ *know* how to calm my nerves. Everyone has given me ~~advise~~ *advice,* but I can't seem to relax enough to speak without turning red. At the beginning of the semester, everyone was a little nervous and shy at the podium. But now that everyone else has conquered the problem, I ~~fill~~ *feel* very self-~~conscience~~ *conscious* whenever I give a speech. I hope my classmates don't ~~dessert~~ *desert* me before I can conquer my embarrassment too. I guess I couldn't ~~of~~ *have* picked a worse time in my life to take a speech class.

WORDS OFTEN CONFUSED, SET 2 (PP. 18–23)

Exercise 1

1. through
2. You're
3. whose, too, to
4. past, there
5. peace, quiet, their
6. through, they're
7. there, lose, their, right, personal
8. where
9. Then, to, than
10. Whether, you're, quite

Exercise 2

1. were
2. There, weather
3. led
4. past, whether
5. passed
6. past, there
7. quiet
8. lose, two, right
9. through, past
10. piece, lead, weather

Exercise 3

1. women
2. piece
3. write, were, personal
4. principle
5. than
6. where, were
7. right
8. woman
9. then
10. passed, through

Exercise 4

1. whether, write
2. who's, You're, your
3. right, through, quite
4. led, too, write, personal
5. past
6. Personnel
7. They're, past, than
8. woman, principal
9. where
10. lose, than, lose

Exercise 5

1. principle, your
2. than, to
3. past, quiet
4. there
5. write
6. woman
7. through
8. women, right
9. threw
10. whether, lose

Proofreading Exercise

Now that the ~~whether~~ *weather* is nice, my kids and I have decided to repaint the outside of our house. We are going to paint it ourselves. But it isn't going to be an easy job since many of the shingles have come ~~lose~~ *loose* over the years. In the ~~passed~~ *past* before we moved in, the house had been repainted without the scraping and sanding necessary, so big chunks of paint have just started falling off onto the grass. We worry that ~~their~~ *there* is ~~led~~ *lead* in the old paint, but we can't decide ~~weather~~ *whether* to call in a professional. One of our neighbors, a woman ~~who's~~ *whose* house was just remodeled, told us, "~~Your~~ *You're* going to regret doing it yourselves. After what I've been ~~threw~~ *through*, I would strongly recommend hiring a professional. That's the only way to guarantee your ~~piece~~ *peace* of mind."

THE EIGHT PARTS OF SPEECH (PP. 26–29)

Exercise 1

pro adv v n
1. I really love cookies.

pro v adj adj n
2. They are my favorite snack. (The pronoun *my* is playing its adjective part here.)

pro v pro prep adj n conj n
3. I prefer the ones with chocolate chips or nuts.

n v adv conj pro v adj
4. Cookies taste best when they are fresh.

adv pro v n conj n prep n
5. Sometimes, I have cookies and milk for breakfast.

adv adj adj n v adj n
6. Now some fast-food restaurants offer fresh-baked cookies.

adj n v adj conj pro v adv adj
7. Oatmeal cookies are delicious when they are still warm.

n v adj n prep adj n
8. Companies release new versions of traditional cookies.

adj n prep n adv v adj n
9. One variety of Oreos now has chocolate centers.

interj v pro adj
10. Wow, are they yummy!

Exercise 2

adj adj n v adj prep adj n prep n
1. Tall office buildings are dangerous for migrating birds at night.

adj adj n v n
2. The buildings' lighted windows confuse the birds.

pro v prep adj n conj v adj n
3. They fly toward the glowing windows and lose their way.

adj n v adj n
4. Bird experts studied this phenomenon.

n v adj n prep n
5. McCormick Place is a tall building in Chicago.

n v n adj n adv prep adj n
6. Scientists counted the number of bird deaths there for two years.

n prep n v prep adj n
7. Hundreds of birds flew into the lighted windows.

adv adj n prep adj n v adj n
8. Only one fifth of that number hit the dark windows.

n v adj n prep adj n prep n prep n
9. Scientists suggest a lights-out policy for tall buildings from midnight to dawn

prep adj n
during migration periods.

n v prep n prep n conj prep n prep n
10. Birds migrate from March to May and from August to November.

Exercise 3

n adv v adj n prep n
1. Jan Demczur recently donated several objects to the Smithsonian Institution.

n v adj n prep n
2. Demczur was a window washer at One World Trade Center.

pro v prep n prep n conj n v n
3. He was in an elevator of the building when terrorists attacked the tower.

prep n prep adj adj n n v adj adj n
4. With the help of his squeegee handle, Demczur saved several people's lives.

n conj pro prep n v n prep n
5. Demczur and the others in the elevator used the handle as an ax.

pro v n prep adj n prep n
6. They cut an opening from the elevator shaft into the building.

n conj adj adj n v adv conj n v
7. Demczur and his five elevator-mates escaped just before the tower fell.

adj adj n v n n
8. Such survival stories give people hope.

n v adj n prep adj n
9. The Smithsonian is the nation's place for rare artifacts.

adj adj n conj adj adj n v adv prep n prep

10. Demczur's squeegee handle and his dusty clothes are now on display at

n

the Smithsonian.

Exercise 4

n v n conj n

1. Plants need water and sunlight.

adv adj n v adv

2. Sometimes house plants wither unexpectedly.

n adv v pro adv adj n conj adv adj n

3. People often give them too much water or not enough water.

pro v n prep adj n adv

4. I saw an experiment on a television show once.

pro v adj n

5. It involved two plants.

adj n v adj n prep n conj n

6. The same woman raised both plants with water and sunlight.

n v prep adj adj n

7. The plants grew in two different rooms.

pro v prep adj n conj v adj n prep pro

8. She yelled at one plant but said sweet things to the other.

adv adj n v adv conj adj pro v

9. The verbally praised plant grew beautifully, but the other one died.

n v n adv

10. Plants have feelings too.

Exercise 5

pro adv v adj n prep adj n

1. I recently read some facts about movie kisses.

adj pro v prep n prep n prep n

2. The first one occurs in a film by Thomas Edison in 1896.

n prep adj adj n v n

3. The title of that short film is *The Kiss.*

adj adj n v n prep n

4. A longer movie kiss holds the record for time.

prep adj n n v n prep adj adj n

5. In a 1941 film, Jane Wyman kisses Regis Toomey for three full minutes.

n v prep adj n prep adj n conj pro adv v pro
6. Mae West flirts with many men in her movies although she never kisses one
prep pro
of them.

n v n prep adj n prep pro
7. *Don Juan* (1926) is a movie with many kisses in it.

n v adv adj n prep pro
8. John Barrymore delivers nearly two hundred of them.

prep adj n adj n v prep adj n prep n
9. In that movie, one kiss occurs for each minute of film.

interj pro v adj n prep n
10. Gee, I love trivial facts like these.

PARAGRAPH EXERCISE

adj n v adv adj n adv pro v adv conj pro v
Your eyelids blink regularly all day long. They stop only when you sleep.
n v adj adj n prep n conj pro v prep
Blinking protects your delicate eyes from injury. When something flies toward
pro adv adj n v adv conj v adj n
you, usually your lids shut quickly and protect your eyes.

n adv v n prep adj n pro v adj n adv conj
Blinking also does a kind of washing job. It keeps your eyelids moist. If
n prep n v prep adj n adj adj n v pro adv adj n
a speck of dirt gets past your lids, your moist eyeball traps it. Then your eyes
v prep n adj n v conj n v adv prep adj n
fill with water, your lids blink, and the speck washes out of your eye.

CONTRACTIONS (PP. 31–35)

Exercise 1

1. who's
2. I'm
3. You're
4. that's
5. It's
6. wouldn't, we'd
7. They're
8. wasn't
9. that's
10. hasn't (*Its* is used twice as a posessive.)

Exercise 2

1. they've, who's
2. They're, they've
3. they've
4. couldn't
5. There's
6. it's
7. We've
8. no contractions
9. they've
10. There's

Exercise 3

1. we'd
2. didn't, I'd
3. couldn't, hadn't
4. wasn't
5. didn't
6. weren't, they're
7. isn't, didn't, I'd
8. no contractions
9. we'd
10. we're, couldn't

Exercise 4

1. hasn't
2. he'd, might've
3. it's
4. wasn't
5. didn't, they're
6. hasn't, it's
7. wouldn't
8. they'd
9. What's, they've, hasn't
10. It's

Exercise 5

1. there's, I'm
2. I've
3. We've, haven't
4. We'll, can't
5. she's, we've
6. it's
7. aren't
8. we're, we'll
9. That's, I'll, it's
10. there's

Proofreading Exercise

~~Ive~~ *I've* just learned about a new web site created to allow people to share ~~there~~ *their* books with complete strangers. ~~Its~~ *It's* called BookCrossing.com, and when ~~your~~ *you're* finished reading a book, it can be ~~past~~ *passed* on to a ~~knew~~ *new* reader just by leaving it on a park bench, at a cafe, or wherever you like. Before you pass it on, you just register the book on the web site, get its ID number, and tell ~~wear~~

where you're going to leave it. Then you place a note or a sticker in the book with ~~a~~ *an* identification number and the web address telling the person ~~whose~~ *who's* going to find it what to do next. This way, people can keep track of the books they decide to "release into the wild," which is how the web site phrases it. The best part about "bookcrossing" is it's anonymous, and ~~its~~ *it's* free!

POSSESSIVES (PP. 37–42)

Exercise 4

1. Roosevelt's
2. no apostrophes
3. Berryman's, Teddy's
4. bear's, President's
5. Roosevelt's
6. Steiff's
7. company's
8. Smithsonian's, bear's, office's
9. bear's
10. Taft's

Exercise 5

1. The Simpsons'
2. show's, "The Simpsons' House Giveaway"
3. Homer, Marge, Bart, Lisa, and Maggie's
4. house's, series'
5. contest's
6. Howard's, The Simpsons' House's
7. property's
8. Las Vegas' (or Las Vegas's)
9. Simpsons'
10. Ned Flanders', Principal Skinner's, Apu's, Chief Wiggum's

Proofreading Exercise

My ~~brothers'~~ *brother's* friends are nicer to me than he is. When Wes had a party for his birthday last weekend, his ~~friend's~~ *friends* Jonathan and Chris tried to convince Wes to let me stay home instead of making me go to our ~~moms'~~ *mom's* bowling tournament. Wes's reaction surprised them. He stormed out of the living room and slammed the door so hard it nearly came off ~~it's~~ *its* hinges. Of course, I ended up watching a bowling tournament, but I appreciated Jonathan and ~~Chris~~ *Chris's* efforts on my behalf.

REVIEW OF CONTRACTIONS AND POSSESSIVES (PP. 42–44)

1. There's, Valentine's
2. I'm, You're
3. America's, that's
4. Necco's, they've
5. heart's (or hearts'), it's
6. company's, cookie's
7. candy's
8. country's
9. New Year's, year's, Valentine's
10. they'll

Bowling for Values

Growing up as a child, I didn't have a set of values to live by. Neither my mother nor my father gave me any specific rules, guidelines, or beliefs to lead me through the complicated journey of childhood. My parents' approach was to set me free, to allow me to experience life's difficulties and develop my own set of values.

They were like parents taking their young child bowling for the first time. They hung their values on the pins at the end of the lane. Then they put up the gutter guards and hoped that I'd hit at least a few of the values they'd lived by themselves.

If I had a son today, I'd be more involved in developing a set of standards for him to follow. I'd adopt my mom and dad's philosophy of letting him discover on his own what he's interested in and how he feels about life. But I'd let him bowl in other lanes or even in other bowling alleys. And, from the start, he'd know my thoughts on religion, politics, drugs, sex, and all the ethical questions that go along with such subjects.

Now that I'm older, I wish my parents would've shared their values with me. Being free wasn't as comfortable as it might've been if I'd had some basic values to use as a foundation when I had tough choices to make. My children's lives will be better, I hope. At least they'll have a base to build on or to remodel—whichever they choose.

RULE FOR DOUBLING THE FINAL LETTER (PP. 46–47)

Exercise 1

1. topping
2. clipping

3. intending
4. meeting
5. picking
6. buying
7. asking
8. calling
9. mapping
10. targeting

Exercise 2

1. digging
2. reviewing
3. dealing
4. clogging
5. clicking
6. unhooking
7. quizzing
8. pushing
9. aiming
10. delivering

Exercise 3

1. snipping
2. buzzing
3. mixing
4. flapping
5. tampering
6. performing
7. conferring
8. gleaming
9. clipping
10. permitting

Exercise 4

1. patting
2. spanning
3. feeding
4. playing
5. occurring
6. brushing
7. gathering
8. knotting
9. offering
10. hogging

Exercise 5

1. helping
2. flexing
3. assisting
4. needing
5. selecting
6. wishing
7. cooking
8. constructing
9. polishing
10. leading

PROGRESS TEST (P. 48)

1. A. you're
2. B. principal
3. B. Woods'
4. A. affects
5. A. its
6. B. (would) have
7. A. than
8. A. Who's
9. B. led
10. B. advise

SENTENCE STRUCTURE

FINDING SUBJECTS AND VERBS (PP. 59–62)

Exercise 1

1. Cats are extremely loyal and determined pets.
2. They form strong attachments to their families.
3. One cat recently showed her love for the Sampson family very clearly.
4. The Sampsons made a temporary move and took Skittles, the cat, with them.
5. The Sampsons and Skittles spent several months 350 miles away from home.
6. Before the end of their stay, Skittles disappeared.
7. The family returned home without their beloved cat and considered her lost.
8. Seven months later, there was a surprise on their doorstep.
9. Skittles somehow navigated her way home but barely survived the 350-mile trip.
10. This incredible story proves the loyalty and determination of cats.

Exercise 2

1. There are a number of world-famous trees in California.
2. One of them is the oldest tree on the planet.
3. This tree lives somewhere in Inyo National Forest.
4. The type of tree is a bristlecone pine.
5. Scientists call it the Methuselah Tree.

6. They place its age at five thousand years.
7. The soil and temperatures around it seem too poor for a tree's health.
8. But the Methuselah Tree and its neighbors obviously thrive in such conditions.
9. Due to its importance, the Methuselah Tree's exact location is a secret.
10. Such important natural specimens need protection.

Exercise 3

1. Your brain has two halves—a right side and a left side.
2. But one side of your brain is stronger in different ways.
3. Scientists refer to this fact as "hemispheric lateralization" and test it this way.
4. (You) Open your eyes and hold up your thumb with your arm far out.
5. Next, (you) point your thumb at something on the other side of the room.
6. (You) Keep both eyes open but cover the thing with the image of your thumb.
7. One at a time, (you) shut one eye and then the other.
8. Your thumb moves to the right or left or stays the same.
9. For most people, the thumb jumps to the right with a closed right eye.
10. Very few people experience the opposite effect and are left-eyed.

Exercise 4

1. Amateur talent shows celebrate the performer or "ham" in all of us.
2. Schools and charities organize these events and raise funds for their organizations.
3. There are singers, dancers, comics, and acrobats in nearly every community.
4. They are not always good singers, dancers, comics, and acrobats, however.
5. In fact, crowds often love the worst performers in talent shows.
6. A sense of humor in the audience and the performers helps enormously.
7. Otherwise, participants feel embarrassment instead of encouragement.
8. Laughing with someone is not the same as laughing at someone. (*Laughing* is a noun—not a verb—in this sentence.)
9. Amateur performers need courage and support.

10. Every celebrity started somewhere, perhaps even in a talent show.

Exercise 5

1. The word *toast* has a couple of different meanings.
2. We toast pieces of bread and eat them with butter and jam.
3. People also make toasts to the bride and groom at weddings.
4. There are Old French and Latin word roots for *toast.*
5. Both *toster* (Old French) and *torrere* (Latin) refer to cooking and drying.
6. *Toast* as the word for cooked bread slices arrived in the 1400s.
7. The story of *toast*'s other meaning makes sense from there.
8. In the 1600s, there was a tradition in taverns.
9. Revelers placed spicy croutons in their drinks for added flavor.
10. Then they drank to the health of various ladies and invented the other meaning of *toast.*

Paragraph Exercise

My most valuable possession at the moment is a pair of chopsticks. These chopsticks are not worth a lot of money. In fact, they are the disposable kind and still have the white paper wrapper on them. Their value lies in my memories of an evening with someone very special. It happened almost a year ago. As a favor to my friend Tressa, I agreed to a blind date with her cousin Marcus. Marcus and I met at a restaurant, ate sushi, and talked for hours. That night was the start of a wonderful relationship. On my way out of the restaurant that evening, I looked for a souvenir. There was a tall glass of take-out chopsticks by the door. I grabbed a pair and treasure it to this day.

LOCATING PREPOSITIONAL PHRASES (PP. 64–68)

Exercise 1

1. (In New Zealand), Maurice Bennett is a man (with a strange claim) (to fame).

2. (During the summer) (of 2002), Bennett created a portrait (of Elvis) (for the twenty-fifth anniversary) (of Presley's death).
3. (At sixty-two square feet), Bennett's rendition (of the King) was unusual enough due (to its size). [or (due to its size).]
4. Adding (to the portrait's interest), Bennett made it (from 4,000 pieces) (of toasted bread).
5. The toast varied (in color) (from burned black toast) (to warmed white toast and four other shades) (in between these two extremes).
6. The burned toast was perfect (for Presley's black hair).
7. The lighter pieces formed the features (of Elvis's face).
8. Bennett worked (on his Elvis portrait) (for a couple) (of months).
9. He used a special oven, toasting nearly one hundred pieces (of bread) (at a time).
10. Now back (to his normal life), Bennett is the owner (of a supermarket).

Exercise 2

1. Most (of us) remember playing (with Frisbees) (in our front yards) (in the early evenings) and (at parks or beaches) (on weekend afternoons).
2. Fred Morrison invented the original flat Frisbee (for the Wham-O toy company) (in the 1950s).
3. Ed Headrick, designer (of the professional Frisbee), passed away (at his home) (in California) (in August) (of 2002).
4. Working (at Wham-O) (in the 1960s), Headrick improved the performance (of the existing Frisbee) (with the addition) (of ridges) (in the surface) (of the disc).
5. Headrick's improvements led (to increased sales) (of his "professional model" Frisbee) and (to the popularity) (of Frisbee tournaments).
6. (After Headrick's re-design), Wham-O sold 100 million (of the flying discs).
7. Headrick also invented the game (of disc golf).
8. (Like regular golf) but (with discs), the game is played (on specially-designed disc golf courses) (like the first one) (at Oak Grove Park) (in California).

9. (Before his death), Headrick asked (for his ashes) to be formed (into memorial flying discs) (for select family and friends). [*To be formed* is a verbal.]
10. Donations (from sales) (of the remaining memorial discs) went (toward the establishment) (of a museum) (on the history) (of the Frisbee and disc golf).

Exercise 3

1. My family and I live (in a house) (at the top) (of a hilly neighborhood) (in Los Angeles).
2. (On weekday mornings), nearly everyone drives (down the steep winding roads) (to their jobs) or (to school).
3. (In the evenings), they all come back (up the hill) to be (with their families).
4. (For the rest) (of the day), we see only an occasional delivery van or compact school bus.
5. But (on Saturdays and Sundays), there is a different set (of drivers) (on our roads).
6. (On those two days), tourists (in minivans) and prospective home buyers (in convertibles) cram our narrow streets.
7. (For this reason), most (of the neighborhood residents) stay (at home) (on weekends).
8. Frequently, drivers unfamiliar (with the twists and turns) (of the roads) (in this area) cause accidents.
9. The expression "Sunday driver" really means something (to those) (of us) (on the hill).
10. (In fact), even "Saturday drivers" are a nuisance (for us).

Exercise 4

1. (Through NASA's space-exploration projects), we learn more (about everything) (from our fellow planets) (to our sun and moon).
2. *Galileo* already discovered a layer (of ice) (on Europa), Jupiter's moon, and (in 2003) will look (for signs) (of life) (beneath the ice's surface).
3. (With the help) (of the *Hubble Space Telescope*), NASA retrieved pictures (of

the planet Uranus)—its system (of rings) and its weather patterns.

4. NASA launched *Cassini* (in 1997) to study Saturn, (with an expected arrival time) (of 2004). [*To study* is a verbal.]
5. (In an effort) to put an American (on Mars) (by 2020), NASA will use information (from *Mars Surveyor* 2001).
6. NASA's *Pluto-Kuiper Express* will study Pluto, the most distant planet (in our solar system).
7. (With the *Contour Mission*) (in 2002), NASA hopes to learn (about the origin) (of comets). [*To learn* is a verbal.]
8. The *Terra* satellite will look (at changes) (in Earth's weather) (as part) (of NASA's Earth Observing System).
9. The *Genesis* probe will fly (around the sun) and gather new information (about its unique properties).
10. Finally, the mission (for the *Lunar Prospector*) is to discover habitable places (on the moon). [*To discover* is a verbal.]

Exercise 5

1. An engraved likeness (of Pocahontas), the famous Powhatan Indian princess, is the oldest portrait (on display) (at the National Portrait Gallery).
2. (In 1607), Pocahontas—still (in her early teens)—single-handedly helped the British colonists (in Virginia) to survive. [*To survive* is a verbal.]
3. Later, (in 1616), Pocahontas traveled (to England) (after her marriage) (to John Rolfe) and (after the birth) (of their son).
4. She visited the court (of King James I) and impressed the British (with her knowledge) (of English) and (with her conversion) (to Christianity).
5. (For her new first name), Pocahontas chose Rebecca.
6. (During her seven-month stay) (in England), she became extremely ill.
7. (At some point) (before or during her illness), Simon Van de Passe engraved her portrait (on copper).

8. The portrait shows Pocahontas (in a ruffled collar and ornate Anglicized clothes) but (with very strong Indian features).
9. Successful sales (of prints) (from the portrait) illustrate her fame abroad.
10. Pocahontas died (on that trip) (to England) (at the age) (of twenty-two).

Paragraph Exercise

(In the broad blue reaches) (of the Pacific Ocean) lies a strand (of islands) (like small green gems) strung (on a wavering line). (From northwest) (to southeast) they stretch (for about 1,500 miles), following the course (of an ancient cleft) (in the ocean floor) thousands (of feet) below.

(In the warm Pacific waters), coral reefs have formed (on some) (of the lava rock), and there is a sprinkle (of small coral islets), mostly uninhabited, (among the larger volcanic islands). . . . Now the fiftieth state (in the Union), (with a total area) (of 6,407 square miles), Hawaii adds a new and shining star (to the flag) (of the United States).

UNDERSTANDING DEPENDENT CLAUSES (PP. 72–76)

Exercise 1

1. The Breathalyzer is a machine that measures a person's blood alcohol level.
2. Police officers use the device when they suspect that a driver is drunk.
3. Robert F. Borkenstein was the man who invented the Breathalyzer.
4. Before Borkenstein created the portable measuring device, officers took suspects' breath samples in balloons back to a laboratory where the samples went through a series of tests, but that process had too many variables to be reliable.
5. Borkenstein's Breathalyzer solved the problem because all testing occurred at the scene.
6. The Breathalyzer was so reliable and became so feared that one man went to

extremes to avoid its results.

7. While this man waited in the back of the police car, he removed his cotton underwear and ate them.

8. He hoped that the cotton cloth would soak up all thc alcohol that he had in his system.

9. When the desperate man's case went to court, the judge acquitted him.

10. The judge's decision came after whole rows of spectators in the court laughed so hard and for so long that they could not stop.

Exercise 2

1. The world is a miserable place when you have an upset stomach.

2. Whether you get carsick, airsick, or seasick, you probably welcome any advice that comes your way.

3. Did you know that motion sickness is most common when people are between the ages of seven and twelve?

4. Motion sickness happens to some people whenever the brain receives mixed messages.

5. If the inner ear feels movement but the eyes report that there is no movement, the brain gets confused.

6. This confusion results in dizziness and the feeling that all is not well.

7. Experts suggest that you sleep well and eat lightly before you travel if you want to avoid motion sickness.

8. When you travel by car, you should sit in the middle of the back seat and look

straight out the windshield.

9. Likewise, the best seat on an airplane or a boat is one that allows a view of the clouds or horizon so that your ears and eyes give your brain the same messages.
10. Whenever the queasy feeling comes in spite of your best efforts, it may dissipate if you sip small amounts of water.

Exercise 3

1. Jo Ann Altsman is a woman who is lucky to be alive.
2. When she had a second heart attack, no other person was there to help her.
3. Because she was in such pain, she couldn't move or easily call for help.
4. She did have two pets that she looked to as she lay on the floor of her home in what she considered her final moments.
5. She wondered if her dog might help, but he only barked at her.
6. Then Altsman's 150-pound potbellied pig LuLu took action when it became obvious that no one else could help her master.
7. The pig somehow made it through the little door that allows smaller pets to go in and out.
8. As she went through the opening, LuLu tore big scratches on her tummy, but she persisted.
9. While she whined loudly for help, LuLu walked to the nearest highway and waited for a car.
10. The man who stopped followed LuLu to Altsman's house, and he called for an ambulance.

Exercise 4

1. On June 8, 1924, two British men, George Mallory and Andrew Irvine, disappeared as they climbed to the top of Mount Everest.
2. When a reporter earlier asked Mallory why he climbed Everest, his response became legendary.
3. "Because it is there," Mallory replied.
4. No living person knows whether the two men reached the summit of Everest before they died.
5. Nine years after Mallory and Irvine disappeared, English climbers found Irvine's ice ax.
6. But nothing else of Mallory's or Irvine's was found until a Chinese climber spotted their bodies in 1975.
7. He kept the news of his sighting secret for several years but finally told a fellow climber on the day before he died himself in an avalanche on Everest.
8. In May 1999, a team of mountaineers searched the area where the Chinese man reported seeing something, and they found George Mallory's frozen body still intact after seventy-five years.
9. After they took DNA samples for identification, the mountaineers buried the famous climber on the mountainside where he fell.
10. Mallory and Irvine were the first climbers to try to get to the top of Everest, and the question remains whether they were on their way up or on their way down when they met their fate.

Exercise 5

1. I read an article that described the history of all the presidents' dogs.

2. Our first president, George Washington, cared so much about dogs that he bred them; Washington even interrupted a battle to return a dog that belonged to a British general.

3. Abraham Lincoln, whose dog's name was actually Fido, left his loyal pet in Illinois after the Lincolns moved to the White House.

4. Teddy Roosevelt had lots of dogs but met and adopted Skip, the one that he loved best, as the little terrier held a bear at bay in the Grand Canyon.

5. FDR's pooch was always with him; he was a black Scottie named Fala, and they say that Roosevelt was so devoted to this pet that he made a U.S. Navy ship return to the Aleutians to pick Fala up after the diplomatic party accidentally left the dog behind.

6. Warren G. Harding's Laddie Boy was the most pampered of the presidential dogs since the Hardings gave him birthday parties and ordered a specially made chair for Laddie Boy to sit in during presidential meetings.

7. Soviet leader Nikita Khrushchev brought with him Pushinka, a dog that he gave to John F. Kennedy's daughter Caroline.

8. At a filling station in Texas, Lyndon Johnson's daughter Luci found a little white dog, Yuki, whom President Johnson loved to have howling contests with in the Oval Office.

9. Of course, Nixon had his famous Checkers, and George Bush Sr. had a spaniel

named Millie, who wrote her own best-selling book with the help of Barbara Bush.

10. And just when it seemed that all presidents prefer dogs, Bill Clinton arrived with Socks, a distinctively marked black-and-white cat.

Paragraph Exercise

Years and Months

As the earth orbits the sun, the seasons change. They change from winter to spring to summer and back to winter. The changing seasons were probably the first calendar that people used. The four seasons gave them a length of time that we call a year. One year is the time that it takes the earth to journey once around the sun.

While it orbits the sun, the earth also spins. During one orbit, the earth spins about 365 1/4 times. To put it another way, there are about 365 1/4 days in a year. A fraction of a day is awkward. So we do not use it. In a calendar, there are three years of 365 days. Then there is leap year—a year with 366 days. The extra day is the result of the four fractions.

The seasons were one early calendar. The phases of the moon were another. People saw that the face of the moon changed. It took about 30 days for the moon to go from full moon to full moon. This meant that people could measure time by the moon. They found that during the four seasons, the moon went through its phases 12 times. That is how the year came to be divided into 12 months.

CORRECTING FRAGMENTS (PP. 79–83)

Exercise 1

Possible revisions to make the fragments into sentences are *italicized.*

1. Most people have at least one couch in their home. (sentence)
2. *It may be* old-fashioned or modern, leather or fabric, comfortable or uncomfortable. (fragment)
3. *It doesn't matter what shape* a couch is in. (fragment)
4. There are always slipcovers to cover an ugly couch. (sentence)
5. And some couches really need slipcovers. (sentence)
6. *There is* a contest by the makers of Sure Fit slipcovers. (fragment)
7. People submit photos of their couches to Sure Fit headquarters in New York. (sentence)
8. *These people hope* to win the company's yearly "Ugly Couch" contest. (fragment)
9. A $10,000 living room makeover *goes* to the person with the ugliest couch. (fragment)
10. Visitors to the company's website vote for one of ten semi-finalists to receive the big prize. (sentence)

Exercise 2

Changes used to make the fragments into sentences are *italicized.*

1. *Cats have* some amazing abilities. (fragment)
2. *One of them is* to survive falling from tall trees or the windows, roofs, and balconies of high buildings. (fragment)
3. Strangely, cats often have fewer injuries when they fall farther. (sentence)
4. From a height of one or two stories, *they often walk* away without injuries. (fragment)
5. The trouble comes when cats fall between three and six stories. (sentence)
6. Scientists *have discovered* that at seven stories and above the results are the same as at the lower levels. (fragment)
7. The timing of a cat's fall determines the outcome. (fragment, omitted "*Meaning that*")
8. Cats' inner ears help them turn themselves right side up while falling. (sentence)
9. Extremely flexible spines and leg positions *help* too. (fragment)

10. Some part of the process must be disrupted at the medium heights. (sentence)

Exercise 3

Answers may vary, but here are some possible revisions.

1. Finding a parking space on the first day of classes seems impossible. I drive endlessly around campus looking for an empty spot.
2. With the hope that the situation will improve, I always spend forty dollars for a parking permit.
3. My old car's engine doesn't like the long periods of idling. It stalls a lot and won't start up again easily.
4. In order to get a space close to my first class, I always follow anyone walking through the parking lot closest to the science building.
5. I am usually disappointed by this method, however. Most people are just walking through the parking lot to get to farther lots or to the bus stop.
6. I was really lucky on the first day of the semester two semesters ago. I drove right into a spot vacated by a student from an earlier class.
7. Maybe I should get up before dawn myself, for that's a fool-proof way to secure a perfect parking place.
8. Every morning, I see these early birds in their cars with their seats back. They sleep there for hours before class but in a great spot.
9. I don't think I can solve the problem this way. I find it hard to get out of bed in the dark.
10. Due to the rise in college populations, campus parking problems will most likely only get worse.

Exercise 4

Answers may vary, but here are some possible revisions.

1. We were writing our in-class essays when suddenly the emergency bell rang.
2. Everyone in the class looked at each other first and then at the teacher. He told us to gather up our things and follow him outside.
3. The series of short rings continued as we left the room and noisily walked out into the parking lot beside the main building.
4. The sunlight was very warm and bright compared to the classroom's fluorescent lights, which always make everything look more clinical than natural.
5. As we stood in a large group with students and teachers from other classes, we wondered about the reason for the alarm.

6. I have never heard an emergency alarm that was anything but a planned drill.
7. Without the danger of injury, a party atmosphere quickly developed since we all got a break from our responsibilities.
8. I've noticed that the teachers seem the most at ease because they don't have to be in control during these situations.
9. After we students and the teachers chatted for ten minutes or so, the final bell rang to signal the end of the drill.
10. When we sat down at our desks again, the teacher asked us to continue writing our essays until the end of the hour.

Exercise 5

Answers may vary, but here are some possible revisions. (Additions are in *italics.*)

1. *I am surprised* whenever I see a seagull up close.
2. After lunch on Tuesdays, our club meets in the gym.
3. After we turned in our research assignments, *the librarians celebrated.*
4. Traveling overseas requires a lot of planning.
5. The pizza arrived within thirty minutes of our call.
6. That was the hardest question on the test.
7. *I have discovered* that people often stretch the truth.
8. Briefly discuss this topic with the person next to you.
9. Even though "wet paint" signs were still on the walls, *people leaned against them.*
10. *The book explains* how a series of paragraphs becomes an essay.

Proofreading Paragraph

Here is one possible revision to eliminate the five fragments.

When a ten-year-old girl named Stephanie Taylor heard about the shooting death of a police dog in New Jersey, she decided to do something to protect the dogs who worked for the police in Oceanside, California. That's where Stephanie lived with her family. She raised enough money to buy bullet-proof vests for all of Oceanside PD's K-9 (canine) officers. Stephanie was glad to know that the dogs who served and protected her neighborhood were being protected themselves.

CORRECTING RUN-ON SENTENCES (PP. 86–90)

Exercise 1

Your answers may differ depending on how you chose to separate the two clauses.

1. Mary Mallon is a famous name in American history, but she is not famous for something good.
2. Most people know Mary Mallon by another name, and that is "Typhoid Mary."
3. The sentence is correct.
4. The sentence is correct.
5. Mary Mallon was the first famous case of a healthy carrier of disease, but she never believed the accusations against her.
6. Mallon, an Irish immigrant, was a cook; she was also an infectious carrier of typhoid.
7. By the time the authorities discovered Mallon's problem, she had made many people ill. A few of her "victims" actually died from the disease.
8. A health specialist approached Mallon and asked her for a blood sample; she was outraged and attacked him with a long cooking fork.
9. Eventually the authorities dragged Mallon into a hospital for testing, but she fought them hysterically the entire time.
10. The lab tests proved Mallon's infectious status, and health officials forced Mary Mallon to live on an island by herself for twenty-six years.

Exercise 2

Your answers may differ depending on how you chose to separate the two clauses.

1. Frank Epperson invented something delicious and refreshing, and it comes on a stick.
2. In 1905, Epperson was an eleven-year-old boy. He lived in San Francisco.
3. The sentence is correct.
4. The sentence is correct.
5. There was a record-breaking cold snap that evening, and the drink froze.
6. In the morning, Frank Epperson ate his frozen juice creation; it made a big impression.
7. Epperson grew up and kept making his frozen "Epsicles"; they came in seven varieties.
8. The sentence is correct.
9. Epperson's kids loved their dad's treat, and they always called them "pop's sicles."
10. So Popsicles were born, and people have loved them ever since.

Exercise 3

Your answers may differ since various words can be used to begin dependent clauses.

1. When I went to an optometrist for the first time last Tuesday, I discovered that I need glasses.
2. Even though I've noticed some blurriness when I read, I thought my eyes were just tired.
3. To my surprise, I need bifocals, which I consider something that only old people wear.
4. Since my insurance policy covers only the lenses, I have to pay for the frames myself.
5. Now I have a dilemma because I need bifocals, but I don't have the money for good-looking frames.
6. People will start calling me "Ma'am" soon if I can't afford "cool" frames.
7. Although my mother gets a good deal at the glasses place in the mall, I definitely don't want to go there.
8. The sentence is correct.
9. Her wire frames start above her eyebrows and end in the middle of her cheeks; they are way too big.
10. I want glasses with small frames in a great color so that I can still look my age.

Exercise 4

Your answers may differ since various words can be used to begin dependent clauses.

1. Now that I've been learning about sleep in my psychology class, I know a lot more about it.
2. Sleep has five stages, which we usually go through many times during the night.
3. As the first stage of sleep begins, our muscles relax and mental activity slows down.
4. The sentence is correct.
5. Because stage two takes us deeper than stage one, we are no longer aware of our surroundings.
6. The sentence is correct.
7. Next is stage three, in which we become more and more relaxed and are very hard to awaken.
8. Stage four is so deep that we don't even hear loud noises.
9. The fifth stage of sleep is called REM (rapid eye movement) sleep because our eyes move back and forth quickly behind our eyelids.

10. Although REM sleep is only about as deep as stage two, we do all our dreaming during the REM stage.

Exercise 5

Your answers may differ depending on how you chose to separate the clauses.

1. In 1999, the BBC released its documentary series called *The Life of Birds.* Sir David Attenborough was the host.
2. The series took nearly three years to complete as the crew filmed in more than forty countries and shot about two hundred miles of film.
3. The BBC spent fifteen million dollars making *The Life of Birds,* a cost that included Attenborough's traveling the equivalent of ten times around the world.
4. The BBC takes such shows very seriously; this one about birds comes after the BBC's amazing documentary called *The Private Life of Plants.*
5. For the plant series, BBC filmmakers even invented new ways to film plants and record the sounds they make, and a lot of the filming had to take place under artificial conditions. However, for the bird series, the BBC wanted a more realistic feeling.
6. All of the filming was done in the birds' own habitats so that it showed their natural behavior, some of which had never been seen or filmed before.
7. To capture these rare moments, filmmakers had to live with birds in the wild, but it was not a very safe environment at times.
8. A tree full of BBC filmmakers was struck by lightning in an Amazon rain forest; they were covered with insects in Jamaica, and Attenborough had to speak to the camera in total darkness in a cave in Venezuela.
9. Makers of the series were especially proud of their bird of paradise footage, which they shot in New Guinea.
10. It turned out to be one of their biggest disappointments because the priceless film was erased by an especially powerful x-ray machine at the airport.

REVIEW OF FRAGMENTS AND RUN-ON SENTENCES (P. 91)

Your revisions may differ depending on how you chose to correct the errors.

With all of the attention on cleanliness lately in advertising for soaps and household cleaning products, people are surprised to hear that we may be too clean for our own good. This phenomenon is called the "hygiene hypothesis," and recent studies support its validity. For instance, one study shows the benefit on children of living with two or more pets. Babies may grow up with healthier immune systems and be less allergic if they live with a dog and a cat or two dogs or two cats. The old thinking was that young children would become more allergic living with many pets, but they don't. Somehow the exposure to pets and all their "dirty" habits gives youngsters much-needed defenses. There is sometimes as much as a seventy-five percent lower allergy risk, according to this study.

IDENTIFYING VERB PHRASES (PP. 93–97)

Exercise 1

1. Kris Kliszewicz, a successful businessman (in England), has been raising money and interest (around the world) (for a pet project).
2. Kliszewicz wants to build a theme park which will allow people to immerse themselves (for a day) (in the life and times) (of Shakespeare).
3. Kliszewicz is planning to call the new history-based theme park "Shakespeare's World."
4. He has decided (on the perfect location) (for the first) (of these parks)—(on the outskirts) (of Shakespeare's hometown), Stratford-upon-Avon.
5. (At Shakespeare's World), troupes (of roaming actors) will perform scenes (from Shakespeare's plays).
6. According (to Kliszewicz), visitors will see the sights and hear the sounds that Shakespeare saw and heard.
7. There will be cobblestoned streets complete (with bakeries and butcheries), fields full (of animals and farming peasants), and tradespeople who will demonstrate Tudor crafts.
8. Some Shakespeare scholars are not convinced that a Shakespeare theme park is a good idea.
9. But Kliszewicz believes that people might enjoy learning more (about Shakespeare) (without the purely academic treatment) that he is given (in classrooms).
10. The idea (of Shakespeare's World) is also getting some attention (in China, Russia, and America), which Kliszewicz plans to make future sites (for Shakespeare's World).

Exercise 2

1. Loyal viewers have been devoted (to the television series *Star Trek*) since its first episode aired (in September) (of 1966).
2. (Until recently), no one could have imagined the amount (of money) that fans would pay (for memorabilia) (from the original series and beyond).
3. (In June) (of 2002), an auction was held (for prime pieces) (of the show's sets, costumes, and documents).
4. Just one memo (from Leonard Nimoy) (to Gene Roddenberry) (about the portrayal) (of Spock) fetched $9,775 even though the pre-auction estimate was only $400-$600.
5. A command tunic that was worn (by the character) (of Sulu) (in the first season) sold (for $16,100).
6. The highest bid (of all) went (to Captain James T. Kirk's command chair and platform) that was featured (in every episode) (of the original *Star Trek* series).
7. Estimates (of the chair's worth) (before the auction) ranged (from $100,000) (to $150,000).
8. (By the time) [that] the auction ended, Kirk's command chair had become the highest-priced object (in the history) (of television).
9. (To everyone's surprise), the winning bid (for the chair) was a phenomenal $304,750.
10. Even the control panel (from the bridge) (of the *U.S.S. Enterprise*) sold (for over $40,000).

Exercise 3

1. I have always wondered how an Etch A Sketch works.
2. This flat TV-shaped toy has been popular since it first arrived (in the 1960s).
3. Now I have learned the secrets (inside this popular toy).
4. An Etch A Sketch is filled (with a combination) (of metal powder and tiny plastic particles).
5. This mixture clings (to the inside) (of the Etch A Sketch screen).

6. When the pointer that is connected (to the two knobs) moves, the tip (of it) "draws" lines (in the powder) (on the back) (of the screen).
7. The powder (at the bottom) (of the Etch A Sketch) does not fill in these lines because it is too far away.
8. But if the Etch A Sketch is turned upside down, the powder clings (to the whole underside surface) (of the screen) and "erases" the image again.
9. Although the basic Etch A Sketch has not changed since I was a kid, it now comes (in several different sizes).
10. Best (of all), these great drawing devices have never needed batteries, and I hope that they never will [need batteries].

Exercise 4

1. (During my last semester) (of high school), our English teacher assigned a special paper.
2. He said that he was becoming depressed (by all the bad news) (out there), so each (of us) was assigned to find a piece (of good news) and write a short research paper (about it).
3. I must admit that I had no idea how hard that assignment would be.
4. Finally, I found an article while I was reading my favorite magazine.
5. The title (of the article) was a pun; it was called "Grin Reaper."
6. I knew instantly that it must be just the kind (of news) my teacher wanted.
7. The article explained that one woman, Pam Johnson, had started a club that she named The Secret Society (of Happy People).
8. She had even chosen August 8 (as "Admit You're Happy Day") and had already convinced more than fifteen state governors to recognize the holiday.
9. The club and the holiday were created to support people who are happy so that the unhappy, negative people around will not bring the happy people down.
10. As I was writing my essay, I visited the Society (of Happy People) web site and, (for extra credit), signed my teacher up (for their newsletter).

Exercise 5

1. Most people do not connect bar codes and cockroaches (in their minds).
2. We do expect to see bar codes (on products) (in supermarkets and shopping malls).
3. And we might not be surprised to see a cockroach (by a trash can) (behind the supermarket or shopping mall).
4. But we would definitely look twice if we saw a cockroach (with a bar code) (on its back).
5. (In 1999), however, that is just what exterminator Bruce Tennenbaum wanted everyone to do.
6. Tennenbaum attached bar codes (to one hundred roaches) and released them (in Tucson, Arizona), (as a public-awareness campaign).
7. When people found a bar-coded bug, they could return it (for a hundred-dollar prize).
8. One (of the roaches) was tagged (with a unique bar code) that was worth fifty thousand dollars (to any lucky person) who found it.
9. Many (of the citizens) (of Tucson) were searching (for these "prizes,)" and some (of the tagged roaches) were found.
10. But Tennenbaum should have put a tracking device (on the fifty-thousand-dollar bug) because it was never seen again.

Review Exercise

"Goose pimples" are tiny bumps that sometimes come out (on your skin) when you are cold or frightened. If you look closely (at the bumps), you will see a hair (in the middle) (of each one). A tiny muscle is attached (to each hair) (inside your skin). When you get scared or chilled, each (of these muscles) tightens up and gets short. The muscles pull the hairs and make them [to] stand straight up. The skin (around each hair) is pulled up, too. The result is little bumps. We call these bumps goose pimples because they look just (like the bumps) (on the skin) (of a plucked goose)!

USING STANDARD ENGLISH VERBS (PP. 99–104)

Exercise 1

1. walks, walked
2. learn, learned
3. are, were
4. has, had
5. do, did
6. needs, needed
7. has, had
8. am, was
9. studies, studied
10. is, was

Exercise 2

1. are, were
2. does, did
3. has, had
4. opens, opened
5. have, had
6. counts, counted
7. are, were
8. do, did
9. look, looked
10. is, was

Exercise 3

1. do, don't
2. had, decided
3. was, played
4. talked
5. asked, was
6. was
7. were, were
8. enjoyed, liked
9. started, stopped
10. am, plan

Exercise 4

1. changed, want
2. had
3. signed, turned
4. was, were
5. did, were, did
6. observed, had
7. watched, helped
8. had
9. imagined, had
10. needs, are, am

Exercise 5

1. Yesterday my English teacher *assigned* a narration essay.
2. The sentence is correct.
3. The sentence is correct.
4. They *were* about holiday traditions in different families.

5. In one essay, the writer *explained* the tradition of Thanksgiving at her house.
6. I *liked* the part about making pies for the adults and candy for the kids.
7. The second essay *outlined* the steps another family goes through to prepare for Chinese New Year.
8. That one *had* even more details about food and gifts for the children.
9. The sentence is correct.
10. I *started* my rough draft last night; it's about my dad's obsession with Halloween.

Proofreading Paragraph

Most people believe that they *have* the best pets. I think that we have the cutest pet hamster in the world. Her name is Toots. We *named* her after the little dog that *dies* in the movie *Lassie Come Home.* Our Toots *doesn't* look like that dog, but she *has* something about her that reminds us of it. The dog in the movie *protects* her owner from some really mean men. When the men try to beat the man who *owns* her, Toots is so brave. She *jumps* in front of her owner and saves him. Our hamster is small but fearless too, so we *named* her Toots.

USING REGULAR AND IRREGULAR VERBS (PP. 109–113)

Exercise 1

1. cook
2. cooked
3. cooking
4. cook
5. cook
6. cooked
7. cooking
8. cooking
9. cooked
10. cooking

Exercise 2

1. buy, bought
2. know, knew
3. is, are
4. agree, agree
5. told, telling
6. sit, sat
7. having, have
8. got, getting
9. need, need
10. am, are

Exercise 3

1. took, supposed
2. did, earned

3. called, told, feel
4. thought, was
5. leaving, drove, saw
6. felt, knew, tell
7. tried, went (or got)
8. been, undo
9. wishes, take
10. used, called, does

Exercise 4

1. use, puts
2. does, do
3. transfers, spend
4. is, like, choose
5. does, wants
6. trusts, is
7. imagine, made
8. talking, asked, worries
9. looked, said, lived, understand
10. wonder, is

Exercise 5

1. lying, fell
2. was, done
3. wearing, shielded
4. lain, woke, realized, happened
5. felt, started
6. passed, turned, began
7. describe, experienced
8. was, felt, saw
9. looked, taped, was, protected, wearing
10. had, felt

PROGRESS TEST (P. 114)

1. A. incorrect verb form (Darryl *used* to teach preschool.)
2. B. fragment (Delete "Because" or combine A. and B. to make one sentence.)
3. A. missing comma to prevent misreading (When I returned, the radio was playing.)
4. A. incorrect verb form (were *supposed*)
5. B. incorrect verb form (will . . . *use*)
6. B. fragment (*We* even *tried* a little handsaw. . . .)
7. A. run-on sentence (We had to wait for the bus, so we played a guessing game.)
8. B. fragment (*I didn't need* to take a breath either.)
9. B. incorrect verb form (Last week they *saw* the newest thriller.)
10. A. run-on sentence (Our new car is huge; our old car was tiny by comparison.)

MAINTAINING SUBJECT/VERB AGREEMENT (PP. 117–121)

Exercise 1

1. wrinkles
2. is
3. absorbs
4. absorb
5. soak, have
6. swells, expands
7. result
8. doesn't
9. block
10. take, get

Exercise 2

1. is, call
2. is, are, has
3. is, are, is
4. was, takes, connects
5. believes, are
6. happens
7. hypothesizes, control
8. gives
9. is
10. think, produces, activates

Exercise 3

1. collects
2. has, is
3. is
4. includes
5. has
6. was
7. stems
8. stays
9. are
10. was

Exercise 4

1. are, involve
2. suffer
3. are
4. come, lead
5. start, works, plays
6. starts
7. are
8. cause
9. is
10. warn

Exercise 5

1. is
2. has
3. starts
4. puts, wants
5. likes
6. have, looks
7. let, wants
8. have
9. helps, turn
10. am, is

Proofreading Exercise

I make friends easily. There *are* only a few people who can resist my charming personality once I *get* started talking. For this reason, I have developed many casual friendships with the people I see regularly. But my friends at school *are* very different from my friends at work. At school, most of the single students *sit* around and *talk* after class. Sometimes, we go out for coffee and pleasantly discuss our futures. At work, however, there *are* too many pressures to relax and talk with my coworkers. I call my work friends on the phone before or after work, but we hardly ever *have* a chance to mingle on the job or even during our breaks. My friends at work *love* to gossip. Whenever my coworkers call, either they or I *start* to tell the latest tale, and we all *have* a good laugh. I have fun with both my classmates and my coworkers. They're just different kinds of fun.

AVOIDING SHIFTS IN TIME (PP. 123–124)

1. There is an old joke that people *tell* about being on the "see-food diet." When they are asked what the "see-food diet" means, the jokers *reply*, "Whenever I *see* food, I eat it." There is a kernel of truth in this old joke, according to scientists. When the human brain sees food, it *sends* out a chemical that *gives* people pleasure. That substance *is* called dopamine, and it is probably the way that the brain *tempts* the body to eat so that it doesn't starve. Unfortunately, there is so much food around most of us in our modern society that it makes people want food even when they *don't* need it.

2. The paragraph is correct.

3. I really enjoyed my winter break this year. It was too short, of course, but I *made* the most of the time I had. My extended family had a reunion at my aunt's house in St. Louis. I didn't pack enough coats and sweaters, but the loving atmosphere *kept* me warm. Once I *was* back in the same room with my cousins, we goofed off just the way we used to when we were kids. One night my four closest cousins and I *stayed* up after everyone else *was* in bed. We played board games and ate buttery popcorn and got the game pieces all greasy just like the old days. Overall, my trip to St. Louis with its late-night game marathon *was* the highlight of my winter vacation.

RECOGNIZING VERBAL PHRASES (PP. 125–130)

Exercise 1

1. [Mixing light of different colors] sometimes produces [surprising] results.
2. It is an entirely different process from [mixing colored paints].

3. For example, [mixing red and green paints] produces a dark brown color.
4. But [mixing red and green light] produces yellow light.
5. [Mixing paints] is an example of a process [called color subtraction].
6. [Mixing colored light] is an example of color addition.
7. White light is made up of [colored] light.
8. When [looking at a rainbow], you are seeing sunlight.
9. The band of color in a rainbow is called a spectrum, [containing seven basic colors]—red, orange, yellow, green, blue, indigo, and violet.
10. Light of these colors can be recombined [to form white light].

Exercise 2

1. Email has begun [to be the most popular form of [written] communication].
2. In the [beginning], people searched for a way [to show emotion].
3. It was time [to invent a new type of punctuation], now [known as "emoticons."]
4. Scott Fahlman proposed two of the first emoticons in the early 1980s [to show when something was meant [to be funny or not]].
5. [Called the "smiley" and the "frown,"] these combinations of colon, hyphen, and parentheses look like this :-) and :-(.
6. In an effort [to document computer history], Mike Jones, Jeff Baird, and others worked hard [to retrace the steps of the first uses of the smiley and the frown].
7. They found them [used by Scott Fahlman] in a [posting] to a computer bulletin board in 1982.
8. These and other emoticons have continued [to help people express themselves online].
9. So when you finish [typing your next joke in an email], don't forget [to add a :-).]
10. [Frowning] : - (is seen by some as questionable net etiquette and is consequently not as common.

Exercise 3

1. The idea of [home schooling children] has become more popular recently.

2. Many parents have decided [to teach kids themselves] instead of [sending them off to public or private school classrooms].
3. There are many different reasons [to choose [home schooling]].
4. In Hollywood, for instance, child actors often are forced [to drop out of traditional schools due to their schedules].
5. The [home schooling] option allows for one of their parents, or a special teacher, [to continue] [to instruct them on the set].
6. Other parents simply want [to be directly involved in their child's [learning]].
7. Many school districts have special independent study "schools," [offering parents the structure and materials] that they need [to provide an appropriate curriculum on their own].
8. Children do all of their [reading] and [writing] at home, with their parents [guiding them along the way].
9. The family meets with the independent study school's teacher regularly [to go over the child's work] and [to clarify any points of confusion].
10. Many parents would like [to have the time] [to home school their children].

Exercise 4

1. It's easy [to give someone the bubonic plague these days]—in tie form, that is.
2. A microscopic picture of the plague is just one of the "decorations" [adorning the Infectious Awareables collection of ties] [sold by Roger Freeman].
3. Freeman was a dentist before [becoming a tie salesman].
4. The diseased ties have started [to become popular].
5. There are ties [showing cholera, staph, ebola, and malaria], [to name just a few].
6. Makers decided [to label the ties with information about the conditions] [pictured on their surfaces] and [to donate five percent of their proceeds to research].
7. Freeman took over [selling the stock of ties] after [being given a herpes tie as a present].
8. Freeman loves the disease patterns [seen through a microscope].

9. Their vivid colors and abstract shapes make them perfect [to use as tie designs]; and they're also being used [to decorate scarves and boxer shorts].
10. The Infectious Awareables ties are priced reasonably, [selling for around forty dollars apiece].

Exercise 5

1. John Steinbeck, author of *The Grapes of Wrath,* was the first native of California [to receive the Nobel Prize for literature].
2. [Calling his hometown of Salinas "Lettuceberg,"] Steinbeck's [writing] made the area famous.
3. At the time, not everyone liked the attention [brought by his portrayals of life in *Cannery Row* and other works].
4. Steinbeck's father was the treasurer of Monterey County for ten years, [working also for the Spreckels company].
5. John Steinbeck tried [to find satisfaction in his birthplace], [enrolling in and quitting his studies at Stanford University many times].
6. Finally, Steinbeck moved to New York, [distancing himself from his California roots].
7. Steinbeck won the Nobel Prize in 1962, [revealing the literary world's esteem for his work].
8. Not [writing anything of the caliber of the Salinas stories] while [living in New York], Steinbeck did return to California before he died in 1968.
9. In 1972, the Salinas library changed its name, [to be known thereafter as the John Steinbeck Library].
10. And the house Steinbeck was born in became a restaurant and then a full-[fledged] museum [chronicling the life of Salinas' most [celebrated] citizen].

Paragraph Exercise

Toast reached its central position on the breakfast table only after a [marketing] war between makers of bread and makers of cereals—and a great deal of inventiveness on the part of toaster designers. Electric toasters did not come on the market until several decades after Americans started [to use electric lights]. Some utility companies, in fact, discouraged efforts [to introduce home appliances of any kind]—they were too busy [competing with gas companies for the [lighting] business].

In most cities in the late 19th Century, electricity was available in homes only at night, [to power light bulbs]; during the day the generators shut down. Not until 1903 was the superintendent of the power plant in Ontario, California, Earl Richardson, able [to persuade his bosses] [to run the generators all day Tuesday]—the traditional [ironing] day—[to allow people [to use the electric iron] he had invented].

By 1910, however, a variety of irons, toasters, and other gadgets were in production. Early toasters consisted of [heating] elements with wire racks for the bread; like the coal stove racks they sought [to replace], they often burned the toast—and the fingers that had [to turn the slices over].

[Burned] fingers were the first problem inventors set out [to solve].

Sentence Writing

Your sentences may vary, but make sure that your verbals are not actually the main verbs of your clauses. You should be able to double underline your real verbs, as we have done here.

1. I found a line of ants [marching across the kitchen counter].
2. [Diving into the deep end of the pool] is fun.
3. I enjoy [waxing my car on a cool day].
4. [Keeping up with my journal entries] takes about an hour a day.
5. I waited until after class [to ask my art teacher a question].
6. I was hoping [to sit next to a friend at graduation].
7. He was trying [to understand algebra].
8. The officer wanted [to look under the seat of my friend's car].

9. [Closed for vacation], the school seemed [deserted].
10. [Written in pencil], my rough draft was a mess.

CORRECTING MISPLACED OR DANGLING MODIFIERS (PP. 131–134)

Answers may vary. Corrections are in *italics.*

Exercise 1

1. *After I had looked out the window several times,* my bus arrived.
2. The sentence is correct.
3. I used a flashlight *to light my way as I fixed the circuit breaker.*
4. My counselor said that, *before I take algebra,* I should take pre-algebra.
5. The sentence is correct.
6. Our tutor *slipped on a piece of chalk and fell.*
7. The sentence is correct.
8. The sentence is correct.
9. *I have a new nephew; my mother sent me his picture* as an attachment to an email.
10. The sentence is correct.

Exercise 2

1. *The blue rug in the hallway* needs to be replaced.
2. I found a puppy *while I was sweeping up the alley.*
3. Full of enthusiasm, *the violinist gave a thrilling performance.*
4. Written in pink ink, *the teacher's comments were easy to read.*
5. The sentence is correct.
6. With a smile on her face, *the teacher told a funny story.*
7. I finally paid the bills *that had been sitting on my desk for two weeks.*
8. The sentence is correct.
9. Checking her answers carefully, *Cheryl finished her homework.*
10. *Before I called the doctor,* my ankle started to feel better.

Exercise 3

1. The sentence is correct.
2. The sentence is correct.
3. *In the store,* she kicked her mother by accident.
4. *Looking outside the house,* the inspector found a few termites.
5. The sentence is correct.
6. *I saw the mother bird* flying around in a circle above the tree.
7. The sentence is correct.
8. The sentence is correct.
9. The sentence is correct.
10. The sentence is correct.

Exercise 4

1. *After I got a headache from the fumes,* the ferry finally made it across the river.
2. *That carnival sold cotton candy full of empty calories, but it was the best I'd ever tasted.*
3. *Two months after we moved out,* our old apartment is still empty.
4. *In her email message,* she promised to return the library books.
5. *Sitting in small groups,* the students took the notes.
6. *Before we said goodnight,* the porch light burned out.
7. Our hostess showed us her favorite room; *it was decorated beautifully.*
8. *I saw a tiny gray mouse* scampering along the baseboards of the cabin.
9. The sentence is correct.
10. All along the highway, volunteers *wearing special T-shirts* planted trees.

Exercise 5

1. Feeling the excitement of the first day of school, *I left my backpack behind.*
2. We saw the new movie that everyone is talking about; *it was full of surprises.*
3. My cousins and I, *wearing our pajamas,* always wrapped our gifts on the night before the holiday.
4. *Now that he practices for an hour a day,* his tennis has improved.
5. *Rising and falling several times a year,* the price of gasoline fluctuates.
6. The sentence is correct.

7. *Hiking in the nearby mountains,* they discovered a new trail.
8. She felt pressure *from her parents* to get good grades.
9. The sentence is correct.
10. The sentence is correct.

Proofreading Exercise

Corrections are *italicized.* Yours may differ slightly.

Hoping to become famous and wealthy, a man in Edinburgh, Scotland, has invented a device. *Located just above the trunk and visible from behind,* the device is a variation on the center-mounted brake light used in the design of many new cars. Instead of just a solid red brake light, however, this invention displays to other drivers *words* written in bold, red-lighted letters.

With simplicity in mind, *the inventor limited the machine's vocabulary* to three words: "Sorry," "Thanks," and "Help." After making an aggressive lane change, *we could use the machine* to apologize. Or after being allowed to go ahead of someone, we could thank the considerate person responsible. Of course, *with the use* of the "Help" display, we could summon fellow citizens for assistance.

And there is no need to worry about operating the device while driving. With three easy-to-reach buttons, *we could activate the messages* without taking our eyes off the road.

FOLLOWING SENTENCE PATTERNS (PP. 137–141)

Exercise 1

S LV Desc Desc
1. Cakes can be plain or fancy.

S S AV Obj
2. Most grocery stores and almost all bakeries sell cakes.

S AV
3. They range (in price) depending (on size, occasion, and amount of decoration).

   [*Depending* begins a verbal phrase.]

S AV
4. A cake (with a "Happy Birthday" inscription) will usually cost thirty (to fifty)

   Obj
   dollars.

S LV Desc
5. Wedding cakes, however, are often very expensive.

S AV Obj

6. An elaborate wedding cake may cost several hundred or even a thousand dollars.

S LV

7. The multi-layered traditional white wedding cake still seems the most popular

Desc

kind.

S AV Obj

8. These delicate structures need special care (during transportation).

S AV Obj

9. Some couples order two or more smaller cakes (for the occasion).

S AV Obj Obj

10. People sometimes save a slice or section (of their wedding cake) (as a memento).

Exercise 2

S AV Obj

1. ((In 1998), Sotheby's auction house sold a piece (of 60-year-old wedding cake) (for an amazing price).

S AV

2. It had belonged (to the Duke and Duchess) (of Windsor).

S AV

3. (On June 3, 1937), the famous couple married (in France).

S AV Obj

4. (On the day) (of their wedding), they put a piece (of cake) (in a pink box) and

AV Obj

tied a pink bow (around it).

S AV Obj S AV

5. They identified its contents (as "a piece of our wedding cake"); they initialed and

AV Obj S AV Obj

dated the box, and they kept it (as a memento) (for the rest) (of their lives).

S S AV LV Desc

6. This couple's relationship, which began (in the 1930s), was one (of the most famous love affairs) (in history).

S AV Obj

7. The Duke (of Windsor) gave up the throne (of England) to be (with Wallis

S AV

Simpson), the woman that he loved. [*To be* begins a verbal phrase.]

S LV Desc

8. Unfortunately, she was a divorced American woman and could not, therefore,

AV Obj S AV

marry the king (of England), so he abdicated.

S

9. The pre-auction estimate (for the box) containing the piece (of their wedding

LV Desc

cake) was five hundred (to a thousand) dollars. [*Containing* begins a verbal phrase.]

S AV S LV

10. When the gavel came down, the high bid (by a couple) (from San Francisco) was

Desc

$29,900.

Exercise 3

S LV Desc

1. Tumbleweeds are nature's seed scatterers.

S AV AV

2. They grow (to the size) (of a bush) and then break off (at ground level).

S AV Obj S AV

3. As the wind blows them (across the open spaces), the tumbleweeds scatter their

Obj

seeds.

S AV Obj S AV Obj

4. But tumbleweeds can cause problems when they encounter structures.

S AV

5. (For instance), thousands (of tumbleweeds) blew (into one woman's yard) (in

AV AV

Colorado), buried her house, and trapped her.

S AV S AV

6. She called (for help), and firefighters worked (for half an hour) to cut a path (to her door). [*To cut a path* begins a verbal phrase.]

S AV Obj

7. (On another occasion), tumbleweeds caused a commotion (in South Dakota).

S AV

8. Members (of a family) awoke (in the middle) (of the night) (to the sound) (of someone) ringing their doorbell frantically. [*Ringing their doorbell frantically* is a verbal phrase.]

S AV Obj S LV Desc
9. When they opened the door, they were very surprised.

S LV Desc
10. The mysterious visitor was an 18-foot-high pile (of tumbleweeds) leaning (against the doorbell). [*Leaning* begins a verbal phrase.]

Exercise 4

S LV Desc
1. My sister Belinda is allergic (to many things).

S AV Obj
2. She gets hives (from mold and pollen).

S AV Obj
3. (Of course), milk upsets her stomach.

S S LV Desc
4. Strawberries and raspberries are many people's favorite fruits.

S AV Obj
5. But they give Belinda a rash (on her face and arms).

S AV Obj
6. The doctor has made a list (of Belinda's allergies).

S AV Obj
7. Soon she'll be receiving allergy shots.

S AV Obj
8. The shots should reduce Belinda's sensitivity (to these substances).

S AV
9. Everyone (in my family) is hoping (for the best).

S LV Desc
10. (With luck), Belinda will feel better soon.

Exercise 5

S LV Desc S LV
1. Giuseppe Verdi's opera *A Masked Ball* is a classic, and performances (of it) are
Desc
usually spectacular.

S AV
2. But two British men, Richard Jones and Anthony McDonald, staged a truly

Obj
unique offering (of Verdi's opera) (for the Bregenz Festival) (in Austria) (in the summer of 1999).

S LV Desc
3. The most amazing part (of the Austrian production) was the stage, shaped (like an open book). [*Shaped* begins a verbal phrase.]

S AV S AV Obj
4. The stage floated (on a lake), and the audience watched the performance (from seats) (on the shore).

S LV Desc S AV
5. This floating book was also huge; its surface covered more than eight thousand
Obj
square feet.

S AV Obj AV Obj
6. Actors crossed a bridge (to the stage) and then walked great distances (during the opera).

S S S LV Desc
7. The size, shape, and location (of the stage) were unique enough.

S S AV Obj
8. Then Jones and McDonald stunned audiences (with an eighty-foot prop) (next to the stage).

S LV Desc S LV Desc
9. The prop was a human skeleton, and just one (of its fingers) was the same height (as an actor) (on the stage).

S AV AV Obj
10. (During each performance), the towering skeleton even moved and pushed one (of the actors) (across the stage).

Paragraph Exercise-3

S LV Desc S AV
Color is perhaps the most powerful tool (at an artist's disposal). It affects our
Obj AV Obj
emotions (beyond thought) and can convey any mood, (from delight) (to despair).
S LV Desc Desc AV Obj AV Obj
It can be subtle or dramatic, capture attention or stimulate desire. [Used more
S AV Obj
boldly and freely today than ever before], color bathes our vision (with an infinite variety) (of sensations),(from clear, brilliant hues) (to subtle, elusive mixtures).

S LV Desc
Color is the province (of all artists), (from painters and potters) (to product designers and computer artists).

AVOIDING CLICHÉS, AWKWARD PHRASING, AND WORDINESS (PP. 145–149)

Your answers may differ from these possible revisions.

Exercise 1

1. Inventing is an American pastime.
2. NASA recently invented a substance which has been recognized by the Guinness Book of World Records.
3. Sentence 3 may be omitted or combined (as it is here) with 2.
4. NASA's record-breaking substance is a solid made of 99.8% air.
5. Sentence 5 may be omitted.
6. It achieved the Guinness World Record distinction as the "least solid object in the world."
7. Sentence 7 may be omitted.
8. The substance is called an aerogel, which is a light, strong material used to build airplanes and spaceships.
9. NASA's new aerogel looks like a frozen cloud.
10. We may be used to inventions by now, but this new aerogel is truly impressive.

Exercise 2

1. One man has done something unique.
2. Irv Gordon has driven his cherry red Volvo P1800 over two million miles.
3. Gordon set a new world record for the amount of miles an individual has driven his own car.
4. Gordon has loved his Volvo since the day he bought it in 1966.
5. He purchased it after another new car broke down on the way home from the dealership.
6. Once Gordon had purchased his Volvo, he couldn't stop driving it.
7. Within the first two days, Gordon drove it 1500 miles.
8. Volvo celebrated its 75th anniversary at the same time that Gordon's odometer passed the two-million-mile mark.

9. Gordon wants to drive his car another million miles.
10. Although Gordon and his Volvo are getting older, this retired science teacher knows how to maintain his precious machine.

Exercise 3

1. After Irv Gordon celebrated his record-breaking mileage, he took his famous '66 Volvo to Europe and put even more miles on it.
2. The Volvo company invited Gordon to participate in its 75th anniversary celebrations in several European countries.
3. Unluckily, Gordon suffered three mishaps during his European tour.
4. The first misadventure happened in Sweden.
5. While Gordon was biting into a crayfish, one of the fillings came out.
6. He couldn't find a dentist for a week as he drove through Holland and Germany.
7. Once Gordon reached England, a Volvo mechanic helped him find a dentist.
8. Then a hydraulic lift at the mechanic's shop smashed Gordon's toe and broke it.
9. After a dentist had fixed his tooth and doctors had treated his toe, Gordon was attending a rugby match when a bee stung him on the eyelid.
10. Gordon must have looked pitiful as he drove his celebrated Volvo onto the ship to return from their European vacation.

Exercise 4

1. An article in *Discover* (Sept. 1999) explains that ancient Egyptians used makeup in many different ways.
2. First, they painted their faces to make themselves attractive.
3. Egyptians seemed to be as vain as we are.
4. Surprisingly, Egyptian men also wore makeup.
5. French scientists and beauty experts have studied the contents of vessels found inside the tombs of kings and queens of the Nile from as early as 2700 B.C.
6. From these remains, scientists have identified the ingredients that Egyptians used in their makeup.
7. The ingredients include goose fat, lettuce, animal blood, crushed beetles, cinnamon, and a few artificial ingredients.
8. Like us, the Egyptians knew enough about chemistry to create these artificial substances.
9. Finally, the Egyptians may have used makeup as medicine.

10. Two of their makeup's artificial ingredients, laurionite and phosgenite, may have helped cure eye problems that resulted when the Nile flooded the valley and contained bacteria that infected people's eyes.

Exercise 5

1. This year I'll get an eight-hundred-dollar tax return.
2. I used to do my own taxes.
3. I would wait for my W-2 forms, fill out the short form, and receive a small refund.
4. Then my mom convinced me to get serious about my taxes.
5. Sentence 5 may be omitted if combined with Sentence 4.
6. I asked my friends at work for any recommendations, and Jason gave me a phone number.
7. I called Helen, Jason's tax preparer.
8. Helen explained that I could control the amount of taxes withheld from my paycheck.
9. Before speaking with Helen, I was ignorant about taxes.
10. And there may be more that I don't understand.

Proofreading Exercise

Nobody in my family is "normal." The oddest of all is my Uncle Crank. His real name is Frank, but ever since I was young, Uncle Frank has been called Uncle "Crank" because his arm doesn't bend the right way at the elbow. It turns like the crank of an old car in silent films. My uncle is proud of his unique arm, but I wish the doctors had fixed it so that Uncle "Crank" could have just been normal Uncle Frank.

CORRECTING FOR PARALLEL STRUCTURE (PP. 152–156)

Your answers may differ from these possible revisions.

Exercise 1

1. I like coffee and tea.
2. I've heard that coffee is bad for you, but tea is good for you.
3. It must not be the caffeine that's bad because both coffee and tea have caffeine.

4. The sentence is correct.
5. All teas are supposed to be healthy, but green tea is supposed to be the healthiest.
6. The sentence is correct.
7. I love orange pekoe tea with tons of milk and sugar.
8. The sentence is correct.
9. I know that all coffee comes from coffee beans, but I didn't know that all tea comes from *Camellia sinensis* leaves.
10. The sentence is correct.

Exercise 2

1. Both men and women fought as soldiers in the Civil War.
2. The women disguised themselves as men, could fight as stubbornly, and enlisted for the same reasons as their male counterparts.
3. They signed up to be soldiers for excitement, for revenge, for financial gain, and for relatives' sakes.
4. The sentence is correct.
5. The sentence is correct.
6. In fact, her real name was Mary Ann Clark, and her real identity was a single mother of two children.
7. The Union soldiers who captured Clark gave her a dress, her freedom, and orders to return to her life as a female in society.
8. After she left the Union camp, Clark ditched the dress, rejoined her fellow Confederate soldiers as a woman, and received a promotion to lieutenant.
9. Letters from soldiers on both sides of the war—from men and women—support the historical findings of the two writers of the book *They Fought Like Demons: Women Soldiers in the American Civil War.*
10. The coauthors of the book, Lauren Cook and DeAnne Blanton, have been able to prove that there were between 250 and 400 undercover female soldiers who fought in the Civil War.

Exercise 3

1. Nearly anyone who has grown up in America during the last century remembers putting a baby tooth under a pillow and finding a quarter or two in its place in the morning.
2. The tradition and significance of leaving a tooth for the Tooth Fairy are hard to trace.

3. One person who is trying to understanding the myth and who collects everything to do with it is Dr. Rosemary Wells.
4. Dr. Wells runs the Tooth Fairy Museum in Deerfield, Illinois, and she knows as much as anyone else about the elusive tooth taker.
5. The sentence is correct.
6. Since then Wells has gathered books, written essays, assembled an art collection, and received gifts about the Tooth Fairy.
7. One of the most intriguing things about the story is that, unlike Santa Claus, the Tooth Fairy does not have any specific "look" or even a particular gender.
8. Wells has discovered a few ancient rituals having to do with lost teeth, such as tossing the tooth into the air or pitching it at a rat.
9. Both European and Mexican children have the story of the "Tooth Mouse" that comes to take away discarded baby teeth.
10. The sentence is correct.

Exercise 4

1. I was washing my car two weeks ago and noticed a few bees buzzing around the roof of my garage.
2. I didn't worry about it at the time, but I should have.
3. The sentence is correct.
4. The sentence is correct.
5. They flew in a pattern as if they were riding on a roller coaster or over waves.
6. The sentence is correct.
7. There was nothing I could do but wait in my car until they went away.
8. Finally, the bees flew straight up into the air and disappeared.
9. Once inside my house, I opened the phone book and called a bee expert.
10. The sentence is correct.

Exercise 5

Your revisions may differ.

1. Experts give the following tips to those who want to get the most out of a doctor visit.
2. First, avoid getting frustrated if you have to wait a long time in the reception area or the exam room.
3. Always answer the doctor's questions first; then ask a few of your own.

4. Inquire about a referral to a specialist if you think you need one.
5. Find out about other treatments besides the one the doctor first recommends.
6. Ask about any tests that the doctor orders and determine how to get in touch with the doctor about the results.
7. Take the time to ask about prescrition drugs' side effects and optional medicines.
8. Try to be calm in your discussions with the doctor.
9. Finally, be prepared to wait in a long line at the pharmacy.
10. If you follow these suggestions when visiting a doctor, you will be more informed and feel more involved in your own treatment.

Proofreading Exercise

Your revisions may differ.

Shirley Temple was born in 1928 and discovered in 1931 when she was just three years old. Someone recognized her natural talent at a dance lesson and asked her to be in movies. She starred in many films that are still popular today. Among them are *Heidi, Rebecca of Sunnybrook Farm,* and *Curly Top.* Directors loved Shirley's acting style and her ability to do a scene in only one take, but not everyone trusted Shirley Temple. Graham Greene was sued when he claimed that Shirley was really about thirty years old and a dwarf. Little Shirley's parents helped with her career and earned money for their efforts. In the early days, the studios paid her mother several hundred dollars a week to put fifty-six curlers in Shirley's hair each night. That way, her famous ringlets would always be perfect and consistent. Shirley's father managed her money, so much money that at one point Shirley Temple was among the ten highest paid people in America. It was 1938, and she was only ten years old.

USING PRONOUNS (PP. 161–165)

Exercise 1

1. I
2. she
3. she and I
4. I, I
5. she and I
6. she
7. I
8. her
9. she
10. her

Exercise 2

Your revisions may differ.

1. its
2. its
3. its
4. their
5. One day last week, the passengers had to gather their belongings . . . .
6. their
7. their
8. The passengers did their best to hide their annoyance . . . .
9. As the passengers stepped off the bus at the end of the line, the driver thanked them for their patience and understanding.
10. it

Exercise 3

Your revisions may differ.

1. its
2. she
3. Each of the new employees receives a locker in the employee lounge.
4. their
5. Every member of the audience had an opinion of the play and expressed it in the volume of the applause.
6. he
7. me
8. You and he
9. she
10. their

Exercise 4

Your revisions may differ.

1. My burrito exploded as I was cooking it in the microwave.
2. The student didn't understand what the librarian was saying and told her so.
3. The decorations blew away while we were putting them on the tables.
4. Our cat sleeps all the time, so she is a boring pet.
5. Samantha asked her friend, "Why wasn't I invited to join the debate team?"

6. The sentence is correct.
7. He finished printing his book report, turned off the printer, and put his report in his folder.
8. Max told his brother, "My bike has a flat tire."
9. Buying my parking pass early gave me one less thing to worry about.
10. Irene's mom lets Irene break school rules by using her cell phone on campus.

Exercise 5

1. The Howells purchased new lawn chairs, but the chairs were too fancy for them.
2. The sentence is correct.
3. I initialed the changes on the contract, put the top back on my pen, and handed the contract to the real estate agent.
4. Study groups help students a lot.
5. As we placed the jars in pans of boiling water, the jars shattered.
6. I always enjoy receiving good news.
7. The sentence is correct.
8. Dan's tutor advised Dan to rewrite his essay.
9. Many people visit amusement parks to experience the thrilling rides.
10. The committee members interviewed the applicants in the members' offices.

Proofreading Exercise

Corrections are *italicized.*

My daughter and *I* drove up the coast to visit a little zoo I had heard about. *The zoo was a hundred miles away, and the drive took* about two hours. Once *she* and I arrived, we saw the petting zoo area and wanted to pet the baby animals, but *the zoo employees* wouldn't let us. They said that it was the baby animals' resting time, so we couldn't pet them. Then we got to the farm animals. There was a prize-winning hog. *When the huge pig was lying down, it was as big as a couch.* My daughter liked the hog best of all, and as she and I drove home in the car, *that big pig* was all she could talk about.

AVOIDING SHIFTS IN PERSON (PP. 166–167)

1. Americans have always had more than they actually need. Americans have gotten used to having as much food, water, and clothes as they want. Restaurants throw away plates and plates of food every day. If people don't want something, they throw it in the trash. But a lot of people have started to think differently.

Recycling doesn't just involve aluminum cans and plastic bottles. Americans can recycle food, water, and clothes if they think more creatively and responsibly than they've been doing in the past. People can change the society's view of recycling by just doing it.

2. The paragraph is correct.

3. If I had a choice to live in the city or the country, I would choose the city. I would choose the city because I am surrounded by other people there, and it feels friendly. The country is too quiet. There is dirt everywhere, flies flying around in the sky, bugs—which I hate—crawling on the floor inside and out. The city is a place where the lights are always on. Yes, I deal with pollution, smog, and crowds, but it just feels like home to me. A city house can be any size, shape, and color. All the houses in the country look the same to me. No matter who the country people are, they have a white house and a big red barn. I have to admit that I have only been to the country a couple of times to visit my relatives, but the city would have to be the place for me.

REVIEW OF SENTENCE STRUCTURE ERRORS (PP. 168–170)

Your corrections may differ.

1. B. wordy (Dill pickles have a snappy flavor.)
2. B. cliché (I don't like being forced into things.)
3. B. shift in time (We all think that it *is* going to be really effective.)
4. B. incorrect pronoun (One of the tour guides gave my friend and *me* a map. . . .)
5. A. not parallel (Students *who study hard and who don't miss class*. . . .)
6. A. pronoun agreement error (Everyone in the room *looked surprised.*)
7. A. subject/verb agreement error (Each of my classes *challenges* me in a different way.)
8. A. not parallel (She buys *old, run-down* houses that need to be painted.)
9. B. run-on sentence (There are seven of them, and they're all adorable.)
10. A. wordy (Real poverty is unimaginable to most people.)
11. B. incorrect pronoun (*He and I* agreed that I needed a tutor.)
12. A. fragment (The *teacher took too long* to explain the assignment on Friday.)
13. B. awkward (They escape from backpacks and purses *and disappear forever.*)
14. B. shift in person (*Even when they know the facts,* they won't admit they're wrong.)
15. A. dangling modifier (*After I rested on the couch,* the television. . . .)

Mother Tells All

I have learned the most memorable lessons about myself from my children. A mother is always on display; she has nowhere to hide. And children are like parrots; they repeat whatever they hear. If I change my mind about something, they will remind me of every word I said.

For example, last summer I told my kids that I planned to take an exercise class and lose about forty pounds. I did lose some weight, and I attended an exercise class. But I started to feel like a balloon losing air. I decided that I did not want to lose any more weight or exercise anymore. I expected my children to accept my decision.

When I stopped, one of my sons said, "Mom, you need to go back to exercise class." Then they all started telling me what to eat, and I felt horrible. I had given up these things because I wanted to, but my words were still being repeated like a nonstop alarm clock. Finally, my kids got bored with the idea of my losing weight. Sometimes, when one of them makes a joke about my "attempt" to lose weight, it hurts me that they don't understand.

From this experience, I have learned not to tell my children about a plan unless I am going to finish it. Otherwise, they will never let me forget.

PUNCTUATION AND CAPITAL LETTERS

PERIOD, QUESTION MARK, EXCLAMATION POINT, SEMICOLON, COLON, DASH (PP. 173–177)

Your answers may vary slightly, especially in the use of optional pieces of punctuation (the exclamation point and the dash).

Exercise 1

1. Have you ever heard someone describe a beer-gone-bad as "skunky"?
2. The comparison is obvious; the beer smells like skunk spray.
3. Now scientists at the University of North Carolina at Chapel Hill can explain this phenomenon.
4. The ingredients in beer have one main enemy: light.

5. A beer that gets too much light undergoes a chemical change; the result is a smell that is very similar to that of a skunk.
6. That is why beer usually comes in colored bottles.
7. Consumers like the colored beer bottles; however, dark bottles are more expensive.
8. Therefore, beer makers would like to use clear bottles; they would cost less and be easier to recycle.
9. New discoveries about the chemical changes in beer due to light might allow makers to avoid the problem in the future.
10. Then beers could be sold in clear bottles; they would be less expensive; they would be more environmentally friendly, and they would never smell "skunky" again.

Exercise 2

1. Wasn't the company's holiday party nice this year?
2. At first, I wasn't sure that I wanted to go; now I'm glad I did.
3. The music—especially the harp music—made everyone so calm and contented.
4. The twinkling lights in the trees on the patio gave off a beautiful light.
5. Even the cubicles around our desks looked festive.
6. The boss announced our new Employee of the Year: Ted Haynes.
7. With so many of us doing the same job, there is a lot a competition; however, all that was put aside for the party.
8. The boss's husband is nicer than I thought he would be; I enjoyed meeting him.
9. I talked with coworkers that I haven't had any fun with in a long time—even Charlie!
10. I hope that everyone will still be in a holiday spirit once we get back to work on Monday.

Exercise 3

1. Have you ever heard of Dare Wright?
2. She was a photographer who created some of the most interesting children's books of the 1950s, 60s, and 70s.
3. Wright's main series of books began when she published *The Lonely Doll* in 1957; it was the story of Edith—the lonely doll—and two teddy bears who came to live with her.
4. The way that Dare Wright illustrated her books was unique: she photographed the doll and two bears as if they were real people living in an apartment of their own in New York City.

5. One of the bears who came to live with Edith was strict, bossy, and older than Edith; that was Mr. Bear.
6. The other bear was carefree, daring, and younger than Edith; that was Little Bear.
7. Dare Wright's stories were edgy and often involved Edith and Little Bear getting into real trouble; in one book they even get kidnapped at knifepoint by a bear called Big Bad Bill.
8. Wright's black-and-white photographs give the books an artistic look that makes them highly prized by book collectors today.
9. Most of Dare Wright's books are out of print; however, a few of the *Lonely Doll* books have recently been reissued—some even colorized!
10. It's been nearly fifty years since Dare Wright started her *Lonely Doll* series; however, they are still being appreciated by children and adults alike.

Exercise 4

1. Nancy Cartwright is a well-known actress on television; however, we never see her when she is acting.
2. Cartwright is famous for playing one part: the voice of Bart Simpson.
3. Besides her career as the most mischievous Simpson, Cartwright is married and has children of her own—a boy and a girl.
4. Wouldn't it be strange if your mother had Bart Simpson's voice?
5. Cartwright admits that she made her own share of trouble in school.
6. But the similarities between her and her famous character end there.
7. Bart is perpetually ten years old; Cartwright is in her forties.
8. Bart is a boy; Cartwright is obviously a woman.
9. It's no surprise that Cartwright is very popular with her children's friends.
10. When they yell for her to "Do Bart! Do Bart!" she declines with Bart's favorite saying: "No way, man!"

Exercise 5

1. Other nations have given America gifts that have become part of our national landscape; for example, France gave us the Statue of Liberty.
2. In 1912, Japan sent the United States three thousand cherry trees as a goodwill gesture.
3. The Japanese wanted to share their own tradition of Sakura Matsuri; that is the spring celebration of the beauty of the cherry blossoms.
4. During cherry blossom time, there are picnics and field trips wherever the cherry trees are blooming in Japan.

5. Of the three thousand cherry trees that Japan sent to America, only 125 remain; they bloom in Washington, D.C., every spring.
6. Thanks to the National Park Service, the lost Japanese trees have been replaced with ones grown in America; however, the original gift trees are the most prized of all.
7. New technology has allowed scientists to take clippings from the original Japanese cherry trees and grow new ones; consequently, the gift will live on.
8. Every spring in Washington, D.C., thousands of people come to join in the Japanese enjoyment of cherry blossom time; in America it's called the Cherry Blossom Festival.
9. And beginning in 2001, the first five hundred offspring of the gift trees will be planted; they will continue to grow next to the originals.
10. The Statue of Liberty stands in New York Harbor; the cherry trees bloom in the capital; both were gifts from other nations that add to the beauty of our own.

Proofreading Exercise

The ingredients you will need for a lemon meringue pie are lemon juice, eggs, sugar, cornstarch, flour, butter, water, and salt. First, you combine flour, salt, butter, and water for the crust and bake until lightly brown; then you mix and cook the lemon juice, egg yolks, sugar, cornstarch, butter, and water for the filling. Once the filling is poured into the cooked crust, you whip the meringue. Meringue is made of egg whites and sugar. Pile the meringue on top of the lemon filling; place the pie in the hot oven for a few minutes, and you'll have the best lemon meringue pie you've ever tasted!

COMMA RULES 1, 2, AND 3 (PP. 179–184)

Exercise 1

1. During the past few weeks, I have fallen behind schedule on several projects.
2. I'm not sure how the time got away from me, but it did.
3. When I first received my assignments to prepare a speech, create a photo collage, and write a response to a newspaper article, I thought I could find the time to finish them all.
4. The sentence is correct.
5. That was a good idea, wasn't it?
6. However, my planning got all messed up when my car started acting strangely.
7. Unfortunately, I spent last Tuesday sitting in a car repair shop lobby instead of gathering the facts for my speech.

8. As soon as my car was fixed, I rushed over to pick up the pictures for my collage, but the photo place had already closed.

9. The sentence is correct.

10. Now I've fallen so far behind on the speech, the collage, and the newspaper response that I don't think I will finish any of them in time.

Exercise 2

1. Most people don't know how coffee is decaffeinated, do you?

2. I just discovered that there are three methods used to decaffeinate coffee, but one of them is the most popular.

3. The most popular method is called water processing, and it draws the caffeine from the coffee beans into a water solution that removes most of the caffeine.

4. After going through the water processing method, the coffee may be a little less flavorful, but at least the process is "natural."

5. To decaffeinate coffee another way, manufacturers add a chemical solution to the beans and then steam them to remove the leftover chemicals.

6. Compared to the water processing method, the chemical method is more "scientific" and removes more of the caffeine.

7. Finally, there is the method that infuses coffee beans with carbon dioxide gas to get rid of the caffeine.

8. Since carbon dioxide is safe, plentiful, and non-toxic, this process is also popular.

9. The carbon dioxide method may be the most expensive of the three ways to decaffeinate coffee, but it also removes the most caffeine.

10. Whenever I drink a cup of decaf in the future, I'll wonder which method was used to remove the caffeine.

Exercise 3

1. When I was in high school, I was lucky to have a great English teacher.

2. Her name was Mrs. Kern, and she always tried to make us learn more than one thing at a time.

3. If we read a story in her class, we had to do research about the writer too. (*or* writer, too.)

4. We a read short play, chose parts to memorize, and gave a performance of the play in front of class.

5. The sentence is correct.

6. She was trying to teach us how to follow directions, how to explain something clearly, and how to think about what she called our "tone of voice" when we wrote.

7. We had to write a real letter of complaint about a product, a service, or an experience that was unsatisfactory to us.
8. Then we sent out two copies of our letters, one to the company we were complaining to and one to Mrs. Kern's school address.
9. If we explained our complaint well and if the tone of the letter was appropriate, we would receive a response from the company, Mrs. Kern assured us.
10. When the big envelope from my company arrived, I learned that she was absolutely right, for in it was a letter of apology, a bumper sticker, and a coupon for a lifetime discount at the company's stores.

Exercise 4

1. When the government issued the Susan B. Anthony dollar coin, it met with some disapproval.
2. People didn't dislike the person on the coin, but they did dislike the size and color of the coin.
3. It was nearly the same size as a quarter, had a rough edge like a quarter's, and was the same color as a quarter.
4. It differed from a quarter in that it was faceted around the edge, was lighter in weight, and was worth four times as much.
5. Due to these problems, the Susan B. Anthony dollar has been replaced by a new dollar coin.
6. Like the Anthony dollar, the new coin holds the image of a famous American woman.
7. She was the young Native American guide and interpreter for the Lewis and Clark expedition, and her name was Sacagawea.
8. The story of Sacagawea's life tells of hardship, suffering, and illness, but it also tells of incredible knowledge, courage, and strength.
9. While the men on the famous expedition had only themselves to worry about, Sacagawea assisted the men and made the treacherous journey from North Dakota to the Pacific with her baby strapped to her back.
10. Although the same size as the previous dollar coin, the Sacagawea dollar has a smooth, wide edge, and it is gold.

Exercise 5

1. The sentence is correct.
2. They were supposed to cure disease, lengthen life, and protect innocence.
3. Part of their appeal comes from how rare they are, for emeralds are even rarer than diamonds.
4. Geologists have been mystified by emeralds because they are produced through

a unique process—the blending of chromium, vanadium, and beryllium.

5. These are substances that almost never meet, nor do they often combine—except in emeralds.
6. In South Africa, Pakistan, and Brazil, emeralds were created by intrusions of granite millions to billions of years ago.
7. These areas are known for their beautiful gems, but emeralds from Colombia are larger, greener, and more sparkling.
8. The sentence is correct.
9. Instead of the granite found in other emerald-rich countries, the predominant substance in Colombia is black shale.
10. Even though these lustrous green gems can now be synthesized, a real emerald always contains a trapped bubble of fluid, and this minuscule natural imperfection is known in the gem business as a "garden."

Proofreading Exercise

When Niels Rattenborg studied the brains of mallard ducks, he made an interesting discovery. Rattenborg wondered how ducks protected themselves as they slept. The ducks slept in rows, and these rows were the secret to their defense. To his surprise, Rattenborg found that the two ducks on the ends of the row did something special with the sides of their heads facing away from the row. Instinctively, the ducks on the edge kept one eye open and one half of their brains awake as they slept. The rest of the ducks slept with both eyes closed and both sides of their brains inactive. The two guard ducks were able to frame the ducks in the middle, watch for danger, and sleep almost as soundly as their neighbors.

Sentence Writing

Here are some possible revisions. Yours may differ.

I enjoy skiing in the winer, but I like hiking in the summer better.

Although tutors will not "fix" a student's writing, they will explain how to clarify ideas, add stronger details, and improve organization.

Mark and Mary don't know what to do, for they are getting married, and Mark's last name is Perry, but Mary doesn't want to be called Mary Perry, so she might keep her own last name instead.

COMMA RULES 4, 5, AND 6 (PP. 186–192)

Exercise 1

1. This year's company picnic, I think, was better than last year's.

2. The sentence is correct.
3. The sentence is correct.
4. Certainly, we had better weather this year.
5. The sentence is correct.
6. Mr. Saunders, who brought the huge umbrellas for everyone to sit under, was the star of the day.
7. Marcus and Jonathan, who catered the party, did a great job; there was a variety of food, and it was all delicious.
8. The sentence is correct.
9. The desserts, I have to say, were better last year.
10. The sentence is correct.

Exercise 2

1. We trust, of course, that people who get their driver's licenses know how to drive.
2. The sentence is correct.
3. The sentence is correct.
4. Mr. Kraft, who tests drivers for their licenses, makes the streets safer for all of us.
5. The sentence is correct.
6. Therefore, we may understand when we fail the driving test ourselves.
7. The driver's seat, we know, is a place of tremendous responsibility.
8. The sentence is correct.
9. The sentence is correct.
10. No one, we believe, should take that responsibility lightly.

Exercise 3

1. The sentence is correct.
2. The sentence is correct.
3. My daughter's friend Harry doesn't get along with her best friend, Jenny.
4. My daughter's best friend, Jenny, doesn't get along with one of her other friends, Harry.
5. The tiger, which is a beautiful and powerful animal, symbolizes freedom.
6. The sentence is correct.

7. The sentence is correct.
8. Kim and Teresa, who helped set up the chairs, were allowed to sit in the front row.
9. My car, which had a tracking device, was easy to find when it was stolen.
10. The sentence is correct.

Exercise 4

1. Arthur S. Heineman, a California architect, designed and built the world's first motel in the mid-1920s.
2. He chose the perfect location, the city San Luis Obispo, which was midway between Los Angeles and San Francisco.
3. Heineman, an insightful man of business, understood the need for inexpensive drive-in accommodations on long motor vehicle trips.
4. Hotels, which required reservations and offered only high-priced rooms within one large structure, just didn't fulfill the needs of motorists.
5. Heineman envisioned his "Motor Hotel," or Mo-Tel, as a place where the parking spaces for the cars were right next to separate bungalow-style apartments for the passengers.
6. Heineman's idea was so new that, when he put up his "Motel" sign, several residents of the area told him to fire the sign's painter, who couldn't even spell the word *hotel.*
7. The sentence is correct.
8. Heineman's Milestone Mo-Tel, the world's first motel, opened in San Luis Obispo in 1925.
9. Before Heineman's company, the Milestone Interstate Corporation, could successfully trademark the name "Mo-Tel," other builders adopted the style and made *motel* a generic term.
10. Much of the original Milestone Mo-Tel building, now called the Motel Inn, still stands on the road between L.A. and San Francisco.

Exercise 5

1. Frozen "TV" dinners, which were first sold by Swanson & Sons in 1954, had only one original variety—turkey on cornbread with sweet potatoes, peas, and gravy.
2. The sentence is correct.
3. Campbell Soup Company, seeing the success of the TV dinner concept, bought the Swanson brand in 1955.
4. The sentence is correct.

5. These women's families, who had been used to complete home-cooked meals, needed a fast alternative.
6. Clarke Swanson, who inherited his father's business, brought the TV dinner concept to life.
7. The sentence is correct.
8. The sentence is correct.
9. The sentence is correct.
10. The frozen TV dinner, which was born in the 1950s, lives on as a billion-dollar industry today.

Proofreading Exercise

Do you know, Ryan, that there is a one-unit library class that begins next week? It's called Library 1, Introduction to the Library, and we have to sign up for it before Friday. The librarians who teach it will give us an orientation and a series of assignment sheets. Then, as we finish the assignments at our own pace, we will turn them in to the librarians for credit. Ms. Kim, the librarian that I spoke with, said that we will learn really valuable library skills. These skills, such as finding books or articles in our library and using the Internet to access other databases, are the ones universities will expect us to know. I, therefore, plan to take this class, and you, I hope, will take it with me.

Sentence Writing

Here are some possible combinations. Yours may differ.

Chili, which can be made with beans or meat, tastes best when it's spicy.

Chili with beans or meat tastes best when it's spicy.

The Hudsons, I believe, have a new dog that barks all night.

I believe that the Hudsons have a new dog that barks all night.

Kevin, my roommate who won a $100 lottery prize, acts as if he has won a million dollars.

My roommate Kevin won a $100 lottery prize but acts as if he has won a million dollars.

COMMA REVIEW EXERCISE (PP. 191–192)

I'm writing you this reminder, Tracy, to be sure that you don't forget our plans to visit the zoo this Saturday. [4] I know we're sisters, but lately you have let our plans slip your mind. [1] When we were supposed to go to the flea market last week, you forgot all about it. [3] I'm taking this opportunity therefore to refresh your memory. [5] I can't wait to see the polar bears, the gorillas, the giraffes, and the elephants. [2] And I have made special plans for a behind-the-scenes tour of several of the exhibits by Max Bronson, the zoo's public relations officer. [6] See you Saturday!

QUOTATION MARKS AND UNDERLINING/ITALICS (PP. 194–198)

Exercise 1

1. "Do you need any help?" my sister asked.
2. In her book *Gift from the Sea*, Anne Morrow Lindbergh writes, "The beach is not the place to work; to read, write or think. . . . One should lie empty, open, choiceless as a beach—waiting for a gift from the sea."
3. Sir Laurence Olivier had this to say about Shakespeare's most famous work: "*Hamlet* is pound for pound . . . the greatest play ever written."
4. In 1999, singer Weird Al Yankovic released a parody of *The Phantom Menace*; it was sung to the tune of "American Pie."
5. "Civility costs nothing and buys everything," observed Lady Mary Wortley Montagu (1689–1762).
6. Forrest Gump made many sayings famous, but "Life is like a box of chocolates" is the most memorable.
7. My teacher wrote "Good Work!" at the top of my essay.
8. The first time a contestant won a million dollars on the television quiz show *Who Wants To Be a Millionaire?* was in November 1999.
9. Karen asked, "Where will you be at noon?"
10. My family subscribes to *Newsweek*, and we all enjoy reading it.

Exercise 2

1. Have you read the book *Who Moved My Cheese*?
2. Anton Chekhov once said, "Any idiot can face a crisis—it's this day-to-day living that wears you out."
3. I gulped when my counselor asked, "How many math classes have you had?"
4. "Let's start that again!" shouted the dance teacher.

5. Last night we watched the Beatles' movie <u>A Hard Day's Night</u> on DVD.
6. Paul McCartney's song "Yesterday" still makes my mom cry whenever she hears it.
7. Abraham Lincoln stated, "I like to see a man proud of the place in which he lives. I like to see a man live so that his place will be proud of him."
8. "Time is the only incorruptible judge" is just one translation of Creon's line from the Greek play <u>Oedipus Rex</u>.
9. Don't you hate it when your dentist asks "How are you?" as soon as he or she starts working on your teeth?
10. My favorite essay that we've read this semester has to be "I Want a Wife" by Judy Brady.

Exercise 3

1. "Marks" is a poem by Linda Pastan.
2. I'll never understand what "No news is good news" means.
3. "Can you help me find an article on spontaneous human combustion?" the student asked.
4. Whatever happened to <u>The Book of Lists</u>?
5. <u>O Pioneers</u> is the title of Willa Cather's most famous novel.
6. "Let's begin," the relaxation expert said, "by closing our eyes and imagining ourselves in an empty theater."
7. Television series like <u>1900 House</u> and <u>Frontier House</u> have made PBS a real competitor for reality-TV-hungry audiences.
8. "I can't keep this a secret anymore," my neighbor told me. "Your son has a tatoo that he hasn't shown you yet."
9. A few days after Emily Dickinson's eight-year-old nephew Gilbert died of typhoid fever, the <u>Amherst Record</u> included a beautiful tribute to him entitled "Death of a Promising Boy."
10. I was shocked when my high school English teacher told us, "Most of Shakespeare's stories came from other sources; he just dramatized them better than anyone else did."

Exercise 4

1. George Sterling described San Francisco as "the cool, grey city of love."

2. One of the most famous actresses of the early twentieth century was Mary Pickford; movie producer Samuel Goldwyn had this to say about working with her: "It took longer to make Mary's contracts than it did her pictures."
3. Goldwyn himself was no easier to get along with: "He would not acknowledge rejection, according to one biographer. He could not be insulted. He could not be deterred. He could not be withstood."
4. When someone suggested that Walt Disney run for mayor of Los Angeles following the success of Disneyland, Disney declined, saying, "I'm already king."
5. Disney knew what it meant to succeed; having dropped out of high school and having moved to Los Angeles with less than fifty dollars in his pocket, he empathized with Mickey Mouse, a character he described as "a little fellow doing the best he could."
6. Mark Twain said of California, "It's a great place to live, but I wouldn't want to visit there."
7. There is a French expression "*L'amour est aveugle; l'amitié ferme les yeux,*" which translates as follows: "Love is blind; friendship closes its eyes."
8. "Let's keep our voices down," the librarian said as we left the study room.
9. Box-Car Bertha, renowned woman of the rails, suggested that "Nobody can hurt you but yourself. Every experience you have makes you all the more fit for life."
10. "Pain is inevitable," said M. Kathleen Casey, "Suffering is optional."

Exercise 5

1. In Booker T. Washington's autobiography Up from Slavery, he describes his early dream of going to school.
2. "I had no schooling whatever while I was a slave," he explains.
3. He continues, "I remember on several occasions I went as far as the schoolhouse door with one of my young mistresses to carry her books."
4. Washington was incredibly attracted by what he saw from the doorway: "several dozen boys and girls engaged in study."
5. "The picture," he adds, "made a deep impression upon me."
6. Washington cherished this glimpse of "boys and girls engaged in study."
7. It contrasted directly with his own situation: "My life had its beginning in the midst of the most miserable, desolate, and discouraging surroundings."
8. "I was born," he says, "in a typical log cabin, about fourteen by sixteen feet square."

9. He explains, "In this cabin I lived with my mother and a brother and sister till after the Civil War, when we were all declared free."

10. As a slave at the door of his young mistress's schoolhouse, Booker T. Washington remembers, "I had the feeling that to get into a schoolhouse and study in this way would be about the same as getting into paradise."

Paragraph Exercise

I've been reading the book How Children Fail by John Holt. I checked it out to use in a research paper I'm doing on education in America. Holt's book was published in the early 1960s, but his experiences and advice are still relevant today. In one of his chapters, "Fear and Failure," Holt describes intelligent children this way: "Intelligent children act as if they thought the universe made some sense. They check their answers and their thoughts against common sense, while other children, not expecting answers to make sense, not knowing what is sense, see no point in checking, no way of checking." Holt and others stress the child's self-confidence as one key to success.

CAPITAL LETTERS (PP. 200–204)

Exercise 1

1. Hidden beneath the church of St. Martin-in-the-Fields in London is a great little place to have lunch.
2. It's called The Café in the Crypt, and you enter it down a small staircase just off Trafalgar Square.
3. The café is literally in a crypt, the church's resting place for the departed.
4. The food is served cafeteria style: soups, stews, sandwiches, and salads.
5. You grab a tray at the end of the counter and load it up with food as you slide it toward the cash register.
6. Although the café is dark, the vaulted ceilings make it comfortable, and you can just make out the messages carved into the flat tombstones that cover the floor beneath your table.
7. One of London's newspapers ranked The Café in the Crypt high on its list of the "50 Best Places to Meet in London."
8. The Café in the Crypt can even be reserved for private parties.

9. The café has its own gallery, called—what else?—The Gallery in the Crypt.

10. So if you're ever in London visiting historic Trafalgar Square, don't forget to look for that little stairway and grab a bite at The Café in the Crypt.

Exercise 2

1. Now that DVDs are more popular than VHS tapes, I am updating my movie library.

2. My friends say that I shouldn't waste my money on repeat titles.

3. But my friend Jake is on my side because he and I are usually the ones who watch movies together.

4. Even though I have good VHS copies of famous films such as *Chinatown, Jaws,* and *Blade Runner,* the DVD versions offer behind-the-scenes footage and original trailers that VHS tapes don't include.

5. Of course, I'm aware that another technology will replace DVDs before too long.

6. Then I guess I'll just have to commit to that new format.

7. There are always collectors who want the old stuff.

8. In fact, I know someone who has a collection of video discs and 8-track cassette tapes.

9. I may be leaning that way myself.

10. I haven't disposed of my VHS duplicates yet, and I've been buying old record albums at thrift stores.

Exercise 3

1. When my art teacher asked the class to do research on Frida Kahlo, I knew that the name sounded familiar.

2. Then I remembered that the actress Selma Hayek starred in the movie *Frida,* which was about this Mexican-born artist's life.

3. Frida Kahlo's paintings are all very colorful and seem extremely personal.

4. She painted mostly self portraits, and each one makes a unique statement.

5. One of these portraits is called *My Grandparents, My Parents, and I.*

6. Kahlo gave another one the title *The Two Fridas.*

7. But my favorite of Kahlo's works is *Self-Portrait on the Borderline between Mexico and the United States.*

8. In an article I read in *Smithsonian* magazine, Kahlo's mother explains that after Frida was severely injured in a bus accident, she started painting.

9. Kahlo's mother set up a mirror near her daughter's bed so that Frida could use herself as a model.
10. In the *Smithsonian* article from the November 2002 issue, Kahlo is quoted as saying, "I never painted dreams. I painted my own reality."

Exercise 4

1. Sir Laurence Olivier was one of the most famous British actors of the twentieth century.
2. He was well known for playing the leading roles in Shakespeare's plays.
3. He performed in London, on such stages as the Old Vic Theatre and St. James's Theatre, and for several years, he was director of the National Theatre.
4. Of course, Olivier also played to audiences in cities around the world, such as New York, Los Angeles, Moscow, and Berlin.
5. Among Olivier's most celebrated roles were Henry V, Othello, Richard III, and King Lear.
6. Though we can no longer see him on stage, we can still watch the film versions of his classic performances.
7. Olivier also directed many plays and some of his own films.
8. He directed the 1948 black-and-white film version of *Hamlet* and received the Academy Award for Best Actor for his performance in the title role.
9. One of Olivier's most treasured memories was of a single live performance of *Hamlet* in Elsinore, Denmark; it was scheduled to have been played outside but had to be moved inside at the last minute, causing all the actors to be especially brilliant under pressure.
10. American audiences might remember Sir Laurence Olivier best for his portrayal of the tempestuous Heathcliff in the movie *Wuthering Heights,* but he was a Shakespearean actor at heart.

Exercise 5

1. My mom and dad love old movie musicals.
2. That makes it easy to shop for them at Christmas and other gift-giving occasions.
3. For Mom's birthday last year, I gave her the video of Gilbert and Sullivan's comic opera *The Pirates of Penzance.*
4. It isn't even that old; it has Kevin Kline in it as the character called the Pirate King.
5. I watched the movie with her, and I enjoyed the story of a band of pirates who are too nice for their own good.

6. Actually, it is funnier than I thought it would be, and Kevin Kline sings and dances really well!
7. Dad likes musicals, too, and I bought him tickets to see the revival of *Chicago* on stage a few years ago.
8. He loves all those big production numbers and the Bob Fosse choreography.
9. Thanks to Baz Luhrmann and others, movie musicals are making a comeback.
10. *Moulin Rouge* and the film version of *Chicago* are just two recent examples.

REVIEW OF PUNCTUATION AND CAPITAL LETTERS (P. 204)

1. The Hollywood "Walk of Fame" is a famous landmark in Southern California.
2. Have you ever seen Woody Allen's early films, such as Bananas or Take the Money and Run?
3. They've remodeled their house, and now they're ready to sell it.
4. "How much will the final exam affect our grades?" the nervous student asked.
5. We have reviewed your policy, Mr. Martin, and will be sending you a refund soon.
6. The two students who earn the most points for their speeches will face each other in a debate.
7. Ms. Thomas, the new English 4B teacher, recently received a national poetry award.
8. Even though I am enjoying my French class, I believe I should have taken Spanish first.
9. You always remember Valentine's Day and our anniversary, but you forget my birthday!
10. The most memorable saying from the original Toy Story movie is when Buzz Lightyear exclaims, "To infinity and beyond!"
11. My sister subscribes to Architectural Digest magazine, and my whole family loves to look through it when she's finished reading it.
12. Finding low air fares takes time, patience, and luck.
13. My friend is reading the novel Thousand Pieces of Gold in her English class.
14. I wonder how much my art history textbook will cost.
15. Bill Gates, founder of Microsoft, is one of the richest people in the world.

COMPREHENSIVE TEST (PP. 205–206)

1. (c) When you step inside, the alarm panel will beep.
2. (shift in person) People should avoid driving over potholes because *no one knows* what's at the bottom of them.
3. (//) *My cell phone and her doorbell were ringing* at the same time.
4. (s/v agr) Either the pastry chef or her assistants *have* made the pie crusts.
5. (apos) *Someone's* bicycle has been parked on the corner of our block for two days.
6. (ww) The twins spent *their* allowance on new computer games.
7. (awk) *I need more information before we apply* for that loan.
8. (cap) My favorite season is fall, but my kids like summer best of all.
9. (pro) The company president gave my coworker and *me* a bonus for finding the lost files.
10. (wordy) The worst part about camping is the lack of running water.
11. (ro) The lawn needs mowing, and the weeds need pulling.
12. (cs) I consider myself smart; however, I know that my mom is smarter.
13. (dm) My sister *used her computer to enlarge* a precious family photograph.
14. (frag) If I had the instruction sheet to put the bookcase together, *I could do it.*
15. (s/v agr) Each of the trees *was* lightly dusted with snow. (or *All* of the trees were . . .)
16. (mm) *After I took a 10-minute break,* my manager asked me to restock the shelves.
17. (ww) The test was more difficult *than* I expected; I'm sure I didn't do well.
18. (awk) We students *inquired about the newspaper story.*
19. (wordy) I returned the DVD to the store; it had been overdue for two days.
20. (pro ref) Everyone in town *put out flags* in support of the rescue crews.

WRITING

ORGANIZING IDEAS (P. 225)

Exercise 1 Thesis or Fact?

1. FACT
2. FACT

3. THESIS
4. FACT
5. THESIS
6. FACT
7. FACT
8. THESIS
9. THESIS
10. THESIS

TRANSITIONAL EXPRESSIONS (PP. 227–228)

Exercise 2 Adding Transitional Expressions

I have been planning to take a cruise with my husband and maybe my kids for several years now. *However,* I haven't decided what kind of cruise to go on yet. *First,* there are the romantic couple cruises to the Caribbean. But then I might worry about my children while we're away. *Next,* there are the breathtaking sights of Alaskan cruises. I've seen pictures of cruise ships passing right next to glaciers, although that seems a little dangerous. *Finally,* there are the family cruises that cater to everyone's desire for adventure and fun. While the kids play one of the numerous supervised activities, the adults can relax and enjoy each other's company. *In conclusion,* I think I've talked myself into a cruise for the whole family this summer!

WRITING ABOUT WHAT YOU READ (PP. 242–244)

Assignment 17

100-Word Summary of "Elvis on Celluloid"

Elvis Presley's film career disappointed many people but none more than Elvis himself. Elvis had dreams of becoming a real actor. He wanted people to let him show his serious side. But because he was such a popular celebrity, Elvis was forced to make a lot of silly musicals just so that everyone could watch him sing. His films were really popular then, and they still are today. But that never mattered to Elvis and his family and friends. It doesn't seem to impress critics either since most of them think of Elvis's movies as just fluff without any substance.

Index